Yugoslavia

the Former and Future

Yugoslavia

the Former and Future

Reflections by Scholars from the Region

Payam Akhavan
General Editor

Robert Howse
Contributing Editor

THE BROOKINGS INSTITUTION/WASHINGTON
and
THE UNITED NATIONS RESEARCH INSTITUTE
FOR SOCIAL DEVELOPMENT/GENEVA

Copyright © 1995 by

THE UNITED NATIONS RESEARCH INSTITUTE FOR SOCIAL DEVELOPMENT (UNRISD)
Palais des Nations CH-1211 Geneva 10, Switzerland

Library of Congress Cataloging-in-Publication data

Yugoslavia, the former and future : reflections by scholars from the region /
Payam Akhavan, general ed., Robert Howse, contributing ed.
    p.   cm.
Includes bibliographical references and index.
ISBN 0-8157-0254-X (alk. paper). — ISBN 0-8157-0253-1 (pbk. : alk. paper)
    1. Yugoslavia—History.   2. Yugoslavia—Ethnic relations.   3. Nationalism—Yugoslavia.
4. Yugoslav War, 1991- — Causes.
I. Akhavan, Payam
DR1282.Y84   1995
949.7—dc20   95-7556
                                                                                                      CIP

9 8 7 6 5 4 3 2 1

The paper used in this publication meets the minimum
requirements of the American National Standard for
Information Sciences—Permanence of Paper for Printed
Library Materials, ANSI Z39.48—1984

Set in Garamond Book

Composition by AlphaTechnologies/mps, Inc.,
Mechanicsville, Maryland

Printed by R. R. Donnelley and Sons, Co.,
Harrisonburg, Virginia

Contents

Tables

Preface

Payam Akhavan

*"Mankind is groaning, is dying to be led to unity,
and to terminate its age-long martyrdom"*

Shoghi Effendi

THIS BOOK is a unique collection of essays, written entirely by authors
from the former Yugoslavia, searching for a better understanding of the
events that led to the calamitous disintegration of the Yugoslav federation. It is by no means an authoritative account or chronicle of the war,
which is still raging, nor is it an exclusively academic treatment of the
subject divorced from the pain and suffering that some of the authors
themselves have experienced. For the peoples of the region, it is intended as a much needed dialogue aimed at understanding the mixture of
forces, events and personalities that exploded into such a cataclysm, and
at the same time an opportunity to reflect on the way out of this gloom to
a brighter and more prosperous future. For the wider international readership, the book provides an important glimpse into the minds of leading
scholars who are concerned with reconciliation and reconstruction in
their homeland. There have been countless articles, commentaries, and
books on the subject by erudite and less erudite writers, but surprisingly
few sources reflecting the thoughts of scholars from the region directly
affected by the conflict. The authors of this collection of essays are
leading scholars from Bosnia-Herzegovina, Croatia, Serbia, and Slovenia
who have been carefully selected because of their integrity and dedication to furthering understanding and friendship among all peoples. This
then is an opportunity to become familiar with the perspectives of some

of the finest thinkers in the former Yugoslavia who, at a time of great confusion and suffering, have made a courageous effort to dissociate themselves from the provincial and destructive intellectual currents in their midst and to search for answers to perplexing and difficult questions that concern us all.

The choice of the title—*Yugoslavia, the Former and Future*—is deliberately provocative. Of course, Yugoslavia is referred to in a broad sense and not as a specific political entity. Despite their great diversity, despite the fratricidal wars they have experienced, the peoples of this region, for better or worse, have much more in common with one another than with other peoples. Even as they stand at a crossroads between East and West, their common identity is distinct. As history amply demonstrates, it was in their union, a union of South Slavs, that they realized their long-sought emancipation from the imperial powers, both of the East and the West. Despite the various claims that this union either was Serb-dominated or, alternatively, was detrimental to the Serbs, the South Slavs' formative experiences with liberation and nation-building are inseparable. Indeed, in an increasingly interdependent world, the future of the different peoples of the region will only reinforce the reality of their inseparability in all spheres of human activity, be it economic, political, or cultural. This is a hard and inescapable fact, which has momentarily been lost in the psychosis of nationalism; hence the title, *Yugoslavia, the Former and Future.* In the midst of a "cataclysm of infantile regression" (to use the pithy terminology of Dr. Asbjørn Eide) when avenging battles from the Middle Ages takes precedence over social development, when even the "civilized" arbiters of world affairs have regressed to a state in which they cynically pursue narrow self-interest rather than facing with resolve the challenges of an emerging new world order, a coherent vision of a better future becomes a highly valuable commodity.

Indeed, in many respects, the disintegration and prospective reintegration of Yugoslavia represents a microcosm of the disequilibrium that the world at large is experiencing. We stand at a critical historical juncture: between an old divisive world view, which fails to grasp the common interest and inextricable destiny of all peoples, and a new unifying world view, which rests on an unshakable consciousness of the interdependence and oneness of the human race. We live in an age of paradox, where integration and disintegration, construction and destruction, exist side by side on an intensifying and unprecedented scale. As seemingly intractable problems, gross injustices, and centuries-old rival-

ries evaporate in a fleeting historical moment, so do the hideous spec-
ters of the past haunt us; as *apartheid* is buried in South Africa, it
resurfaces in southern Europe. Through this turmoil and confusion,
humankind is confronted with the formidable challenge of building a
new world civilization based on universal values, a challenge that demands a fundamental reassessment of the spiritual and moral foundations of human society.

While every effort should be made not to ignore or to obfuscate basic
moral issues through a sterile analysis of events, it must be recognized
that the Yugoslav conflict, as with most things in life, is a highly complex and multifaceted phenomenon. As spectators to the travail and
suffering of other peoples, we often overlook the peculiarities or gravity
of events, what they represent to the actors who are directly involved,
and trivialize or belittle the complexity of a situation so that it can easily
fit into our conception of things. In reality, however, there is never an
easy explanation, at least on the intellectual plane. Despite the desire for
theoretical or conceptual coherence, there are many and often contradictory ways of approaching social phenomena. This collection of essays
clearly reflects many common perspectives while at the same time it
contains many inconsistencies. It is for the interested reader to reflect
on these and to reconcile the differing approaches that are conditioned
by the perspective as well as cultural experience, academic field, and
even the personal peculiarities of the authors. Some adopt the view that
Yugoslavia was a multiethnic society in which the Serbs occupied a
position not unlike that of Croats, Muslims, and other ethnic groups;
others characterize the Yugoslav federation as an instrument of Serbian
hegemony; and yet others suggest that the Serbs were the biggest victims in the socialist years. Some believe that the Yugoslav National Army
used force "to save Yugoslav socialism from nationalism and Western
imperialism," while others simply suggest that ethnicity and the dominating role of the Serbs among the military is more important than
communist ideology in explaining the role of the army. The truth is
often a mixture of different factors, and at this stage perhaps it is more
important to reflect with an open mind without immediately producing
all the answers. I do believe, however, that there is at least one basic
theme running through most of the essays, a theme that is most important at a time when stereotyping the Yugoslav conflict as a tribal war has
been in vogue. I choose to call this theme "demystification." There is a
certain mystique to history and nationalism in a land of exotic peoples
and traditions, even a certain romanticism. Familiarity with the hard

facts, however, more or less illustrates that behind the façade of ethnic conflict and historical destiny one will almost always find a shameless opportunist or two, or even an entire political elite of "ex-communist democratic dictators," who benefit from deception, mass hysteria, fear, hatred, and war. Indeed, these are the fundamental instruments by which such "national saviours" elevate themselves to great heights of power at the expense of their peoples' lives and hopes.

The first chapter "Historical Elements for Understanding the 'Yugoslav Question,' " is a broad, concise, and interesting overview of the historical currents leading to the disintegration of Yugoslavia. Professor Dušan Nečak traces the unification of the South Slavs and the origins of the "Yugoslav idea" from the period of Habsburg and Ottoman imperial disintegration to the creation of the Kingdom of Slovenes, Croats, and Serbs in 1918, leading finally to the creation of the Socialist Federal Republic of Yugoslavia in 1946 and to its disintegration in the 1990s. He identifies unitary tendencies in the idea of Yugoslavia as "three tribes belonging to one nation," the subsequent emergence and significance of strong federalist currents, and attempts at the containment of nationalism through communist ideology. He observes:

> The multiethnic composition of the Yugoslav federation created a certain awareness of national problems among the leaders. They were not able to define a suitable relationship between "nation" and "class." As in other communist states, interethnic tensions were managed on the surface through ideological restraints while social conflict developed and intensified underneath. When Yugoslavia was swept by the wave of social and political change brought about by the demise of communism in Eastern Europe, these tensions surfaced and eventually erupted into a bloody ethnic and religious war. The postcommunist "redefinition" of Yugoslavia in the form of a new federation was no longer feasible, and recognition of the full political independence of those constituent republics seeking national sovereignty became inevitable.

Professor Nečak recognizes, however, that this solution was not without serious drawbacks.

> With the exception of Slovenia, which had a fairly homogeneous ethnic composition and well-established relations with its autochthonous Italian and Hungarian minorities, the dominant nations in other repub-

lics of Yugoslavia became embroiled in conflicts with national minorities. . . . At a critical point in the disintegration of the Yugoslav federation toward the end of 1991, it became clear that the impending
international recognition implied the relegation of the Serbs in Croatia
to the status of a national minority. In the case of Croatia, where strong
nationalist currents among the majority prevailed, statehood was interpreted as absolute control by the ruling ethnic group. Unfortunately,
when the delicate political compromise that was required could not be
attained, tensions quickly erupted into violence, especially in the regions of Krajina and Slavonia, where the Serb-dominated Yugoslav
National Army (JNA) played a decisive role in the outcome of the
conflict. A similar pattern of disintegration occurred in Bosnia-
Herzegovina, where both Serbia and Croatia vied for their respective
spheres of influence through a ruthless war, largely at the expense of
the Bosnian Muslim population.

Looking to the future, he does not hold much hope.

If to this already dismal equation we add the precarious situation of
ethnic Albanians in Kosovo and western Macedonia, an increasingly
aggressive Serbian nationalism drawing strength from a perceived or
well-grounded feeling of national isolation and peril, and the nationally
divided population of Montenegro, which vacillates between adherence to Serbia or Montenegro, the just and lasting resolution of the
Yugoslav question seems very distant. The nations of Yugoslavia have
faced a decision on their common destiny on several occasions in
history, but the forces of division and disintegration have always been
stronger than those of unity and consolidation.

He concludes that the political leadership of Yugoslavia

did not accept in time the fact that has been demonstrated many times
before in the history of Yugoslavia, and indeed in the history of the
world: that ethnic conflicts must be acknowledged and promptly managed with a view to their peaceful resolution based on genuine consideration of the legitimate aspirations of different nations. Otherwise, the
only alternative is the resolution of such conflicts through violence and
fratricidal wars.

This essay is a good point of departure for far-reaching questions
about the nature and role of "national consciousness": to what extent
do nations exist in an objective or primordial sense? To what extent is

nationhood purely a matter of subjective perception? Is national consciousness a widespread and natural phenomenon among peoples, or is it essentially defined and articulated by elites? How and to what end is national identity and sentiment galvanized and used? Whose interests does it serve? What are the "legitimate aspirations" of nations and how can conflicting aspirations be reconciled in a multiethnic setting?

Some of these questions are dealt with in the chapter "Resurgence of Ethnic Conflict in Yugoslavia" by Professor Dušan Janjić. The provocative subtitle, "The Demise of Communism and the Rise of the New Elites of Nationalism," is itself instructive. He demystifies nationalism and national consciousness by asserting that the main factor in the disintegration of Yugoslavia "was an underdeveloped political culture and heritage of authoritarianism that diverted democratic aspirations into a purely nationalistic struggle for self-determination." In this way, nationalism was an extension of communism which, because of its inherent divisiveness, was doomed to failure. Having pointed out that the former Yugoslavia was "a hybrid society with coexisting decentralized power of the state and a single party political system including specific forms of self-management," Professor Janjić concludes astutely that the turning point was in 1989.

> That year witnessed and revealed the economic collapse and the bankruptcy of the identifying values of socialism, self-management and Yugoslavia as a confederation under communist rule. Socialist ideology made way for nationalist ideology, homogenization, and hegemony. Since then, all political, social, and other conflicts have been expressed exclusively in nationalist terms. All the existing differences and the complexity of the society were replaced by only one reality: national divisions. This finally led to the civil interethnic conflicts that made it all but impossible to find a formula for the reform of Yugoslav society that was acceptable to all.

Following the capable treatment of the "mystique" of nationalism by Professor Janjić, the next chapter exposes the fictitious nature of the much vaunted federal legal framework of Yugoslavia. "The 1974 Constitution and Constitutional Process as a Factor in the Collapse of Yugoslavia" by Professor Vojin Dimitrijević is an insightful and highly provocative analysis. I am especially honored to have the contribution of Professor Dimitrijević, who is a long-standing advocate of human rights, an active former member of the United Nations Committee on Human

Rights, and among the best international jurists of Yugoslavia. In his candid and creative style, he dismisses the 1974 Constitution as "a monument to pseudo-ideology, false legitimacy, and bombastic mediocrity" and observes:

> In spite of its official depiction, Yugoslavia has in fact never been a true federation. Even with the 1974 Constitution it was, until the death of Tito, a unitary state governed by its centralized Communist party. Top party officials, and above all Tito, were able to make the most important decisions and impose them, regardless of the statutes of the party, not to speak of the constitution. Party members were submitted to the strict discipline of "democratic centralism" and were removable by the decision of the superior party organs, which were obeyed even if they violated the constitution and laws.

Professor Dimitrijević goes on to explain why, despite the demise of communist rule, the consociational framework of the 1974 Constitution failed to accommodate the aspirations of the various national groups:

> the political system in Yugoslavia, behind its constitutional façade, was that of consociationalism, [but] "consociational arrangements were never formalised, and with the demise of the party there were no institutional mechanisms to establish democratic consociationalism." The 1974 Constitution, as well as all others, failed to provide them, even as a fallback position.

The following chapter, "Disparity and Disintegration," by Professor Dragomir Vojnić is a thorough and scientific account of the economic dimension of Yugoslavia's demise. Professor Vojnić, a leading economist, has put together twelve very informative charts that provide a comprehensive statistical overview of disparity among the republics and autonomous provinces of Yugoslavia. These statistics indicate that in 1989, two years before the outbreak of war, the per capita gross product of Slovenia was on top by a large margin, followed by Vojvodina and Croatia. Serbia falls into the middle category, with Montenegro slightly behind and Bosnia-Herzegovina yet lower, and Macedonia and Kosovo at the bottom. The chart also illustrates that these differences had intensified between 1952 and 1989. Other charts provide statistics on various indicators, including demographic structure and the growth of population density, the size of household, and transfers of resources by the

Federal Credit Fund for Development of Economically Underdeveloped Republics and Provinces. In all areas it is evident that from the early years of Yugoslavia, the demographic stress and economic frictions between the various republics and provinces intensified until the dissolution of the federation. These indicators lead Professor Vojnić to conclude that

> a broad spectrum of fundamental differences among the republics and provinces contributed to an eventual process of disintegration. . . . The multifaceted and fundamental differences were, for the most part, historically inherited, although they continued and intensified during the existence of the common Yugoslav state. . . . The differences in the levels of economic development, demographic movements, ethnic structure, civilizational and cultural levels, tradition, habits, psychology, and outlook were key elements in the process of disintegration.

The socioeconomic differences among the republics and provinces are also replicated to a considerable extent among the various ethnic groups *within* some of these same entities, notably in the case of the Krajina and Bosnia-Herzegovina. Of course, other less easily quantifiable factors, such as the differences between the urban and rural populations, also contributed in significant measure to the tensions that ultimately resulted in the disintegration of Yugoslavia. The siege of Sarajevo, for example, is perhaps more typical of a conflict between the urban and rural than it is a purely ethnic conflict among Serbs and Muslims. Certainly, the "ethnic entrepreneurs" (to once again use the terminology of Dr. Eide) and warlords had powerful constituencies among the "less sophisticated" rural population, which could more easily be indoctrinated and manipulated. Nevertheless, it is rather difficult to determine the extent to which ethnicity was used merely as a means of sublimating social and economic grievances or whether the "more sophisticated" urban elites could have transcended differences in a show of multiethnic solidarity in order to contain the mischief of the demagogues among the rural population. Yet, these questions are now part of an unfortunate past, except to the extent that they can provide lessons for another land and another people.

Reflecting on the future of Yugoslavia, Professor Vojnić suggests that

> the only viable solution for . . . the newly independent states is to pursue independent economic policies directed toward eventual inte-

gration into the evolving common European market, taking into account the varying requirements and levels of development of each state.

Indeed, the only viable and reasonable solution at this point may be a relatively independent path to economic development. As the author observes, however,

> there are insufficient statistical and empirical indicators to analyze and evaluate the economic effects of the disintegration of Yugoslavia on its former republics and provinces, because, as newly independent states, only Slovenia and, to a lesser extent, Croatia, which is still at war, function with any degree of economic stability.

Yet, at the same time, Yugoslavia never had the opportunity to develop its economic system past the postcommunist era of transition. It remains to be established that the economic interests of the rich and poor republics and provinces would have been mutually exclusive, that a common Yugoslav market would not provide sufficient incentives for all the actors, or that it would have represented an impediment to integration with the European common market for the more wealthy republics and provinces.

Chapter 6, "Yugoslav Origins of the Post-Yugoslav Situation and the Bleak Prospects for Civil Society," is a thoughtful essay typical of Professor Žarko Puhovski, whom I have known as an independent and critical thinker and a conscientious advocate of human rights. He is a shameless "Yugoslav" who has consistently defied nationalist mythology, even in the hardest of times. In a demystifying and astute fashion, he analyses the role of political elites in the process leading to the disintegration of Yugoslavia:

> For decades society was indoctrinated with collectivist rhetoric. Against this background . . . it was relatively easy to transform one form of collectivist ideology into another. . . . Ethnonational collectivism was almost tailor-made to replace the old ideological schema.

Professor Puhovski's gift lies in expressing highly complex and controversial issues with convincing simplicity. He clearly points out (a lesson worth remembering) that the war could not exist without the death of the "Yugoslav idea":

In ideological terms, there was some (of course, perverse) logic in Serbs killing Croats for Serbia, or Croats killing Serbs for Croatia. On the contrary, there was no logic at all in Yugoslavs killing other Yugoslavs for Yugoslavia.

Looking to the future of Yugoslavia, he observes, using the example of Croatia, that boundaries and territorial integrity are essential for civil society and democracy:

the basic premise of Croatian politics [is] that there are no prospects for real democracy in Croatia except on the basis of the boundaries that Croatia had as part of Yugoslavia at the beginning of the war. It is on this premise that Croatian politics stands or falls. Of course, the majority of nationalists concentrate on the question of boundaries primarily as a symbolic and only secondarily as a pragmatic aim. The small minority of political actors for whom democracy is of central concern also have to support the maintenance of old boundaries, knowing well that with a more or less permanent situation of occupation of parts of Croatian territory, the country will live in a perpetual state of revanchist nationalism without the prospect of arriving at rational political solutions.

As he points out, however, the case of Croatia is not only relevant for direct Serbo-Croat relations,

but also for the prospect of ending the war in Bosnia and Herzegovina. This happens to be the case because the only immediate way to stop the conflict between Serbia. . . and Croatia is to partition Bosnia and Herzegovina between the Serbs and Croats. In any other scenario, the end of the war could have only one of two possible outcomes: Croatia is finally liberated from aggression . . . which means victory for Croatia and defeat for Serbia; or Serbia manages to retain some parts of Croatian territory. . . which means victory for Serbia and defeat for Croatia. In both cases, revanchist sentiments will persist in the region for decades to come.

He recognizes that from a *realpolitik* perspective, the partition of Bosnia and Herzegovina is the obvious "elegant" solution if the post-Yugoslav war is regarded as an essentially Serbo-Croatian conflict (as many observers have suggested). Of course, such a solution is not accepted by anyone who is concerned with justice, not only for the Bosnian Muslims, but also for the principles of equitable conflict resolution. Yet it could be "sold" to international public opinion with two seemingly solid arguments. First, two of the three sides in the Bosnian-Herzegovinian conflict, the Serbs and the Croats, control most of the arms and troops used in the war and can, therefore, almost guarantee at least a cease-fire if not long-term peace. It appears that this is exactly what the international community, tired of watching the repeated horrors of the war and its own impotence, is eager to achieve. Second, increasing propaganda against "Islamic fundamentalism" in the media of the most influential countries of the world gives Serbs and Croats (as Christians) the chance to claim that they are (once again, after their struggle against the Turks) protecting Europe from the Muslim threat.

Nevertheless, he points out that even if this morally undesirable "solution" were to be accepted, it would create a whole new set of problems. So long as ethnonationalism prevails as the basis of legitimacy for the various régimes, ethnic minorities shall be considered as a "natural" obstacle to the creation of a "pure" community of the majority. Accordingly, Professor Puhovski ends on a sober note by reminding us that "there is no room for celebrating the creation of the newly independent states and a lot of need for rethinking the post-Yugoslav situation."

The next essay, "Piecing Together the Balkan Puzzle," is written by Professor Milorad Pupovać, whom I have known as a creative and constructive thinker and activist. Professor Pupovać characterizes the Balkans as "a strait between seas of homogeneity and archipelagoes of lesser complexity." Reflecting on the future, he expresses the multiethnic dilemma in the following way:

While it is not possible to continue the process of constituting nation-states and the accompanying policy of national integration and unification, it is equally impossible to stop this process. It appears then that the Balkan nations have reached a stalemate. None of them will be able to attain their desired objectives with respect to ethnic unification. Any attempt to continue in that direction is possible only through a war that would, for many of them, be their last, and for many others would be a tremendous risk with potentially dire consequences. The only possible way out is a solution based on compromise.

Professor Pupovać identifies the pieces of the puzzle and suggests that any compromise must rest upon the fact that there are two crucial interethnic "questions"

> between the Croats and Serbs on the one hand, and the Albanians and Serbs on the other. It is also crucial to recognize that each of these two questions has a subquestion. The subquestion with respect to Serbo-Croat coexistence relates to the Bosnian Muslims, and in the case of Albanian-Serbian coexistence, it relates to the Macedonians. The first question and its subquestion may be considered as the central question of Yugoslavia, or in other words, the relationship between the two largest nations of the former Yugoslavia—Serbia, and Croatia along with the Bosnian Muslims. The second question and its subquestion may be considered as the central question of the Balkans, since in addition to the Macedonians its resolution involves Serbs and Albanians as well as the Bulgarians and Greeks. Therefore, just as it is crucial to provide answers for the first question and its subquestion in order to achieve peace and stability on the territory of the former Yugoslavia, it is also crucial toward the same end to find a viable solution for the second question and its subquestion.

What follows is an analysis of the different interests involved and ways in which they may be accommodated. He concludes by emphasizing that irrespective of the solutions he has proposed, or any other solution for that matter,

> the resolution of the problems confronting the Balkans will not be possible without mechanisms for reaching compromise . . . preventive diplomacy; negotiation and mediation; international monitoring, especially of human rights, as well as the development of democratic institutions; and the use of United Nations peacekeeping forces. . . . It should [also] be considered that by the time the Yugoslav and Balkan crisis has been contained, its peoples will be impoverished. It is extremely difficult to achieve trust and peace in a poor society with people who have been indoctrinated, and it is even more difficult to build a civil society. Therefore, "sticks" that the international community has used directly or indirectly (that is, economic sanctions) should

be replaced with carrots. In other words, the sanctions should be lifted, and, instead, the doors of international economic, trade, financial, and other organizations should be opened as part of a larger program of active and direct assistance to establish democracy in the tormented Balkan region.

The final chapter by Professor Zoran Pajić of Sarajevo University is a befitting conclusion for this collection of essays. The title itself, "Bosnia and Herzegovina: From Multiethnic Coexistence to 'Apartheid' . . . and Back," is thought provoking. The readers may want to note that it was only good fortune that allowed him to write this article. At the time that I solicited his contribution, he happened to be teaching at the University of Essex in England. Professor Pajić is a "true" Sarajevan; that is to say, the Sarajevo we have come to think of as a pocket of multiethnic society facing the onslaught of fascism, the Sarajevo that has become the embodiment of the struggle of values between civilization and barbarity. In addition to writing scholarly works, he has been a dedicated proponent of human rights. It is ironical that Professor Pajić served as a member of the United Nations Working Group of Experts on Southern Africa: little could he have imagined that one day he would celebrate the dismantling of institutionalized racism in Southern Africa while the ugly head of apartheid was being raised in his own country. Echoing the words of the other authors, Professor Pajić explains the "rule" governing ethnic entrepreneurs:

As a rule, the visionary dream of any nationalist leader is to be in control of his or her own national territory, to establish his or her own legal order and economy, to have his or her own military and police force, and so forth. These are the means by which one transforms oneself from a leader to an autocratic ruler.

The consequence of such "visionary dreams," he points out, is the negation of individual rights by a sort of institutionalized ethnic absolutism.

The process of consolidation of the new states is still in its initial stage, and it would not be fair to draw firm conclusions one way or the other, in particular for those countries that are still in a state of war. Nevertheless, the tendency toward an ethnically "pure" state is easily noticeable. The common starting point in most of the "new and democratic" constitutions is the idea that the *raison d'être of the state is to serve the nation and not the citizens*. This leaves little room for individual rights. An individual is treated as a member of a group, and rights and freedoms are granted and guaranteed only on the basis of such membership. If an individual belongs to a small group that cannot qualify as a "national minority," there is very little possibility of claiming rights on the sole basis of citizenship. Even worse, there are cases where an individual would refuse to be classified as member of a group for different reasons (mixed ethnic background is very common among "Yugoslavs"; there are many cases of intermarriage, and many who dissent from the "national" leaders and would therefore be reluctant to declare their ethnic background). Not belonging to a recognized group, the human being does not belong anywhere, because the state, as the above-mentioned constitutional provisions suggest, is owned in the first place by the "host" ethnic group and in the second place can serve as home for people who can qualify as members of a recognized minority ethnic group, and who are treated as "historical guests."

Stressing that these tendencies are frightening for the future of this part of Europe, he asks,

Is there any hope that the present situation will not lead the whole region into a nightmare, that it will not lead into a new phase of apartheid or strict segregation based on the "ethnic principle" and eventually spread further to the east of the continent? Are there no new ideas on the horizon that could show the way out of the atmosphere of hate, warmongering propaganda, ethnic exclusivity, crime, and mafialike policies? Are there no instruments in the international community—Europe in particular—that can at least secure the implementation of a minimum commitment to international law and principles as spelled out in dozens of resolutions and statements concerning the Yugoslav crisis and the situation in Bosnia-Herzegovina?

In his concluding sentence he notes that it is difficult to envisage how, without international involvement, "the people of Bosnia and Herzegovina can be emancipated from the nationalist trap that they have been dragged into by their own leaders." Indeed, how terribly tragic if the world community countenances the imposition of an artificially induced system of ethnic segregation on the age-old multiethnic complexion of Bosnia-Herzegovina. I chose the essay of Professor Pajić as the last chapter because it so capably captures the essence of the struggle in the former Yugoslavia and what it represents for the world community:

the war in Bosnia-Herzegovina should be considered not as a war of peoples, but rather as a war of values; it is fundamentally a war between fascism, built on national chauvanism and mythology, and solidarity, democracy, and ethnic pluralism, built on recognition of the oneness of humankind. Through the haze of historical, political, and ethnic complexity, this is moral clarity and demystification at its best.

In concluding my remarks, I wish to express my gratitude not only to the authors who have written an outstanding collection of essays, but also to those who provided the inspiration and means for the completion of this book. It was at the kind suggestion of Professor Rudolfo Stavenhagen from the University of Mexico City that I became associated with this initiative in the first place. He had suggested that I put together such a manuscript after we had discussed various concerns and subjects of mutual interest at the Martin Ennals Symposium on Self-Determination in Saskatoon, Canada, in March 1993. It was also with the encouragement, patience, and support of Dr. Dharam Ghai, director of the United Nations Research Institute for Social Development, that I was given the impetus to persevere in completing what proved to be a rather challenging task. Certainly, it was no easy task finding suitable authors because of the present climate of hostilities as well as the practical difficulties involved in communicating with the authors at long distance. On more that one occasion, Dr. Ghai impressed upon me the importance of producing such a work quickly so that it could become part of the current discussion rather than a book of purely historical interest. His sense of urgency was an essential element in the completion of this project, as was his patience and understanding. Finally, I must express my great appreciation to Dr. Asbjørn Eide, director of the Norwegian Institute of Human Rights and Special Rapporteur of the United Nations Sub-Commission on Prevention of Discrimination on Minorities. For several years, he has been an important mentor to me and many others, and his ceaseless struggle to find answers to the difficult problems that ethnic conflict generates is a source of inspiration. I have been under the influence of his approach since the earliest days of my career in the field of human rights. His comments on the manuscript have been particularly valuable.

Last but not least, I should mention the valuable contribution of my friend and colleague, Professor Robert Howse from the University of Toronto Faculty of Law, whose introductory chapter is an indispensable supplement to the collection of essays. Professor Howse provides an outstanding overview of the central factors and issues in relation to the

Yugoslav conflict and challenges the "tribal war" thesis, the acceptance of which he considers as tantamount to a capitulation to the nationalist warmongers. Mention should also be made of his father, Lloyd Howse, who has kindly contributed the historical footnotes for the chapter on the Yugoslav Question.

I also wish to communicate to the readership my "accidental" involvement with the Yugoslav conflict. While an associate at the Danish Centre for Human Rights in Copenhagen, I was appointed to participate in two missions of the Conference on Security and Cooperation in Europe (CSCE) in Croatia and Serbia, in October 1992 and January 1993, respectively. I shall never forget the first time I flew over Vukovar—the "Hiroshima of Europe"—in a UN helicopter. The horror of the devastation and human suffering was something no words could adequately express. As a member of the mission, Ambassador Hans Corell of Sweden, rightfully asked: "Who is to speak for these poor people?" This was a question I was to revisit many times as I joined the United Nations in the capacity of a human rights officer. I spent several months traveling throughout the areas of conflict in the former Yugoslavia and saw all that I needed to see to flee even the mention of war. The sight of so much human suffering strains the limits of human endurance. I cannot pretend to be a historian or scholar on Yugoslavia, but my views are born of a brief but hard experience. Perhaps this is why I am somewhat impatient with a sterile academic treatment of the subject.

I learned much simply through living and conversing with Yugoslavs from all walks of life. Indeed, one of my initial and most valuable experiences was sitting in the home of an illiterate peasant in a remote village, enjoying his warm and generous hospitality, and listening to how completely he had been indoctrinated and misinformed by his "national saviors." He explained how he was friends with all people without regard to religion until the "others" betrayed his trust. He told me grossly exaggerated tales of horrors committed by the "others" on "his people" and of fear for the safety of his loved ones. All that he had been fed by the manipulative media, and I hated to tell this well-meaning man how he had been lied to by his disgraceful "national saviors." I hated to tell him that he had driven out his "threatening" neighbors not to the benefit of "his people" but rather to the benefit of the populists and warlords whose interest "ethnic cleansing" served. He lamented with hurt that his village was not the same without his old friends, but that "it had to be done." It does not take much intelligence or imagination to figure out that ordinary people do not spontaneously decide to slaughter each other on a massive and systematic scale or that exacerbated fear can drive human beings to commit the most inhuman acts. Yet much of this seems to be lost, and we often content ourselves with the thought of "well, they have always killed each other, so what can we do?"

In many respects, I have come to see the tragic conflagration in the former Yugoslavia as a rude awakening for a triumphant West lulled in the complacency of post–cold war euphoria. The sheer barbarity of the war shattered the illusion of a *New Europe* that had finally emancipated itself from the fetters of a dark legacy of nationalist strife and hatred. In addition, just as the Maastricht Treaty came to be identified with the acceleration of European unity, and just as the menace of totalitarianism had been defeated by an awe-inspiring democratic revolution, the Yugoslav war reawakened historical rivalries among the European powers. In response to the carnage in Croatia and Bosnia-Herzegovina, Europe regressed to replaying the balance of power theatrics of the First World War. At a critical historical juncture, when mankind seemingly stood at the threshold of a new world order, such cynical and dithering statesmanship came to be identified with the anticlimax of a tragic drama where the protagonist turns a quintessential moral and historical challenge into a *realpolitik* quagmire.

Of course, whatever the war represented to the world at large, it was first and foremost a tragedy of immense proportions for the peoples of the former Yugoslavia. It was a conflagration that, as it swept through this picturesque land, left a path of horrific destruction and despair. It held in its relentless grasp the destiny of all alike, from the urbane intellectual to the humble peasant. For many, it obliterated the fruits of a lifetime of toil and labor. Indeed, in many places it reduced to rubble the fruits of many centuries of civilization and trampled upon all that was sacred, its evil reach not even sparing the most remote villages and hamlets. It was a plague of instigated hatred that left neighbors thirsting for each others' blood and made of friends ill-wishers. It brought untold suffering to millions and scarred the collective memory of an entire generation, engulfing in its violent vortex the lives and dignity of hapless men and women and shattering the innocent dreams of children. This grim reality is worth remembering lest we betray the suffering of the Yugoslav peoples through callous and haughty intellectualizing. It is above all empathy with the hapless victims of hatred and a resolve to confront their wicked tormentors that is needed, an empathy and resolve that can be projected into a vision of a world community freed from the scourge of war. In his epic *Bridge on the Drina*, the celebrated Yugoslav writer Ivo Andrić asks how those who have been subjected to war and made to suffer the contagion of hate can describe

that swirling current which passed from dumb animal fear to suicidal enthusiasm, from the lowest impulses of bloodlust and pillage to the greatest and most noble of sacrifices, wherein man for a moment touches the sphere of greater worlds with other laws? Never can that be told, for those who saw and lived through it have lost the gift of words and those who are dead can tell not tales. Those are things which are not told, but forgotten. For were they not forgotten, how could they be repeated?

Before all else then, let us not forget the horrors of war lest we allow another people to suffer the same fate. Yet let us not despair at the convulsions that surround us but instead busy ourselves with the immense challenge of building a better world.

The Hague, May 9, 1994

Acknowledgments

The assistance of a number of individuals and institutions was indispensable to this volume. Lloyd Howse contributed the footnotes to chapter 1, providing explanations of historical references and terms. Ari Blicker, Robert Howse's research assistant at the Faculty of Law of the University of Toronto, proofread with care several versions of the manuscript and made numerous helpful suggestions. Adrienne Cruz at UNRISD offered support and advice throughout. The financial and administrative support of the Faculty of Law of the University of Toronto were vital to the timely editing of this book. Our editorial work also benefited from the counsel and encouragement of the staff of the Brookings Institution. Nancy Campbell edited the manuscript, Stacey Seaman proofread the pages, and Robert E. Elwood prepared the index.

Payam Akhavan
Robert Howse

Yugoslavia in 1990–91

A Horizon beyond Hatred?
Introductory Reflections

Robert Howse

W ITH THE COLLAPSE of communist regimes throughout central and eastern Europe at the end of the 1980s, two competing interpretations of the post–cold war future gained prominence and influence in Anglo-American foreign policy circles. The first, propounded by Francis Fukuyama, sought to understand the collapse of communism as the universal triumph of capitalist liberal democracy. While acknowledging the possible resurgence of largely anachronistic conflicts of the past, including ethnic conflicts, as a short-term consequence of the end of communism, Fukuyama suggested that, once the dust had settled, liberal democracy would remain the only credible and viable social and political order in Europe.[1] The alternative interpretation, that of John Mearsheimer, an adherent to the realist school of international relations, predicted a full-scale return to the instability of the past in the wake of the end of cold war bipolarity, including the inevitable resurgence of ethnic conflicts as potentially a major catalyst of instability and competition among the Western and, in particular, the European powers.[2]

Although these two views of the future appear diametrically opposed on the surface, I believe that either could justify the minimalist response of the Western powers to the breakup of Yugoslavia and the resultant civil war. In the Fukuyama view, the Yugoslav conflict was both inevitable and temporary, part of the transition to a new and permanent order of liberal democratic peace. Why sacrifice Western resources and lives

I am grateful to Brian Frost and David Yanowski for helpful comments on an earlier version. This introduction draws on the argument in Robert Howse and Karen Knop, "Federalism, Secession and the Limits of Ethnic Accommodation," *New Europe Law Review*, vol. 1 (1992), pp. 269-320.

to end a conflict that is a necessary growing pain for the new order? After all, Hegel, Fukuyama's model and guide, had described history (that is, historical progress) as a slaughter bench.

In the realist view, national conflicts are inherent in the deep structure of international politics in the post–cold war era. These conflicts cannot be prevented or solved, but rather the major task is to prevent their escalation into unbounded and unstable competition between the major powers. This, for different reasons, suggested a minimalist response to the Yugoslav crisis, a response that would not require a hard choice between the differing traditional allegiances of the European powers in the Balkans (that is, Germany and Croatia, France and Serbia, Russia and Serbia) and would therefore prevent the Yugoslav crisis from escalating into a conflict among the major powers. Of course, an underlying assumption was that decisive intervention would require the intervening powers to choose sides. At the very least, the presence of Serbian enclaves in Croatia and Bosnia meant that there was no obviously legitimate *territorial* solution transcending traditional allegiances and interests of the major powers in the region that could serve as the goal of decisive intervention.

Unless either of these main perspectives on the post–cold war world order have misunderstood the character of nationalism in the contemporary world, we are compelled, whatever our moral sensibilities and instincts, to view the Western response to the Yugoslav crisis as entirely reasonable. As for the sanctions against Serbia, UN intervention in the form of peacekeeping, negotiations, and so forth, these can best be seen as relatively low-cost, politically rational responses to uneducated public opinion, which demands that "something must be done." To decry the failure of these measures is to assume that Western statesmen or policy bureaucrats ever seriously believed that they would lead to a resolution of the war.

In my view, the essays in this volume, all by scholars from the former Yugoslavia with a more or less liberal orientation, are of cardinal importance in reconsidering the various assumptions behind the predominant Western views of the post–cold war order and the place of ethnic conflict and ethnic nationalism in that order (or disorder). The essays offer no quick fixes and are remarkably free of simplistic criticisms of Western policy. Taken together, however, they certainly put into question, on the one hand, the inevitability of ethnic self-assertion degenerating into aggressive nationalism and, on the other hand, the assumption that nationalism is a kind of anachronism, a temporary phase or a product of the "Balkan temperament" rather than a dangerous, permanent ideological alternative to liberal democracy.

First, most of these essays point to causes of the federal breakup and the war that are specific to the social, political, and economic situation of Yugoslavia as it evolved since the death of Tito. The existence of these causes, largely ignored in Western analyses of the Yugoslav crisis, puts in question at the outset the view that conflicting or overlapping territorial claims of different ethnic groups must necessarily result in aggressive nationalism and national conflict and the notion that such conflict is the fate of the Balkans.

Second, many of these essays, and particularly those of Dušan Janjić, Žarko Puhovski, and Zoran Pajić, clearly display the character of nationalism as a totalizing ideology that constructs a collective identity based on ethnicity and makes the nation the absolute principle of politics as well as the governing principle, even in personal and economic relations. Nationalism no less than communism legitimates the exercise of absolute power by an elite or vanguard in the name of a unifying myth that suppresses the diversity of individual interests and identities and justifies endless sacrifice of both prosperity and personal freedom in the name of a collective struggle against an absolute "other" (the other ethnic group or groups rather than the bourgeoisie or the West).

The affinities between nationalism and communism in terms of ideological structure are expressed most succinctly by Puhovski: "Three fundamental elements of postcommunist nationalism have their origins in the old system. Communism was based on an antiliberal ideology that was at the same time collectivist and belligerent in character."

He further notes:

Class struggle was a dominant ideological doctrine, and for decades society was indoctrinated with collectivist rhetoric. Against this background of an indoctrinated "public sphere," it was relatively easy to transform one form of collectivist ideology into another, even if it was distant in content, so long as the collectivist nature of the ideology was preserved. Therefore ethnonational collectivism was almost tailor-made to replace the old ideological schema.

Closely related to Puhovski's analysis of the nature of nationalism as an ideology is the assessment and explanation in several of these essays of the failure of federalism and federal mechanisms, such as minority linguistic and cultural rights, to satisfy ethnic aspirations in Yugoslavia. This failure has been interpreted by some in the West as a failure per se of federalism and as a proof that ethnic aspirations will never fall short of the demand for sovereign control of a defined territory that is ethnically pure. However, there are two strands of analysis running through the essays that put in question this pessimistic perspective. The first is the spirit and context in which federal decentralization and linguistic and cultural guarantees were made: these changes represented a conscious choice by the Tito regime to respond to the pressures for reform that had built up in the 1960s, not through liberalization but through decentralization to the communist power elites in the republics. This choice, and its fateful implications for the future of the Yugoslav federation, is a central theme in chapters by Dušan Janjić and Vojin Dimitrijević.

As Dimitrijević shows, the 1974 Constitution implied a radical decentralization of power to republican (ethnically based) elites. It formally vindicated the nationalist agenda in conferring on each of the republics a supposed right to self-determination and introducing procedures of collective decisionmaking that gave the federal government virtually no scope to act without the consent of the representatives of the republics. This decentralization (and on paper, at least, the restructuring of Yugoslavia as a very loose confederation) constituted a gamble by Tito that the country could be held together through his power brokering among the various communist elites, through the central structure of the League of Communists, through the distribution of economic privileges and perquisites among the various republics and their ruling elites (detailed in Dragomir Vojnić's essay), and through the marginalization of dissident elements who were dissatisfied, for one reason or another, with the outlines of this solution.

In some sense, Tito's choice emanated from the reality that much of his and Yugoslavia's power and prestige flowed from its status as a leader of the nonaligned movement and from the perceived viability of a Third Way between Stalinism and capitalism. If the pressures for reform in the 1960s led to genuine liberalization, the consequence would be the loss of this special status, and with it the raison d'être of Titoism. Yugoslavia would become part of the West, economically, politically, and socially, if not culturally. (It is perhaps also possible, although this is not explored by the authors of these essays, that Tito may have feared the reaction from Moscow to such a choice.)

As some of the authors emphasize, especially Žarko Puhovski and Vojin Dimitrijević, the choice of formal decentralization combined with the accommodation of ethnic elites was in many respects a fateful decision. First, by suppressing the liberal orientation within Yugoslav political circles, Tito marginalized and largely destroyed liberal dissent within Yugoslavia, thereby preventing the development of liberal attitudes and a liberal as opposed to a nationalist-collectivist alternative to communism.

Second, the absence of a liberal foundation for the Yugoslav federation as a multiethnic state based on individual rights made the promotion of multilingualism, minority linguistic and educational rights, and other seemingly generous accommodations of ethnic diversity largely worthless as a check against the emergence of ethnic nationalism. In her essay Albina Nečak Luk notes that, at least at the level of rhetoric, "Cultural pluralism became the basic principle of interethnic relations in Yugoslavia. . . . Such an approach was intended to eliminate both ethnic ghettoization and assimilation and to bring about opportunities for social advancement to members of both minority and majority nations, irrespective of their ethnic origin."

Luk further notes that Yugoslavia was among the multilingual states that based language policy not only on the territorial principle but also on the right of an individual to "maintain and use his or her mother tongue throughout the state." In practice, the Slovene and Macedonian languages never achieved equal status with Serbian and Croatian in federal institutions, education, and the media. I would add that as long as one defined the goal of multilingualism in terms of substantive equality of linguistic *groups* rather than equality of opportunity for *individuals* regardless of mother tongue, multilingualism would fail to satisfy the aspirations of those linguistic groups that constituted relatively small minorities within the population as a whole, simply by virtue of the weight of demographic reality on linguistic practice.

My own experience of official multilingualism and related linguistic, educational, and cultural policies of a pluralist nature during my diplomatic posting in Yugoslavia from 1984 to 1986 led to me to an excessively optimistic assessment of the degree to which the practice of ethnic and religious tolerance had become entrenched in the Yugoslav federation. To use a distinction drawn by Kenneth Anderson, I (as well as many other analysts and supposed Western experts on Yugoslavia) found it all too easy to mistake tolerance for liberalism.[3]

As Zoran Pajić notes in his essay, Yugoslav multilingual and multicultural policies were not simply a sham or a token concession to ethnic identity, as is often now thought or claimed. Many analysts have emphasized Serb domination of the upper echelons of the military. But the federal civil service, including its upper ranks, was representative of all the main linguistic and cultural groups (and indeed Croatians and Slovenes were, if anything, disproportionately represented in many of the key economic or financial posts). Although the role of the Yugoslav and Serb authorities in suppressing the independence movement in the Albanian province of Kosovo is well known, less well known is that the federation also established an Albanian-language university there, just as federal multicultural policy supported Macedonian-language higher education in the republic of Macedonia.

I now believe that the main reason all these seemingly pluralistic policies failed to create a sense of commitment to Yugoslavia as a multicultural state is that they never ceased to be conceived of in collectivist terms: that is, they were viewed as collective rights or privileges brokered by ethnic elites, not as rights of the individual to free self-development in his or her own linguistic and cultural context.[4]

This had at least two main consequences. Viewed in collectivist terms, that is, in terms of group power for each nationality, the rights policies in question were bound to seem a poor second-best to full statehood, however useful they might be in protecting and promoting individual freedom and equality within a liberal multicultural federation. Indeed, as Dušan Nečak suggests in his essay on the historical origins of the Yugoslav question: "All the national programs of the Yugoslav nations in the empire, as well as in the Yugoslav states [before World War II], were based on the principle of national sovereignty and independence, whether within or outside a multinational state." The failure of the Yugoslav communists to transform nationalism into multiculturalism cannot simply be attributed to either the supposedly intractable or immutable character of nationalism as a mode of ethnic self-assertion or the suppression of ethnic conflicts under Tito. What was absent was an essential foundation of liberalism, which *could not* be supplied by the fundamentally collectivist ideology of Yugoslav communism. As Dušan Janjić suggests, "where the collectivity prevails over individuality and individual rights are repressed, the conditions for critical thinking or plural identities are not found. Within such a context, ideological rhetoric and artificial political integration rule the day."

A second, related consequence of conceiving multilingual and multicultural policies as collective rights was that these policies were themselves viewed as the achievement and, in a sense, the property of the ethnic power elites, a proof of their bargaining power at the center. Had they been conceived in liberal terms, these policies might have created a sense that cultural and linguistic security need not depend on ethnically based collective power (that is, that these were rights of Yugoslav citizenship not dependent on collective ethnic self-assertion for their vindication). Instead, as group rights they actually reinforced the sense that only the collective power of one's own ethnic group could provide any guarantee of linguistic or cultural security, thereby supporting what Janjić calls "the monopolization of ethnic politics by the governing strata in the republics."

Dimitrijević notes in his essay on the constitutional and political reforms of the 1970s that Tito's repression of liberal elements "did not involve mass persecution of ordinary citizens, who had more rights than the inhabitants of other 'socialist' countries, including the all-important right to travel abroad." Moreover, at least until the crisis of the 1980s triggered by Yugoslavia's inability to continue to service its foreign debt, the Yugoslav middle class was relatively prosperous and had access to Western clothes, music, and films. Among younger people, at least in urban areas but not exclusively there, a hedonistic, sexually liberated lifestyle was practiced without fear of state repression. Why then, as Fukuyama (and other liberal idealists) would have us expect, did westernization or modernization of personal lifestyles not, in and of themselves, lead to a liberal foundation?

In a moving collection of articles on the war in Yugoslavia, the Croatian journalist Slavenka Drakulić provides the following answer:

> We traded our freedom for Italian shoes. . . . Millions and millions of people crossed the border every year just to savour the West and to buy something, perhaps as a mere gesture. But this freedom, a feeling that you are free to go if you want to, was very important to us. It seems to me now to have been a kind of contract with the regime: we realize you are here forever, we don't like you at all but we'll compromise if you let us be, if you don't press too hard. . . . We didn't build a political underground of people with liberal, democratic values ready to take over the government; not because it was impossible, but on the contrary, because the repression was not hard enough to produce the need for it.[5]

Another dimension of the problem is the complex relationship between modernization and nationalism as an ideology. Nationalism often presents itself as the protection or revival of a tradition, and hence, from the perspective of liberal idealism, may often be viewed (as it was viewed in most of Marxist theory) as an *anachronism*, inherently at odds with modernization and secularization.[6] A contrary perspective, influenced by Alexis de Tocqueville and argued with great effectiveness by Canadian political scientist Stéphane Dion, sees contemporary ethnic nationalism in part as a reaction to the loss of collectively or authoritatively fixed identity and status that goes hand in hand with modernization or, more generally, the phenomenon of the breakdown of authority.[7] Modernization, in giving rise to the opportunity to define, as an individual, one's own identity, allegiances, life plan, and so on, involves or implies a sense of ultimate personal responsibility for one's own choices and future.[8] Depending on the social, political, and economic circumstances in which it arises, such a responsibility may appear as either an opportunity and a liberation or a threat. Under communism in Yugoslavia the middle class was able to enjoy— and here is the connection to Drakulić's point—a degree of personal freedom but without civic or personal responsibility because the ultimate fate of society could be still understood as being in the hands of the communist elites, not of citizens with rights. Any individual shortcomings, in terms of economic or professional success, could ultimately be blamed on the system, for which one had no ultimate responsibility as a citizen.

The Yugoslav experience of gentle, or licentious, communism should teach to contemporary liberals that the triumph of the VCR, to use Fukuyama's phrase, does not mean the triumph of freedom as the reciprocity of civil rights and civic duties. Liberal democratic revolution entails an assumption of responsibility through citizenship. This means viewing one's own and one's community's future as something other than an externally imposed fate. For the Yugoslavs of my age (mid-twenties) with whom I associated in Belgrade and on the Croatian and Slovenian coast, with whom I danced to Bryan Adams and Cyndi Lauper and partied the night away on Western yachts and speedboats, the Yugoslav solution, I realize clearly now, meant that one could live it up, then blame the blues and the hangover on someone else—one's parents, the system, Titoism. Several years later, some of these young people had moved from sex, drugs, and rock and roll to fanatical nationalism. Others escaped the responsibility of liberal revolution in a more benign fashion through departing for Italy and Germany or by simply tuning out. As Kant suggested, not only the brutality of official repression, but also the reluctance to assume ultimate responsibility for one's own life choices, that is, the absence of self-discipline and personal existential courage, can delay the march of liberal enlightenment.[9]

The absence of liberal civic values among the educated, Western-oriented middle class, which is a part of the story largely ignored by the

Western news media, must then significantly qualify the simplified and simplistic image of ignorant peasants and villagers being effortlessly manipulated by thugs and demagogues. Even more misleading is the notion that the resurgence of nationalism merely represented a return to the past. Among the urban middle class, without whose complicity or acquiescence the war could not have continued this long, the much-cited memories of nationalistic crimes during World War II carried little weight. What nationalism provided was an escape *from* the future, a liberal modernist future whose challenges required resources of personal courage, responsibility, and initiative, which few Yugoslavs had the opportunity to develop or practice under the soft despotism of Yugoslav communism.

This theme is central to the final chapter in this volume, by Zoran Pajić. He notes:

> In comparison with the previous life, the future offered by the reform-minded political parties was quite terrifying. Their standard election messages included: "open-market economy," "competition," and "the struggle to achieve European standards." People were simply not ready for such a vision. . . . One might argue that after so many years of a comfortably collective identity within the system, the common man was simply unprepared to take responsibility to exercise his individual freedom. The easiest option was therefore to seek another form of collective identity, another protective shield against the confusion. This was nationalism.

In contrast to the articles that appear regularly in Western newspapers and magazines and claim to have found a solution to the conflict in Yugoslavia, the authors of these essays are universally reluctant to suggest that there are any obvious answers or neat solutions. The most explicit treatments of the prospects for a solution are to be found in the chapters by Žarko Puhovski, Milorad Pupovać, and Zoran Pajić.

According to Puhovski, the only solution to the war in Bosnia that would have a hope of achieving stability, given the territorial ambitions of the two dominant warring powers, would be the partition of Bosnia-Herzegovina between Croatia and Serbia. Puhovski warns, "Of course, such a solution is not accepted by anyone who is concerned with justice, not only for the Bosnian Muslims, but also for the principles of equitable conflict resolution." In the absence of decisive Western support for such an admittedly inequitable solution, Puhovski is not optimistic for the chances of an end to the conflict. He points to the nationalist trap that is identified in several of the essays of this volume: the regimes in Zagreb and Belgrade have increasingly used the war, the nationalist ambitions that are its goal and the fear of other nationalities that is both a cause and effect of war, as the main source of political legitimacy. Without the war, these regimes would eventually have to go through the painful process of liberal democratic transition, taking responsibility for the social and economic disaster that the war has created within each society. The war itself provides an excuse for delaying this process, which could eventually create the conditions for a liberal solution to ethnic conflict based on rights, not force. The nature of the dilemma is well stated by Janjić: "The absence of liberal democracy precludes resolution of the national issue, and an unresolved national question militates against acceptance of liberal democratic institutions."

As Milorad Pupovać suggests, a territorially just solution to the conflict in Yugoslavia is impossible because the principles of justice at issue—national self-determination and territorial integrity—yield conflicting and contradictory claims by different groups that one or the other of these principles gives them some kind of stake in the very same territory. If one places this insight alongside the recognition of the nationalist trap, one cannot but conclude that the futile search for a just territorial compromise through negotiation has actually postponed the one route toward lasting peace: the development of liberal democratic institutions and values in each of the warring societies.[10] If any territorial compromise is going to be in some sense arbitrary, the world community should simply throw its weight behind the compromise that, given the realities of geography and military power, is likely to win for the region a period of relative stability and peace, the essential preconditions for restarting the arrested liberal democratic transition that could ultimately lead to the management of ethnic conflict through rights and democratic institutions rather than through violence and genocide. To insist that the fate of the Bosnian Muslims ultimately depends upon how much territory "their" government controls, or that the fate of the Serbs in Croatia depends upon how closely integrated their community is with Belgrade, is, in fact, to buy into the nationalist myth that fuels the war.

The concern with "rewarding aggression" that one frequently hears in discussions of the Bosnian situation is understandable, given that the recognition of Bosnia (in my view, one of the greatest errors in the entire international response to the crisis) seemed to imply that the borders of this newly independent state represented a kind of legitimate status quo ante disturbed by Serb and Croatian aggression.[11] It is perhaps time to admit the error of the West (and the international community more generally) in providing recognition to the breakaway republics without confronting the difficulty minority problems that this raised in all but the Slovenian case. In any event, how many historical examples are there of borders that were drawn according to principles of territorial justice or whose contours have not been significantly shaped directly or indirectly by force or conquest? That borders can and should reflect abstract principles of justice may well be an illusion largely nourished by nationalism.

Of course, that liberal democracy can take root in Croatia and Serbia once the war has ended represents a kind of wager. It is based on the concept, supported by most of these essays and their interpretation of the development of the Titoist approach to the nationalities problem in the 1960s and 1970s, that the liberal revolution in Yugoslavia was artificially stunted or arrested due to a variety of social, political, and economic factors—factors that made an escape from the responsibility and challenge of liberal democratic reconstruction particularly attractive or compelling and that also placed the various ethnic elites in a position well suited to the mass mobilization of popular fear and hatred.

Why, over time, could these factors not be reversed? Here, I think it bears emphasizing that international guarantees of minority rights and interstate understandings on protection of minorities may be less significant than the various ways—through money and technical advice for the construction of modern liberal economic institutions or measures to build a liberal civil society—that the international community can help to evolve an indigenous liberal culture in the former Yugoslav republics.[12] In reaction to the war and the kind of fanatical nationalism that is its cause and effect, new voices of antinationalist opposition have now come into being. Of course, given the nationalist trap, it is not surprising that these groups, which include the extraordinary and courageous Belgrade Circle, can easily be marginalized as traitors as long as the society remains mobilized by war and isolated by the world community.[13] From this perspective, I agree fully with Milorad Pupovać's suggestion that "the sanctions should be lifted and, instead, the doors of international economic, trade, financial, and other organizations should be opened as part of a larger program of active and direct assistance to establish democracy in the tormented Balkan region." I doubt, however, that any of this will work without a halt to the war first occurring—however imperfect the compromise may be, and however much it may reflect the immediate *rapports de force* among the various warring parties.

Even without much territory of their own, Bosnia's Muslims would be more secure in the context of a liberal democratic Croatia and a liberal democratic Serbia than they are today or will be as long as they cast their lot with the option of armed struggle for territory. I emphasize that this last point is my own, and is not explicitly advocated by the authors of these essays. It is rooted, however, in the analysis in many of these chapters, which has emphasized the absence of a liberal foundation as a cause of the Yugoslav breakup and ultimately the war. It is rooted in Kant's basic insight that states with republican (that is, liberal democratic) constitutions are most unlikely to go to war with each other, an insight that has been empirically verified in modern scholarship.[14]

Of course, as the situations in Belgium and Canada illustrate, liberal democracy does not make nationalism go away. Since, as has been suggested, nationalism is not merely an anachronistic or traditional outlook but also a temptation of escape from the responsibility of self-definition imposed on the individual in late modernity, it will remain attractive (as the primary post-Marxist form of collectivist retreat from self-making) to those who have not developed the moral and intellectual courage or perhaps (because of poverty or other disadvantage) lack the means to take up liberal modernity's promise of autonomous self-development.

So the risk is always there. But the fact remains that no multinational federation with entrenched liberal foundations has broken up, much less dissolved into a violent war of all against all.[15] Liberalism offers what no territorial compromise, no partition, no border arrangement can ever offer. With its vision of civil rights and civic duty rooted in the irreducible sanctity and dignity of the individual as human being, liberalism reveals a genuine horizon beyond hatred and a powerful moral counterprinciple to the sanguinary demands of collectivism.

CHAPTER ONE

Historical Elements for Understanding the "Yugoslav Question"

Dušan Nečak

AMIDST THE SOCIAL and political transformation of eastern Europe in the 1990s, unresolved national questions have been one of the root causes of instability and conflict. The neglect and repression of national aspirations and conflicts contributed as much to the demise of the rigid communist state systems of the eastern bloc as did the other excesses of totalitarianism. According to the Marxist perspective, national questions were symptoms of bourgeois society that would "wither away" with the progressive establishment of communism. Therefore, at least in theory, national questions in Yugoslavia and other East European communist states were considered to have been resolved. The fallacy of this assumption was clearly demonstrated after the demise of communism.

Of course, it is apparent that there was a difference between Yugoslavia and other East European countries. Beginning with the victory of the Yugoslav antifascist resistance in World War II, which gave the communist leadership international recognition and legitimacy, communism in Yugoslavia evolved as a more open and flexible system in comparison with its late-Stalinist variants in other East European countries. Nevertheless, in its essential ideological structure and methodology, so-called Titoism was not different from communism in other states. The multiethnic composition of the Yugoslav federation created a certain awareness of national problems among the leaders. They were not able to define a suitable relationship between "nation" and "class." As in other communist states, ethnic tensions were managed on the surface through ideological restraints, while social conflicts developed and intensified underneath. When Yugoslavia was swept by the wave of social and political change brought about by the demise of communism in Eastern Europe, these tensions surfaced and eventually erupted into a bloody ethnic and religious war. The postcommunist "redefinition" of Yugoslavia in the form of a new federation was no longer feasible, and recognition of the full political independence of those constituent republics seeking national sovereignty became inevitable. This solution, however, was not without serious drawbacks. With the exception of Slovenia, which had a fairly homogeneous ethnic composition and well-established relations with its autochthonous Italian and Hungarian minorities, the dominant nations in other republics of Yugoslavia became embroiled in conflicts with national minorities on their territory.

At a critical point in the disintegration of the Yugoslav federation toward the end of 1991, it became clear that the impending international recognition implied the relegation of the Serbs in Croatia to the status of a national minority. In the case of Croatia, where strong nationalist currents among the majority prevailed, statehood was interpreted as absolute control by the ruling ethnic group. Unfortunately, when the delicate political compromise that was required could not be attained, tensions quickly erupted into violence, especially in the regions of Krajina and Slavonia, where the Serb-dominated Yugoslav National Army (JNA) played a decisive role in the outcome of the conflict. A similar pattern of disintegration occurred in Bosnia-Herzegovina, where both Serbia and Croatia vied for their respective spheres of influence through a ruthless war, largely at the expense of the Bosnian Muslim population. If to this already dismal equation we add the precarious situation of ethnic Albanians in Kosovo and of western Macedonia, an increasingly aggressive Serbian nationalism drawing strength from a perceived or well-grounded feeling of national isolation and peril, and the nationally divided population of Montenegro, which vacillates between adherence to Serbia or Montenegro, the just and lasting resolution of the Yugoslav question seems very distant. The nations of Yugoslavia have faced a decision on their common destiny on several occasions in history, but the forces of division and disintegration have always been stronger than those of unity and consolidation.

Imperial Disintegration and the Unification of the South Slavs

The second Yugoslavia was established during World War II as a federation of South Slav nations and national minorities. The idea of a Yugoslav state is, of course, much older, and the path to its realization was not without problems. A recurring and central question was whether the South Slavic peoples are nationalities or nations in the sociological and political sense, or only constituent parts of an emerging unified Yugoslav nation. A further aspect of this question pertained to the nature of the Yugoslav idea and the Yugoslav movement, and even questions which peoples or nations were South Slavic to begin with.[1] Before the establishment of the first Yugoslav state, pro-Yugoslavia programs were mostly centralist in character, with the federalist concept all too rarely advocated explicitly. Because of the polycentric nature of the Yugoslav movement, however, the tendency toward federalism was always present, and was formally expressed in decisions approaching some form of national self-determination as early as 1848 and 1870.[2]

In historical writing, we can sometimes find the assertion that the existence of the present-day Yugoslav nations is, in fact, the result of an "accidental" national unification of South Slavs in the nineteenth century. The South Slavs had missed the opportunity—which, among others, was exploited by the Italians and Germans and sought by the Poles—to establish independent states through national unification. The idea of this "accidental" national unification as the result of mostly external factors, and the corresponding claim that, in reality, the Yugoslav peoples were only "tribes" of a uniform Yugoslav nation, remained alive in the scholarly community and in Yugoslav political discourse right up to the founding of the second Yugoslavia.

We know from history that the Yugoslav idea orginated in the national programs of the emancipated, politically organized, and distinct peoples of Yugoslavia. It is also true that from the Renaissance onward, the Yugoslav "nations" were aware of their common Slavic linguistic affiliation. However, the national consciousness of these peoples, which developed in the nineteenth century, was even then independent and distinct, as were the Yugoslav idea and the Yugoslav program. The Yugoslav idea did not originate from the desire to live in a community of related nations but rather, above all, as a common defense by the South Slavic Balkan nations against the threat of assimilation from the Germans, Romanians, Hungarians, and Turks. The Yugoslav idea promised the prospect of survival to each of the relatively small national groups (Slovenes, Croats, and Serbs), and a possibility for further development that did not entail the replacement or loss of national consciousness. This fact is essential for understanding the contemporary Yugoslav question. Nevertheless, these elements of national self-preservation became part of the Yugoslav idea when a supranational concept was hidden within it; a concept that was neo-Illyrian, integrative, and Serbian.

At a certain point in history—in particular after 1918, when the rule of the Turkish and Austro-Hungarian empires over the South Slavic nations came to an end—it became possible to realize the Yugoslav idea in the form of a common state.[3] This was due precisely to its apparently contradictory nature; specifically, the unity sought in its name could only be realized on the basis of an equal association of already existing individual nations.[4] The policy, which in the name of "Yugoslavism" restricted national rights and favored one of the national groups or even denied the existence of others, brought the union of Yugoslav nations to collapse for the second time toward the end of the 1980s, particularly because Yugoslavism, in either the national or political sense, was placed above individual national identities. Since World War II, furthermore, the "basic three" nations have been joined by the Macedonians, the Muslims, and the growing number of Albanians in Kosovo, making the Yugoslav question all the more complicated. Accordingly, the conflicts within the union of Yugoslav nations arose not only from the political manipulation and misappropriation of the Yugoslav idea, but also from the social and cultural differences among the Yugoslav nations living within the framework of a single state.

As mentioned, the Yugoslav nations had lived under the rule of the Habsburg and Ottoman empires in the nineteenth century. It was only in 1878 that changed circumstances allowed for the formation of the two independent states of Serbia and Montenegro. These two countries delineated their common boundaries in 1913 by dividing Kosovo, Metohija,[5] and Sandžak[6] between themselves.[7] Furthermore, as a result of the partition of Macedonia, Serbia annexed the so-called Vardar Macedonia. In 1878, Bosnia-Herzegovina was placed under Austro-Hungarian administration and subsequently annexed to the Empire in 1908. The most important event in the political evolution of the Habsburg empire in this period was the introduction of dualism in 1867,[8] at which time the Slovenes were formally separated from the Croats through the delineation of internal boundaries by the central authorities, while the Croats themselves were divided into Dalmatia and Istria. In addition, Croats in the region of Slavonia gained autonomy through the Treaty of 1868 between Croatia and Hungary.[9]

Divided in this way, the Yugoslav nations awaited World War I; one part under the influence of the Eastern cultural sphere and the other under the influence of Western civilization. The religious diversity within and between these two spheres has played an important role in the evolution of the Yugoslav question. The Yugoslav nations that lived in the east, including the Serbs, Montenegrins, Macedonians, Albanians, and Muslims were predominantly Orthodox Christian or Muslim, while the Slovenes and Croats were predominantly Roman Catholic. These religions or, more precisely, their respective churches and religious institutions, played a significant role in the progress and development of the Yugoslav nations. However, they also contributed to the complication and entanglement of relations among the various peoples of Yugoslavia. The adherence of these nations to different religions, the result of complex historical developments, continues to be an important basis for invidious national differentiation as well as social integration and homogenization. In particular, adherence to a religion has always been and remains the ultimate criterion for determination of membership in a national group in the linguistically unified but nationally mixed areas of Bosnia-Herzegovina, as well as parts of Croatia. In the case of Montenegro, adherence to the Serbian Orthodox Church has presented an impediment to the process of Montenegrin national development. Nevertheless, a national Montenegrin identity emerged despite such religious affiliation, although throughout history and until the present, for primarily political reasons, part of the Montenegrin population has renounced its nationality in favor of belonging to the Serbian nation. The difference in traditions that conditioned adherence to these different religions is most clearly reflected in the existence of two alphabets for essentially the same language. Because of the prevailing climate of interethnic hostility, the uniform Serbo-Croatian or Croato-Serbian language has been split into two separate languages of Serbian and Croatian.

After the Enlightenment period, when the idea was advanced that the Serbian identity should be constituted on the basis of a uniform folk language (Dositej Obradović), the notion of the Principality of Serbia became a significant gravitating point (for Montenegro as well) for the resolution of the Serbian question.[10] It was proposed that the entire Serbian population be united in a single state, suggesting a revival of the Dušan empire.[11] This clearly involved the liberation of Serbs in the territories of Old Serbia (Kosovo), Sandžak, Bosnia-Herzegovina, southern Hungary (Vojvodina), Croatia, and any other place where Serbs constituted a significant element of the population, whether in enclaves or dispersed. The proposed liberation and unification of all Serbs inevitably raised the question of the fate of other nations inhabiting the same territories, in particular the Croats, the Slavic Muslims, and the Albanians. In the period from the turn of the century to World War I, Serbian state authorities saw the answer to this question in the annexation of the territories concerned and the expansion of central rule in Serbia. The mistaken belief that Serbo-Croatian linguistic unity also signified national unity made it possible even for liberal elements in Serbia to support this concept of "Greater Serbia," which was first formulated by Ilija Garašanin in 1844.[12] Thus, the demand by the present Serbian leadership for the union of all Serbs in one state, which they consider an indispensable condition to the resolution of the Yugoslav question, is historically rooted. In the latter part of the nineteenth century, the ruling circles in Serbia saw an opportunity for the realization of this goal. It had become possible to annex territories populated by Serbs through a strategic alliance with the anti-Habsburg and anti-Ottoman movements of other nations, but without acknowledging their equal status.[13] When this concept for resolving the Serbian question was expanded to encompass all the territory that was later to constitute Yugoslavia, including Macedonia and Slovenia, and to admit a limited recognition of the national identity of Croats and Slovenes as "tribes" of a unified Yugoslav nation in addition to the Serbs, the Greater Serbia concept attained its Yugoslav variant, which lasted until 1914.[14]

Alongside this concept, another vision was developed in Serbian Social Democratic circles, which sought a simultaneous resolution of the Serbian and Yugoslav questions. Their goal was to establish a Balkan federation, which would not necessarily be confined to the territory of present-day Yugoslavia. On the other hand, one of the most prominent advocates of this idea, Svetozar Marković, promoted the idea of a federal union of Serbia with other territories in which Serbs lived and with Montenegro.[15] He rejected the union of all Serbs in a Greater Serbia and advocated federation not only because of the complicated ethnic structure of Yugoslav territory, but also because he was well aware of the highly particular traditions, national consciousness, and interests of elements of the population in the territories concerned. He emphasized that the federal unification of Serbs could and should occur only in a manner that guaranteed the national rights of all other groups.

Croatian national consciousness was based on historically acquired national rights and on the autonomy gained within the framework of the Hungarian Empire. Like the Serbs, the Croatian national movement also aspired to the unification of all Croatian territories, including Slavonia and Bosnia-Herzegovina. Two particular problems arose: the unification of the Croatian literary language (Croatian literature existed in three dialects—Štokavian, Kajkavian, and Čakavian) and relations with the Serbs in Croatia, who constituted approximately one-quarter of the population. The experiment with Illyrism was not a success and, as a sort of "Yugoslav" movement whose echoes were still heard in the interwar period, it remained essentially a Croatian movement.[16] More successful was the political recognition of the Serbs in Croatia when, together with the Croatians, they founded a coalition against Vienna at the turn of the century. A significant step in the development of the Yugoslav movement was Serbian support for Croatian autonomy and democratization. However, the weakness of this "Yugoslav" policy was made apparent primarily by the fact that it encompassed only Croatian-Serbian relations, and that the relationship was built on the illusion of a Serbo-Croatian national unity and not on the recognition of the individuality of the two nations. This was precisely the factor that made possible the wider political action of those Croatian circles, such as the Croatian Party of Rights, which relied exclusively on Croatian national rights for the resolution of the Croatian national question. This party advocated the historic Greater Croatia, and, in doing so, entered into a direct confrontation with the interests of Greater Serbia when dealing with the question of Bosnia-Herzegovina. Among the ranks of this party, many viewed Greater Croatia as a step toward a Yugoslav federation that would also include the Slovenes, and in which the political rights of Serbs in Croatia would be accommodated. Thus, on the Croatian side, there are historical analogues to today's problems.

The situation of Bosnia-Herzegovina was fundamentally affected by the underlying problem of Serbian-Croatian relations. In historical terms, the Muslims of Bosnia-Herzegovina, who speak Serbo-Croatian as their mother tongue, have consistently emphasized their unique identity and distinguished themselves from both Croats and Serbs. Since World War II, however, their greatest problem has been recognition of their unique character as a nation, since they are claimed by both Serbs and Croats.

In the case of Montenegro, independent statehood offered a sound basis for national independence. Yet until World War I, the national consciousness of the Montenegrins was Serbian in origin, meaning they shared a common belief in the medieval Serbian state and its battle against the Ottoman Turks, and observed the teachings of the Serbian Orthodox Church. Their national consciousness, however, is not identical with that of the Serbs, which developed after the emancipation of the Serbian state. For social and economic reasons, the union of Montenegro with Serbia was of vital importance for the former, although the two dynasties were in strong opposition. Thus, although internally divided, Montenegro joined Serbia directly and without constitutional reservations even before the Yugoslav union of 1918. The Macedonians began their fight for national emancipation in the middle of the nineteenth century. The strongest proponents of independent Macedonian statehood and the development of Macedonian national consciousness were members of the Macedonian National Revolutionary party, which was also the name of the strongest party in the 1990 elections. However, the territory that the Macedonians claimed was subject to the interests of larger neighboring nations, and the Ottoman administrative order was extremely repressive. The nationalist struggle reached its peak in 1903, with the founding of the short-lived Kruševo Republic.[17] The comprehensive repression by the Ottoman Turks, however, pushed the Macedonians to the very edge of existence. The hopes that had been raised by the revolution of the Young Turks were not realized, and the Macedonians lost their last chance in 1913, following the Balkan War. Macedonia was divided among Serbia, Greece, and Bulgaria, and the Macedonian nation was not recognized by any of them. For some extreme nationalists in Serbia today, the very existence of the Macedonian nation, as well as the question of its territorial limits, is still controversial. In neighboring Bulgaria, anti-Macedonian nationalist passions have eased somewhat for the time being, but they are raging among the Greeks, who, because of historical claims, have even refused to recognize the name of the nation.

The Slovene national program originated in 1848 under the name United Slovenia, which at the time contained no Yugoslav element. It was only in 1870 that the Slovenes defined their attitude toward a union with other Yugoslav nations. This took place at the Yugoslav Congress of March 1870 in Ljubljana, in which Slovene and Croatian politicians, as well as a Vojvodina Serb by the name of Laza Kostić, participated.[18] The Congress adopted a declaration stating that the unity of South Slavs had remained "constantly alive throughout all the ages of world events in the emotions of the peoples and makes itself known opposed to other nations as a linguistic unity"; that the Slovenes, Croats, and Serbs who lived within the boundaries of the Habsburg empire and those outside felt the same national needs; and that, for this reason, they joined "all their moral and material power and intended to employ it for their unity in the literary, economic, and political spheres." Judging by the tendencies expressed in the program, the Congress holds a place of great importance in Slovene history. It expressed the desire of the Yugoslav nations to live together in the event of major political changes such as the collapse of the Austro-Hungarian empire.[19] It has to be underscored that the emphasis on cultural and linguistic unity was only of a tactical nature. The pressure of German assimilation on the Slovenes was extremely strong, and the need for a unified political approach against encroaching German influence was urgent. It was clear to all Slovene politicians, as well as to the Croatian National party, which had initiated the Congress, that the Slovene national identity would have to be equally represented and maintained in a Yugoslav political entity. Such ambiguous consent to cultural and linguistic unity in the interest of a strong political alliance and the unity of Yugoslav nations was adopted by various Slovene political currents and individuals on two other occasions: during the wave of neo-Illyrism and the forging of new alliances with the Croatians in the first decade of the twentieth century, and again in the first Yugoslavia when Slovene liberals adopted unitarism in their fight against Slovene clericalism.

Slovenes, along with the Croats and Serbs in the Habsburg empire, were continuously hoping for the federal transformation of the dual monarchy. All the Slovene parties foresaw the joining of Slovene territory in the empire with the Slavic South and the formation of a specific South Slavic entity, although until the end of World War I it was only envisioned within the framework of the Austro-Hungarian empire. The well-founded fear that, in the event of the collapse of the empire, Slovene territories would be threatened by Italy clearly contributed to the position of the Slovene leadership. However, in spite of numerous ideas for the federalization of the Habsburg empire—among which the most notable is the proposal to establish a Slavic entity in the empire on the basis of a trilateral structure—no changes occurred. Or rather, the last Austrian emperor, Karl, was too late in proposing them, as imperial forces had already been defeated and the empire was on the verge of collapse.

It is important to note that the Austrian Social Democrats and their ideological leaders, Karl Renner[20] and Otto Bauer,[21] were particularly aware of the urgency of resolving national questions in order to prevent social conflicts in the state. They formulated the so-called Austro-Marxist model for national self-determination, elements of which are still contained in contemporary perspectives on the national question in the territory of the former Yugoslavia, especially with regard to the status of Serbs in Croatia.[22] The Austro-Marxist thesis, which would have also been suitable for postwar Yugoslavia, was based on the premise that the territory of the Austro-Hungarian empire should be preserved through the depoliticization of the national question. They asked: "How is it possible to unite such large cultural differences within a single proletariat and remain within the framework of a single party, a single program, and single policy?"[23] They proposed that by adopting the "personal principle," whereby each individual could choose his or her nationality, national questions could be reduced to the manageable legal question of cultural autonomy. The Yugoslav national movements, however, could not accept such a limited conception of the nation, which separated the cultural element from national sovereignty and statehood. All the national programs of the Yugoslav nations in the empire, as well as in the Yugoslav states, were based on the principle of national sovereignty and independence, whether within or outside a multinational state. National conflicts could not effectively be suppressed by separating social and political interests from so-called national interests; for instance, leaving the economic fate of one nation to another, supporting unitarism, and reducing a nation to its "cultural core."

The Kingdom of Slovenes, Croats, and Serbs: The First Yugoslavia

The Yugoslav nations formed a common state because of their cultural affinity, the possibility of uniting all national territories in one state, and particularly because of the conviction that a unified state would be easier to defend from the centuries-old imperial encroachment by larger neighboring nations (that is, Germans, Italians, and Hungarians) under whose rule they had lived until the beginning of the twentieth century. The Serbian and Montenegrin nations joined the new Yugoslav state on December 1, 1918, as previously existing states, while the national status of the Slovenes and Croatians was not clearly determined, because they had been part of the Austro-Hungarian Empire until the end of World War I. The most prominent Slovene and Croatian politicians were well aware that their future had to be built on the basis of national sovereignty and statehood. Therefore, it is not surprising that the leader of Slovene clerics and president of the National Council for Slovenia and Istria, Dr. Anton Korošec, in a communiqué from 1918 addressed to the first meeting of the National Council, emphasized ". . . that the state rights that the Slovene nation practiced in its own state [he had in mind the historical Carinthia formed in the early Middle Ages] taken over by foreigners for more than a thousand years will be returned through national self-determination and unite all Slovenes, Croatians, and Serbs in an independent Yugoslav state." In his words, the Slovene nation had chosen the National Council precisely ". . . to be prepared for the historical moment when it would assume jointly with the Croatians and the Serbs all the rights and duties of an independent state."[24]

From the perspective of the Slovenes and Croats, the establishment of the Kingdom of Slovenes, Croats, and Serbs on October 29, 1918, signified the initial realization of national self-determination that would eventually lead to historical circumstances in which both nations could make an independent and sovereign choice about their further national development. This was the goal of the Slovene and Croat nations upon the formation of the Kingdom of Yugoslavia on December 1, 1918. At the same time, the establishment of the Kingdom was a great success for the Serbs since it signified their national unification in a common state in accordance with ideas on the resolution of the Serbian national question that had been prevalent since the nineteenth century. This along with other factors—such as victory in World War I, previous statehood, and an established dynasty—presented Serbian leaders with the opportunity to assume the role of a "Piedmont."[25] As a hegemonic power in the common state, they provided the Slovenes and Croats with a substitute for the Germans and Hungarians during the period of the Empire. For the Slovenes in particular, and to a lesser extent the Croats, the reemergence of such conditions meant a new struggle to preserve national independence. On the other hand, the Macedonians were considered mere inhabitants of South Serbia in the new Yugoslav state, while the Montenegrins became a constituent part of the Serbian nation. For their part, the Albanians gradually became the foremost intrastate enemy of the Serbs.

The Serbian-Albanian conflict in Kosovo, which was the first manifestation of ethnic conflict among the Yugoslav nations in the contemporary period, was already fully in evidence during the period of the first Yugoslavia. Because of the aggressive and systematic colonization of the historically Serbian provinces of Zeta and Raška, the so-called cradle of the Serbian nation, the Serbs felt so threatened that Dr. Vasa Čubrilović (political adviser to the Stojadinović government, a former member of the Serbian nationalist organization Nova Bosna, and later a prominent historian and academic) submitted a memorandum entitled "The Expulsion of the Albanians" to the Royal Government on March 7, 1937, in which he proposed a violent solution to the Albanian question: "It is impossible to repel the Albanians just by gradual colonization; they are the only nation who have not only succeeded in surviving at the centre of our state, in Raška and Zeta, but they have also caused us damage because they have pushed our ethnic borders north and east. . . . The only possibility and method is the brutal power of a well-organized state. . . . We have already stressed that for us the only efficient way is the mass deportation of Albanians out of their triangle." He foresaw the deportation of Albanians from seventeen districts, including the regions of Peć, Vučitrn, Djakovica, Gnjilane, Kačanik, Istok, Debar, and Gračanica.[26]

The Kingdom of Slovenes, Croats, and Serbs was supposedly established exclusively to protect the national interests of the constituent nations. Once this fundamental expectation was not fulfilled, the existence of the state defied its raison d'être. Social injustices only deepened national antagonism, and became a substantial part of the explosive mix of national and class differences that destroyed the first Yugoslavia. The reasons for the collapse of the first Yugoslavia, as with the Habsburg empire, were rooted in an incorrect approach to the national question. The approach was based on a limited national autonomy, which emphasized and protected the cultural characteristics of each nation, while the economic and wider political interests of the Slovenes and Croats were largely transferred to the supranational (that is, Serbian) state. Other groups such as the Macedonians, Muslims, and Montenegrins, were not even recognized as constituent nations. Furthermore, members of the largest national minorities, especially the Albanian, German, and Hungarian minorities, numbering several hundred thousand, had very limited cultural and linguistic rights.

Such an approach to the resolution of the national question, some elements of which could be compared to the Austro-Marxist approach, inevitably led to conflict. This was, as it is today, primarily reflected in the relationship between Serbs and Croats. Not only the Yugoslav politicians, but also a great number of intellectuals justifiably believed that the resolution of the Yugoslav question and the very existence of Yugoslavia depended on the resolution of the Croatian-Serbian conflict. Instead of addressing relations among the nations based on recognition of their equality and sovereignty, the Kingdom of Yugoslavia, particularly during its initial years, spoke of a uniform nation, of a three-part nation, or of one nation of "three tribes." In sum, instead of full recognition of the national independence of the constituent nations in accordance with the historical Yugoslav idea, the policy of the first Yugoslavia was dominated by a centralist approach.

During the period following World War I, the political leadership, as well as the liberal intellegentsia, strongly advocated the integrationist concept of a fusion of Slovenes, Croatians, and Serbs into one Yugoslav nation with a single Serbo-Croatian language.[27] From the royal dictatorship of 1929 onward, day-to-day policies were dominated by a unitarist approach that subordinated national identities in favor of "Yugoslavism." Accordingly, it is no surprise that such policies gave rise to a nationalist reaction. In Croatia, this current developed into the extremist movement Ustaštvo, while in Slovenia the strongest political party, Slovenska ljudska stranka (the clericals), was starkly nationalist, as were all other political groups, with the partial exception of the liberals. The bourgeois Yugoslav politicians realized the destructive power of the unresolved national question too late.

Communism and the National Question under the Second Yugoslavia

The Yugoslav communists, creators of the second Yugoslav state, which originated in the middle of World War II during the antifascist national liberation struggle and the revolution, took the national question into consideration right from the start. The principles adopted by the wartime antifascist parliament of Yugoslav nations (AVNOJ) at Jajce in 1943 offered a realistic prospect for the positive resolution of the Yugoslav national question. The future state was to be a federation of equal nations and national minorities, with the recognition of the Macedonian nation and, later, the Muslim nation as well. In addition, the state would also respect the national integrity of each nation, which would have its own republic. In formal terms, this was undoubtedly a step forward in comparison with the first Yugoslavia, and this approach was incorporated in the first Yugoslav constitution of 1946. In many other aspects, however, this constitution was a copy of the Stalinist Soviet constitution of 1936. It envisaged a highly centralized state founded on the mistaken assumption that, with the gradual realization of communism, the national question would "wither away." The class principle was thus placed above the national principle, and the role of cohesive power in the state apparatus was assumed by the Communist party of Yugoslavia. It was only in 1959, when the Albanian question resurfaced, that top

Communist party leaders had to acknowledge that the national question had not been resolved. They began to regulate the status of national minorities, which then led to the reorganization of relations among the Yugoslav nations.

Until 1968, a process of democratization and decentralization took place in Yugoslavia that was apparent not only in the outward opening of Yugoslavia, but also in changes to the Yugoslav federal system. In that year, constitutional amendments were adopted in order to strengthen the autonomous status of the provinces and to expand the role of the Council of Nations, which was the parliamentary body representing the Yugoslav nations. Both Amendment VII, which awarded the status of constitutive federal elements, although not the status of federal republics, to the autonomous provinces of Kosovo and Vojvodina and the decision that the Albanians had the right to national symbols (that is, a national flag) signify the initial stages of the worst conflicts in the state. Serious Yugoslav historians consider this process "a strengthening of the autonomy of Kosovo and the equality of Albanians" and as an event "which could not pass without tensions, disagreements, and misunderstanding on both sides. . . . Serbian nationalists confronted the changes with the slogans of threatened Serbian identity, and the Albanians deemed them merely a formality and felt that some rights had been given merely to pacify political dissatisfaction among the Albanians."[28] That this perception really existed was apparent during the demonstrations in Priština and many other towns in Kosovo and Macedonia on November 27, 1968, when demonstrators used the slogan "Kosovo, a Republic" as their rallying cry. These demonstrations were a rehearsal for the outburst of Albanian discontent in 1981, which determined the forceful Serbian policies for dealing with the Albanian question— policies that became an important element in the process leading to the disintegration of the second Yugoslavia.

If we add to the adoption of the constitutional changes the simultaneous decentralization of the Communist party, which emphasized the creative role of republican Communist parties as opposed to the federal Communist party (republican party congresses of the period took place before the federal congress), the change in the direction of federalization is even more obvious. All these elements created the foundations for the last Yugoslav constitution in 1974, which again contained elements of a federal system, with the introduction of the consensus principle for decisions concerning the vital interests of individual republics or nations.

The deteriorating economic situation resulting from communist mismanagement exacerbated ethnic tensions. Economic, historical, cultural, and linguistic differences among the Yugoslav nations deepened even more with conflicting interpretations of the constitution, which was considered excessively decentralist by the economically less-developed regions of the southeast, and excessively centralist by the more prosperous regions of the northwest (that is, Slovenia and Croatia). Nations in both parts of Yugoslavia felt threatened economically, which in turn intensified their sense of vulnerability as nations, and their political leadership began to adopt policy measures that disregarded the Yugoslav state as a whole. The principle of limited sovereignty—by which some national sovereign rights were surrendered to the federal state so that, for example, federal laws that prevailed over republican laws and economic, financial, and foreign policy as well as the military were within the competence of the federation—was replaced by the principle of complete sovereignty, with each nation bearing exclusive responsibility for its own fate.

In Serbia, Slovenia, and Croatia, this was accomplished through the adoption of constitutions or constitutional amendments that had the features of constitutions of independent states. Slovenia and, subsequently, Croatia and Bosnia-Herzegovina held referendums on the independence and sovereignty of their respective republics. In the case of Slovenia, the adoption of a series of laws in the economic, fiscal, and military fields allowed the republic to "decouple" itself from the federal state.

These events also had the effect of propelling the Macedonians and Bosnia-Herzegovina toward greater national self-awareness. Up to the point at which the Yugoslav federal state, under the direct influence of the Serbian leadership, decided to intervene militarily in Slovenia on June 26, 1991, the day after the proclamation of its independence, there existed at least some possibility of a loose association among the republics of the former Yugoslav federation. Since then, however, there has not been even the slightest possibility for such an association, as a brutal and savage war, first in Croatia and then in Bosnia-Herzegovina, has shattered the vestige of trust remaining among the Yugoslav nations—a trust that will take several generations to restore.

Clearly, the political leadership of the second Yugoslavia did not accept in time the fact that has been demonstrated many times before in the history of Yugoslavia, and indeed in the history of the world: that ethnic conflicts must be acknowledged and promptly managed with a view to their peaceful resolution based on genuine consideration of the legitimate aspirations of different nations. Otherwise, the only alternative is the resolution of such conflicts through violence and fratricidal wars. In the past, other nations and peoples have shared the tragic fate of the peoples of Yugoslavia, and others may yet suffer the same fate in the future. From this accumulated experience, we can arrive at the conclusion that there is never just one guilty party or just one truth, only that the dead will never discover who was right.

CHAPTER TWO

Resurgence of Ethnic Conflict in Yugoslavia: the Demise of Communism and the Rise of the "New Elites" of Nationalism

Dušan Janjić

T HE RECENT RESURGENCE of ethnic conflict and hatred in the former Yugoslavia can be attributed primarily to the complex ethnic structure of the country, as well as to the prolonged structural crisis of state socialism. Yugoslavia was a highly heterogeneous society (see tables 2-1 and 2-2) consisting of several distinct peoples (that is, ethnic groups as well as "nations" with corresponding republics). These nations evolved and emerged under different social and historical circumstances and were at varying levels of economic, cultural, and political development at the time of their union with one another. With the exception of Bosnia-Herzegovina, each of the constituent republics of the Yugoslav federation was dominated by a single national group. Therefore, conflicts between the republics and the federal authorities as well as conflicts among the republics themselves, including the autonomous provinces of Serbia, invariably turned into interethnic conflicts. Nevertheless, although a necessary precondition for ethnic conflict, ethnic diversity itself is not the essential cause of nationalism and chauvinism in the former Yugoslavia.[1]

An element that generally puzzles analysts is the degree of "ethnification" of all political and social issues in the former Yugoslavia and, in particular, the rapid transformation from political crisis to armed conflict. In general, the process of disintegration occurred over a period of approximately two and one-half years, and was characterized by three distinct stages:

Table 2-1. *Nations, Nationalities, and Ethnic Groups in the Former Yugoslavia*

	Number	Percent
Total population	22,427,585	100
Nations		
Croats	4,428,043	19.7
Macedonians	1,341,598	6.0
Montenegrins	579,043	2.6
Muslims	1,999,890	8.9
Serbs	8,140,507	36.3
Slovenes	1,763,571	7.8
Nationalities		
Albanians	1,730,878	7.7
Bulgarians	36,189	0.2
Czechs	19,624	0.1
Hungarians	426,867	1.9
Italians	15,132	0.1
Romanians	54,955	0.2
Ruthenians	23,286	0.1
Slovaks	80,334	0.4
Turks	101,291	0.5
Ukrainians	12,813	0.1
Ethnic groups		
Romanies	168,197	0.7
Vlachs	32,071	0.1
Yugoslavs	1,219,024	5.4
Other (no declared national affiliation, less than 0.1% of total population	254,272	1.1

Source: 1981 census. Although the latest Yugoslav census was conducted in 1991, a considerable amount of data was not collected as a result of the outbreak of war. Accordingly, the 1981 census continues to be the most accurate source of basic statistical information on the former Yugoslavia.

—The disintegration of the single-party state toward the end of 1989;

—The introduction of the multiparty system through elections between 1990 and 1991; and

—The civil war in Slovenia and Croatia from June 1991 until the outbreak of war in Bosnia-Herzegovina in April 1992.[2]

It was during this last period that Yugoslavia disintegrated into a cataclysmic civil war, which assumed the characteristics of an interethnic conflict between Croats, Muslims, and Serbs.

Throughout this period, Yugoslavia experienced a paradoxical development, with a policy of economic integration on the one hand, and a process of political fragmentation on the other. The process of political liberalization and reform fostered the development of a single Yugoslav

Table 2-2. *Diversity within and among the Republics and Provinces of the Former Yugoslavia*

Republic or province	Total population (thousands)	Population in the agricultural sector (thousands)	1983 GDP per capita as % of Yugoslav average	Major religions	Major languages
Bosnia-Herzegovina	4,124	683	69	Catholic, Orthodox, Muslim	Serbo-Croatian
Croatia	4,601	668	125	Catholic, Orthodox	Serbo-Croatian
Macedonia	1,090	392	65	Orthodox, Muslim	Macedonian, Albanian
Montenegro	584	76	77	Orthodox	Serbo-Croatian
Slovenia	1,892	173	197	Catholic	Slovenian
Serbia					
Serbia proper (excluding provinces)	5,695	1,514	99	Orthodox	Serbo-Croatian
Kosovo Province	1,585	380	28	Muslim, Orthodox	Albanian, Serbo-Croatian
Vojvodina Province	2,035	391	121	Orthodox, Catholic	Serbo-Croatian Hungarian
Yugoslavia	22,425	4,277			

Source: 1981 census.

market across republican boundaries, and, more generally, that market's further integration into Europe and the international division of labor. Despite the strong support of the United States and the European Union, however, the rise of intolerant political demagoguery and the consolidation of regional and ethnic movements, beginning particularly in 1988, became an increasingly serious obstacle to the reform process. The strongest movement of this persuasion was formed in Serbia and Montenegro under the leadership of Slobodan Milošević, followed by a similar movement of an anti-Serbian nature in Slovenia and Croatia. The eventual result was the collapse of economic and political reform, leading to the disintegration of Yugoslavia itself.[3] In political terms, this course of events culminated on June 6, 1991, at a meeting of the presidents of the constituent republics of the former Yugoslavia in Sarajevo. At this meeting, the leaders of Serbia (Slobodan Milošević), Croatia (Franjo Tudjman), and Slovenia (Milan Kučan) rejected as contrary to the interests of their respective republics a plan for the redefinition of the Yugoslav federation proposed by the president of Bosnia-Herzegovina, Alija Izetbegović, and the Macedonian president, Kiro Gligorov.

The federal structure established in the former Yugoslavia by the Constitution of 1974 was jeopardized not through a movement toward confederation, but rather through the disintegration of a single-party and centralist order composed of a political, administrative, economic, and military elite. In sociological terms, it was but a disintegration of a typically neotraditional society. Throughout its political existence, the internal political space of Yugoslavia has been torn apart by conflicting objectives and actions, with occasional social, ethnic, and political eruptions.[4]

In general, the so-called ethnification of the political process was a specific product of the system of state socialism.[5] The most prominent characteristics of that system were as follows:

First, the enormous discrepancy between economic expectations and the actual possibilities for their realization; second, the increasing inability to meet the needs of different strata of society, leading eventually to the disempowerment of an overwhelming majority of citizens; third, the loss of confidence in the prospect for development, reform, and modernization[6] as reflected in the downfall of the federal government under Ante Marković (which confirmed the preference for the option of provincialism, chauvinism, and national totalitarianism); and fourth, the ensuing disintegration of mechanisms for the reconciliation of conflicting interests.

In brief, since the beginning of the 1980s, power in Yugoslav society depended on structures and elements that were tending toward conflict. Taking into consideration this fact, the disintegration of the former Yugoslavia and the civil war in Bosnia-Herzegovina represent the cumulative effect of a multitude of failed policies pursued primarily by domestic actors, and only secondarily by foreign elements.

The Factors of Disintegration and the Interethnic Dimension

National antagonisms were not inevitable or predestined; they had been managed peacefully since the foundation of the Yugoslav state in 1918 until 1941–45, and then until 1991, when they erupted in the form of large-scale armed conflicts.[7] The background for such conflicts was found in explicit—and, to a large extent, converging—national, linguistic, religious, cultural, and historical differences, with national divisions as the axis. Toward the end of the 1980s, these hitherto suppressed antagonisms turned into open conflicts. It was then that the Yugoslav multiethnic "melting pot" began to boil. The main factors underlying this course of development were an underdeveloped political culture and a heritage of authoritarianism compounded by growing nationalism, which diverted democratic aspirations into a purely nationalistic struggle for self-determination. The factors and elements that contributed in a significant way to the conflict included:

—The traditional ethnic cleavages, which remained largely unaltered in the postwar period;
—The fact that Yugoslav nations were "unaccomplished nations," such that the conflicts could be understood as belated movements for national emancipation;
—Increasing social and political uncertainty confronting individuals who, because of an authoritarian political heritage in which the individual rights of citizens were not adequately protected, sought security in the collectivity of the nation;
—The crisis of social values and opportunities that encouraged lawlessness and gave impetus to the search for a solution in ethnocentrism;
—Absence of a fairly powerful federalist democratic alternative so that, for example, the idea of a confederation was linked to the strengthening of bureaucratic centralism, but this time at the level of the nation-state;
—Emerging dissatisfaction with political, economic, and social status, primarily at the national level;
—The unattainability of interethnic harmony, absent at least a certain degree of goodwill and self-restraint on the part of the various ethnic groups;
—Lack of a clear and principled justification for integration into Europe, in contrast to straightforward anti-individualism and anti-cosmopolitan nationalist ideology;
—Inadequate experience with democratic institutions and procedures for the management of conflicts, which was conducive to the use of violence. In effect, the absence of procedures for the management of conflicts created a "might makes right" situation, and thereby sowed the seeds of civil war and the disintegration of Yugoslavia. The resolution of conflicts by means of forced national homogenization challenged the very concept of a multiethnic state, upon which the Yugoslav federation was based; and

—The absence of a coherent policy that could depart from the then existing state of affairs and provide a social and political context conducive to the resolution of conflicts.[8]

For far too long, the unpleasant reality of interethnic tensions was suppressed by the ideological myth of a conflict-free socialist society. The institutional system was not prepared to acknowledge the existence of ethnic conflicts, let alone resolve them. For this reason, the state was inclined to resort to repression when encountering such conflicts, or even the suggestion that such conflicts existed. In reality, however, repression was ineffective and counterproductive, contributing instead to the deepening and proliferation of artificially suppressed conflicts until they eventually undermined the institutional system itself. It would be appropriate to say that, in effect, the system did not disintegrate by the force of opposition, but rather by its own glaring inability to deal with the challenges posed by social reality. It is but a sad irony that in the very period of democratization, Yugoslavia was pushed toward civil war.[9]

The institutionalization of national conflicts in the course of 1970s, and especially in the Constitution of 1974, served to elevate the influence of ethnicity on the articulation of interests. Furthermore, bearing in mind that the institutionalization of national interests was not carried out within a democratic system, the necessary social balance was also lacking. This explains why, subsequently, serious national conflicts were either repressed by force or covered up rather than resolved. The monopolization of ethnic politics by the governing strata in the republics (and provinces) adversely affected interethnic and interrepublican relations and contributed to the formation and expression of the "national interest," while the strengthening of statism provided legal sustenance for "national bureaucratism."

Bureaucratic elitism founded in republican (provincial) statism clad all partisan interests in national attire. Once a national status was obtained, the interest concerned was absolutized and turned into both the internal and external determinant of the nation. Within the nation, it was the interest of the bureaucracy and forces with which it was allied. On the outside, it stood for the "authentic" interest of the nation as designated by the bureaucracy, and, where appropriate, as the interest of its own (that is, national) working class. Without the intervening forces of a free market, the interests of a private sphere of the national bureaucracy became the national interest, and were thrown into the midst of a political game in conflict with the interests of other republics and provinces. The confrontation of absolutized national interests became a self-seeking competition for profit maximization as the single Yugoslav market dissolved into a common market in the international sphere. The republics (and provinces) with the stronger economies tended to expand in the direction of the market, since they could profit from such reforms. At the same time, they used various barriers to protect their national autarchy.[10] Such a course of events in a country as heterogeneous as Yugoslavia contributed significantly to the confrontation of interests and disintegration on a national scale in the form of conflict between nation-states. Through such conflicts the forces of decentralization were unleashed.

The unrestrained consolidation and clash of interests—that is to uncontrolled social change—represented one of the main features o crisis that confronted Yugoslav society. The crisis was also the pro of the state-controlled mode of production and the accompanying tem of a specific bargain for redistributing the social cost of the resui poverty. The indications of this profound crisis became fully apparei the early 1980s, initially in the economic but later also in the poli sphere.[11] It was ultimately the political crisis that led to the collapse the old order. This crisis was the result of the emergence of an auto mous political sphere and the strengthening of noninstitutional political life; in other words, the proliferation of "movements," "protest rallies," "popular gatherings," and "political marches."[12]

The year 1988 marked the beginning of an open and all-inclusive transformation of "classic strikes" into classic political manifestations directed against others, initially rival elites, but thereafter also rival ethnic groups or nations.[13] The most apparent expression of this phenomenon was through the campaign of so-called solidarity with the Serbs and Montenegrins of Kosovo under the direct guidance of the Serbian party and state leadership and, above all, Slobodan Milošević.[14] Subsequently, the movement adopted the term "happening of the people" or "anti-bureaucratic revolution" which focused on Serbia and Montenegro but its impact was spent on changes to the *nomenklatura*.[15] Although this form of political life served as a kind of supplement to the official public life, and even an attempt to retain it with certain minor modifications, it ultimately represented an expression of the crisis, which was growing into agony, increasingly pronounced social despair, and the destruction of existing rights. No new rights were established, but conditions leading toward a civil war were made possible.[16]

Overturning the existing ruling class through the direct pressure of social rage—which, through ideological, political, propaganda, and even police methods, was directed in such a way as to explode in the streets—merged with the tendencies of nationalist populism in an attempt to resolve the problems of systemic inefficiency while using people as a form of pressure group. Of course, these events also include a germ of a democratic consciousness as manifested in the involvement of people wishing to take things into their own hands, to become active creators of their own political destiny. Nevertheless, the political manipulation of these popular gatherings was also very strong. In effect, while relying on the existing practice of political pressure and voluntarism and departures from the proclaimed normative and ideological system, attempts were made to provoke state intervention; to create an emergency that required extraordinary measures or short-cut methods of state intervention. This manipulation led directly to the further disintegration of the Yugoslav society and state. Its natural offspring was a chauvinistic, war-mongering policy that drove people into the abyss of ethnic war. Thus, it could be maintained that in early 1989 the country entered into the final stage of the worst crisis since its inception shortly after World War II. The deepening of the crisis was preceded by the announcement of a number of constitutional amendments that were to be inaugurated by the end of 1988.

The second half of the 1980s was marked by a stronger trend of disintegration of the dominant political party, the League of Communists of Yugoslavia (LCY), into six equally autonomous political parties. That trend culminated in the XIVth Extraordinary Congress of the LCY (January 20–22, 1990). The substantial differences within the party elite and its division into two powerful blocs resulted in the formation of two distinct platforms: centralist-unitarist and decentralist-pluralist, which were by that time already marked as the Serbian and Slovenian positions, respectively.[17]

Following the disintegration of the LCY, social conflicts within the country became increasingly pronounced. During this period, the elites made use of the mass media and other means to promote national homogenization, emphasizing a largely fictitious impending threat to the national interest from other (Yugoslav) nations. That led to increased fragmentation, with political divisions following the line of national divisions to an increasing extent. The long-standing general and structural crisis of society in Yugoslavia turned into a profound political crisis, and eventually into violent and bloody ethnic conflicts. These conflicts could be divided into three different types according to the level of their development and the actors involved:

The first type of conflict comprises those between the constituent federal units or republics that, because of their status as ethnicity-based entities, necessarily became ethnic conflicts. In this context, the most prominent subcategories of conflicts are as follows:

—Direct political conflicts between Serbia and Slovenia, and Serbia and Croatia, as well as the dormant conflict between Serbia and Macedonia;

—Open conflicts between the residual power of the federal state and the constituent federal units (in particular Slovenia, Serbia, and Croatia) over the redistribution of the economic and financial burden of economic reform and the prerogatives of state authority (especially armed forces and foreign policy) that the republics wanted to arrogate to themselves as necessary elements of their emerging status as independent nation-states, although the basic conflict is actually derived from the question of whether to retain Yugoslavia or let it dissolve; and

—Conflicts within federal subunits themselves, which emerge in response to ongoing tendencies of centralization by the dominant ethnic group within the subunit, and reflect efforts to renew the territorial political autonomy of Vojvodina and Kosovo in Serbia and demands for the establishment of Serbian autonomy in Croatia and Bosnia-Herzegovina. These also include demands for autonomy through secession throughout Bosnia-Herzegovina (the so-called Serbian Republic of Bosnia-Herzegovina and the Croatian Republic of Herceg-Bosna) as well as in Serbia (namely, Muslim autonomy in Sandžak and Hungarian personal autonomy in Vojvodina). Furthermore, there were also tendencies toward political and even territorial independence in individual regions (that is, Istria in Croatia and Slovenia, and Dalmatia in Croatia).

In effect, there are at least two types of overall political conflicts within federal units (as can be best observed in Croatia and Serbia). The first kind is that of democratic or popular legitimacy during regime change, which has thus far been avoided in Croatia by peaceful transformation of power from the former regime to the new one through the creation of a pact between the former regime and the forces of opposition. As for Serbia, this conflict was postponed in such a way that the old regime retained power and renewed its legitimacy in multiparty elections.

The second type of conflict is that between national/ethnic collectivities. The most dramatic examples are the conflicts between Serbs and Croats and between Serbs and Albanians.[18]

Conflicts of the third type develop in personal relations, in everyday life. This type is characterized by a domination of collective, national ethnic consciousness and identification, as well as a pronounced polarization of day-to-day life. Many of those overwhelmed by nationalist zeal deploy all of their spiritual forces in the service of their nations; nationalism is regarded as a way to salvation. After many calls to die for the nation comes the one to die for the homeland. A man who must permanently struggle for economic survival is an unsuitable subject for democracy. Being a citizen implies being aware of one's own rights and freedoms as well as of the means to fight for them. State socialism, however, relied on an amorphous mass, dependent on the state for survival, that could be easily manipulated by leaders and "leading roles of the party." To motivate the masses, the leaders had to make people aware of the reasons for their national association and the objectives they wish to realize. To accomplish this, they used the principle of "divide and conquer" by widely disseminating the illusion that the nation, nationalism, and chauvinism offer the way to accomplish humanity and national freedom.

The intensification of these conflicts in Yugoslavia defined the political environment within which the reform was initiated and pursued with decreasing chances of success. Its failure became final with Serbia's breach of Yugoslavia's payments system and its appropriation of 1.7 billion dollars, followed by an escalation of nationalism, interrepublican conflicts, and initiation of an open war.[19]

The so-called Slovenian war resulted in a new and even graver phenomenon: the overall loss of confidence. The primary question was no longer whether Yugoslavia would be a federation or a confederation, but whether there existed any political will or viable social forces interested in a "new beginning." Conflicts at all levels intensified and the psychosis of war ultimately prevailed. Fear and hatred provoked open ethnic conflicts. The spiral of conflicts increasingly relied on the spiral of fear, while the rule of fear accelerated engagement in armed clashes. There was less and less recognition of the fact that civil war was a zero-sum game, and that it could only bring numerous casualties without providing solutions for a single problem.

The Communist *Nomenklatura* and the "New Elites" of Nationalism

The republican elites (Slovenia, Croatia, and Serbia), parts of the federal leadership, and the highest ranks of the military operated on the premise that their political objectives should be realized at any cost. Initially the methods they employed included the internal destabilization o "adversaries" by means of encouraging ethnic conflicts on their terri tory, or by tolerating and allowing the drafting of "volunteers" and mercenaries to be sent to areas affected by ethnic rebellion. Ultimately, such methods escalated into open war. Thus, to a considerable extent, the civil war in Yugoslavia, which gained momentum in the second half of 1991, was the result of the intentional incitement of hatred between nations. It was the consequence of political recklessness on the part of leading personalities who played the key roles in politics during a highly sensitive period of social dislocation and uncertainty. It was also the consequence of a restricted concept of social transformation formulated by national political elites who were interested, above all, in the perpetuation of their own power.

In Yugoslavia, the collapse of state socialism and the initiation of fundamental economic reforms, coupled with the introduction of democratic rules and institutions and political pluralism, resulted in the proliferation of about 200 political parties,[20] the overwhelming majority of which, with their individual national programs, enlisted the support of members and voters exclusively within a particular ethnic community.[21] There was not a single ethnic community that did not form at least one national political party. The first multiparty democratic elections resulted in the election of new governing political elites in all the nation-state republics.[22] Irrespective of differences in names, the victorious parties in all the republics primarily relied on nationalism. The differences between them were to be found in their ideological self-legitimization; some (for instance in Slovenia, Croatia, Bosnia-Herzegovina, and Macedonia) defined themselves as "democratic" while others were "socialist" (that is, in Serbia and Montenegro). Yet their essential similarity is clearly visible in the preference of the present ruling political elites for the old statism and state nationalism;[23] ideological, cultural, and political

chauvinism; and for the strengthening of state ownership and intervention in the economy conducive to militarization and the strengthening
of state control over society.

The communist *nomenklatura* was the most important source of the
"new elites." While nationalism was initially embraced by the communist regime as but one factor of self-identification, it went on to consume
its entire identity. Thus, nationalism, which was once a means of perpet-
uating communism, eventually became the architect of its demise. When
the crisis of political legitimacy intensified, the authorities used nationalism to prove that their absolute rule was in accordance with the interest
and requirements of their ancestral heritage. This was possible because
historically it was not the federal political elite of Yugoslavia that
thrived, but rather the elites of the constituent federal units (republics
and provinces). Members of the elite were dispersed throughout the
existing institutions as well as those that existed only on paper. The
outcome was the reduction of friction within and among the elites
and a strengthening of the spirit of their association at the level of the
constituent republic or province.[24] Thus, Yugoslavia overcame the
totalitarian dynamics of socialist development only to replace them
with totalitarian nationalist regimes. It only confirmed the insight of
Polish philosopher and former dissident Adam Michnik: that when
seeking to defend their own power, the old communist elites themselves resorted to nationalism and chauvinism. Furthermore, the shift
from communism to nationalism was all the more simple since both
communism and nationalism are collectivist ideologies. Nationalism,
chauvinism, and separatism are equally manichean as Stalinism,
which is based on the dichotomy between "us" and the "(class)
enemies" and which expresses its underlying logic in the slogan
"those who are not with us are against us."

The convergence of communist and nationalist elites in Yugoslavia
became apparent at all levels of government. The most prominent and
best-known examples are Milan Kučan and Slobodan Milošević, current
presidents of the small nationalist states of Slovenia and Serbia, respectively, and former members and leaders of the supreme bodies of the
(Yugoslav) League of Communists. Another example is the former communist general and present leader of the Croatian nationalist state,
Franjo Tudjman. However, the real problem now is that all of these
high-ranking members of the former communist nomenclature and current "national leaders" are backed by populist movements and enjoy the
support, confirmed at the elections, of the majority of voters.

The new elite emerged as an amalgamation of a part of the communist nomenclature, intellectuals of the opposition, dissidents, and nationalist intellectuals.[25] The appearance of new personalities within the elite does not signify the destruction of social foundations and the interests upon which they rested. The new elite do not represent clearly defined social and class interests and, just like the old elite, have a life bond with the state and the nation. While the old elite established their position based on the "knowledge of history," the new elite referred to their "knowledge of the deficiencies of communism."

The composition, habits, and behavior of the elite, and especially the political elite, may have considerable influence on the pace and development of a political system.[26] The elite assume particular weight in societies profoundly divided along ethnic and cultural lines, such as Yugoslavia, which was essentially an elite-led, multiethnic society with many of the characteristics of a confederation. In the post-Tito period, the ethnocentric features of its elite grew into an overwhelming state-nationalist chauvinist pattern of rule that proved a decisive factor in the instability and disintegration of Yugoslavia.[27]

Characteristically, the political elites who emerged through such circumstances could not reach agreement among themselves or resolve conflicts in a peaceful and democratic manner. Among other things, this resulted from the fact that all of the elites had similar political programs aimed at the establishment of a sovereign nation-state at the expense of other nations and national interests. The ethnic exclusionism of the elites led them to look upon others as enemies who ought to be destroyed.[28] The magnitude of the ambitions cultivated by these elites and their attempts to round up the whole of their ethnic community within a sovereign national state inevitably collided with each other.

However, the emergence of these elites did not reverse the government's loss of legitimacy; the establishment was still unable to confirm itself as the most reliable vehicle for fulfillment of the basic needs of society. Therefore, the life of the nation was not freed of the events that provoke changes of the old customs and the destruction of public morality. Under such circumstances, nationalism and chauvinism are easily adopted as ideologies of salvation for various social strata. State nationalism is necessarily joined by other forms of nationalism, both existing and newly created, including the "informal" nationalism of marginal social groups. Actually, this tends to be the case where communist nationalism has replaced or, alternatively, formed an alliance with "anticommunist nationalism," which has, for decades, been kept out of

the public sphere, primarily through repression. This kind of nationalism can succeed in consolidating power, but it cannot secure democratic rule. Therefore, it can be concluded that the newly created
nation-states that retain programs and elites of this kind, could not be
considered complete in terms of democracy and modern developments.

Nationalism: the Enemy of Democracy

In a society such as Yugoslavia, nationalism represents a sort of social
cancer and an enemy of democracy. The basis of democracy rests on an
equal treatment of all individuals irrespective of their ethnic or other
origin, while the creation of national states is based on exclusivist
principles such as the legalization of national segregation and rejection
of pluralism. Furthermore, nationalism offers a means of excluding all
but one's own group; and when a state is based on such insularities,
repression, stagnation, lack of creativity, provincialization, and stupidity
are bound to follow. No individual is allowed to depart from the tedium
of the national (actually chauvinistic, prefabricated) mass. Only one who
"comprises all virtues and expresses the will and views of his nation"
can be singled out; this establishment of the national leader or "father of
the nation" is one of the manifestations of state omnipotence.[29] Where
the collectivity prevails over individuality and individual rights are repressed, the conditions for critical thinking or plural identities are not
found. Within such a context, ideological rhetoric and artificial political
integration rule the day.

Strong nationalist attempts at the preservation of ethnic self-identity,
along with the homogenization of nations and confrontation with "others," lead to the use of nondemocratic methods and subjugation of
human rights and freedoms in favor of national or collective rights. This
mindset was adopted by a number of the rulers of small states belonging
to the former Yugoslavia when they decided that the rights to life,
freedom, and human dignity were worth less than the rights to an
independent Slovenia, independent Croatia, and Greater Serbia on one
side, and a "rump Yugoslavia" on the other. In view of their maximalist
objectives, the elites of the emerging states failed to demonstrate any
will for genuine negotiation, compromise, or agreement on a "third"
Yugoslavia. Forgotten were all arguments in defense of Yugoslavia, although they existed, along with the rights of the Slovenian nation to its
own state. Although numerous reasons and interests existed for the

perpetuation of the Yugoslav social and state community, they lost weight in the face of the constitutional and international recognition of Slovenia and Croatia as independent states. Therefore, January 15, 1992, marked the beginning of the end of the Yugoslav community.

A new political, or even economic, association will not be possible for a long time yet. In the most general terms, this reality is the consequence of the weakness of and lack of support for the forces of democracy and modernization in the Yugoslav drama. The member states of the European Community offered their support to nationalism and the forces of war and conflict. This resulted in the beginning of a new era: the emergence of "incomplete" national states, the intensification of national conflicts, and the introduction of new sources of instability and wars.

Yet the problem can also be attributed to the legacy of the nineteenth century nationalist movements. The elites who won the first multiparty elections—inspired by feelings of "democratic exclusivity" and believing themselves to be the very incarnation of democracy, rather than just a temporary majority within it—contributed to the transformation of the loyal and semiloyal opposition into the disloyal opposition. Furthermore, this sort of behavior provoked defensive reactions on the part of nations that could not accept such repression. Finally, the slogan commonly associated with the creation of national states appears to be "now or never." This is exactly why a liberal and democratic Yugoslavia was no more viable than the newly created states themselves.

Nationalism was confirmed as nonacceptance of a liberal-democratic culture, procedures, and institutions. Repressive national populism, in principle, rejects democratic consensus-building and regards liberal federalism, with its requirement of the inviolability of individual rights, as its greatest adversary. The absence of liberal democracy precludes resolution of the national issue, and an unresolved national question militates against acceptance of liberal democratic institutions. Peoples who were, for forty years, denied a democracy wherein they could voice their legitimate interests began to express their grievances with overemphasized emotionalism and manifestations befitting the era of tribalism.

The drama and disintegration of Yugoslavia can also be seen as a struggle for independence of individual Yugoslav republics (a struggle that caused ethnic conflicts). The downfall of the communist model of centralized power (through Communist party rule) necessarily strengthened the tendency toward decentralization. However, this ordinary and necessary process was accompanied by a struggle for total independence unattainable in a modern society, and especially in Europe, where the international integration of states (particularly within the European Union) implied transfer of numerous political decisions to the supranational level. In effect, although political mobilization of ethnic groups most often results in ethnic conflicts (thus giving nationalist movements and ethnic policies a primarily adverse connotation), national and ethnic movements can also provide a positive challenge to the processes of modernization and establishment of states.

Lessons to Be Learned

The question of what Yugoslavia really was, a question that remained unanswered for quite a long time, has been answered by the nationalist rejection of Yugoslavia as even a mere alliance of independent states. Yugoslavia was not accepted as a manifestation of Europeanism through pluralism and regional integration. Generally speaking, discussions about Yugoslavia tend to grossly oversimplify the issues involved, as evinced, for example, by the frequent disregard for the historical context of the Yugoslav crisis.

Yugoslavia's turning point was in 1989. That year witnessed and revealed the state's economic collapse and the bankruptcy of the identifying values of socialism, self-management, and Yugoslavia as a confederation under communist rule. Socialist ideology made way for nationalist ideology, homogenization, and hegemony. Since then, all political, social, and other conflicts have been expressed exclusively in nationalist terms. All the existing differences and the complexity of the society were replaced by only one reality: national divisions. This finally led to the civil interethnic conflicts that made it all but impossible to find a formula for the reform of Yugoslav society that was acceptable to all, and left in its wake material, political, spiritual, and emotional devastation out of which emerged incomplete national states.

CHAPTER THREE

The 1974 Constitution and Constitutional Process as a Factor in the Collapse of Yugoslavia

Vojin Dimitrijević

T HE CONSTITUTION of the Socialist Federal Republic of Yugoslavia, promulgated on February 21, 1974, has often been cited as one of the reasons for the war, or at least as one of the contributing factors leading to Yugoslavia's disorderly and bloody dissolution. This chapter attempts to examine the validity of this claim. From the outset, however, it is necessary to place the constitution in proper historical perspective and to understand the underlying reasons for the manner in which it was formulated.

The Historical and Conceptual Origins of the 1974 Constitution

Under socialism, Yugoslavia was famous for its social and legislative experiments, and for the frequency with which it changed its constitutions and its official name. After the 1946 Constitution, which was a rather uninventive replica of Stalin's Soviet Constitution of 1936, new constitutions with a "self-management" character were adopted in 1953, 1963, and 1974. Furthermore, these constitutions were amended extensively in 1967, 1968, 1971, 1981, and 1988.[1]

Whereas the 1946 Constitution could be explained as the effort of a thoroughly "Bolshevized" Communist party to impose its will and to apply the time-tested Soviet "solutions" to Yugoslavia, starting from the 1953 Basic Law, the communist leadership was at pains to develop an original and self-styled approach with respect to the purpose, justification, organization, and development of a socialist state outside the Soviet-dominated camp of "people's democracies." The story of the Stalin-Tito split is well known and need not be retold here.[2] In this context it is important to note, however, that the ideological differences within the Soviet Communist party (including its international organ, the Cominform, the substitute for the dissolved Communist International) had not preceded the conflict, but were developed by the Yugoslav Communists after 1948. Although branded as traitors and capitalist collaborators by almost all established Communist parties in the world, the Yugoslav leadership, in fact, believed that the wholesale incorporation of Yugoslavia into the Western sphere of influence would be against their Marxist worldview and would eventually result in their loss of power. Thus, the Yugoslav leadership made great efforts to produce an ideological basis for a system that remained socialist and Marxist while appearing to be more humane and democratic, and which at the same time removed the country from the Soviet orbit.

With borrowings from the early Marx, the anarchists, social democrats, and even fascist corporatists,[3] the doctrine of self-management was adopted and put into experimental use in 1950 by legislation instituting workers' councils in enterprises, and was enshrined in all Yugoslav constitutions and relevant statutes after 1953. The practical effects of self-management will be discussed later, but it should be noted at the outset that it became a great public relations success among left-wing intellectuals everywhere. This success, combined with a benevolent attitude on the part of Western security establishments toward the first defector from the Soviet empire, shielded the Tito regime for a long time from serious criticism, both from the liberal left and the conservative right. The nature of dissidence in Yugoslavia and the lack of support for a human rights movement there can be explained by the fact that for a long while communist Yugoslavia was seen as either an attractive social experiment or at least something "much better" than the Soviet Union and its satellites.

Security considerations and Tito's idiosyncratic thirst for recognition and pomp accounted for the related doctrine of nonalignment. As a result, since the late 1950s Yugoslavia has not been isolated from the world community, and, together with its president, enjoyed international prestige far in excess of its power and potential. Yugoslav constitutions since 1963 contain lengthy provisions on international relations, in which the traditional debt to "socialist internationalism" was combined with allegiance to "peaceful coexistence."

The break with the USSR had, however, an effect that was not immediately noticeable. Namely, the rebellion against Soviet dominance was at the same time a departure from the universalist communist dream of a world society where the "national" proletariat would have only one state, devoid of the bourgeois trappings of ethnicity. Already the Soviet Union was not a nation-state but the embryo of a universal workers' state open to new citizens from everywhere. Many communists, including those from pre-war Yugoslavia, had no difficulty imagining themselves and their country becoming a part of the USSR. In 1948, however, Tito and his associates stood up against Soviet and other communists on behalf of the right of every national Communist party to run things its own way or, to put it quite bluntly, to establish its own sovereign dictatorship (of the proletariat). This brand of communism was rightly called "national communism," and it eventually became very popular in Europe and elsewhere, under different guises (such as "euro-communism" in Italy and Spain). However, the nagging question remained as to how a universalist doctrine could be adapted in this manner. In the case of Yugoslavia, the unanswered question was: on whose behalf did Tito stand against Stalin and ruthlessly purge his opponents in Yugoslavia? On behalf of the sovereign state of Yugoslavia, on behalf of its ethnically diverse population, or on behalf of a well-defined nation? The logical next step, to grant to the communist parties in the (ethnic) nations of Yugoslavia independence from the "supranational" League of Communists of Yugoslavia, was eventually taken.

Nationalism was somewhat legitimized among the communists in 1948 and thereafter, intensified in response to the latent and overt nationalism of the rest of the population and noncommunist political actors. It is true that Tito's regime became popular in Yugoslavia only after the rift with Stalin, but the nature of the support was again dubious in socialist or communist terms. It was resistance against foreign domination, which was the first step toward other kinds of nationalism. From the very beginning, Tito and the Yugoslav Communist party met serious and organized internal resistance only from nationalists. In the war, apart from German and Italian units, the Partisans had to fight the Ustashe groups and the army of the "Independent State of Croatia," the forces of the Serb movement of general Mihailović, the Slovene nationalist "White Guard," and the Albanian nationalist bands in Kosovo, among others. This continued long after the seizure of power. Whereas the orderly, rule of law–based opposition of the old political parties was easily quelled in 1945 and 1946, for quite some time the new regime had to fight incursions of nationalist guerrillas, especially in Croatia.

Organized and systematic action abroad against the communist regime in Yugoslavia was undertaken almost without exception by nationalist emigré groups, some of whom engaged in terrorism. On the other hand, nonnationalists among them found it very difficult to organize "all-Yugoslav" groups. Their statements in favor of democracy sounded too abstract, and therefore found little resonance in Yugoslavia itself. Finally, after the definite stabilization of the regime in Yugoslavia, dissidence gradually became increasingly tainted by nationalism. To be sure, the most famous dissident, Milovan Djilas, was a proponent of democracy and modern socialism, but opponents of Yugoslav communism of the same or similar democratic persuasion were increasingly difficult to find.[4] As in some other communist countries, in order to get international support nationalist dissidents masqueraded as democrats. One should remember that at the time, human rights groups were hailing as genuine anticommunist democratic dissidents only people like the present chief ideologue of the ultranationalist Communist (renamed socialist) party of Serbia, Mihailo Marković; the chauvinist and anti-Semitic president of Croatia, Franjo Tudjman; the nationalist-militarist Slovenian minister of defense, Janez Janša; and the fascist Serbian leader Vojislav Šešelj (until recently closely allied with the national communists of Serbia).

Absent the benefit of hindsight, there seems to be no evidence that the communist leadership of Yugoslavia was aware of the dimensions of the national issue, or at least [not] until the late 1960s, and even then it approached the issue from the wrong angle.[5] Initially, the communists were carried away by their success in the liberation war, where their investment in the Yugoslav cause and the "fraternity and unity" of the Yugoslav nations proved to be politically prudent, especially at a time when all of them were treated by the aggressors as racially inferior. In resolutely supporting the federal structure of the state they thought they had done away with the perennial squabbling in pre-war Yugoslavia, where centralism meant Serb domination. This was acceptable to the democratic public opinion, including the remnants of the traditional political parties, which were more concerned with the brutal imposition of communist power via the tested methods of intimidation by secret police and mobs, as well as by rigged elections.

The new rulers believed that the "national question" could be resolved in the Marxist fashion (and it should be remembered that Joseph Stalin was the foremost Marxist authority in the field), while in fact they swept it under the carpet immediately after consecrating their wartime federalist program in the 1946 Constitution. Subjects related to national claims, indeed the history of national conflicts (including the gruesome massacres during the war), became taboo, along with everything the authorities chose to label as "nationalism." For a long while it became impossible to air national grievances openly. As a result, such grievances went into a kind of political underground from which they reemerged in full force, albeit in a primitive and warped form, only after Tito had been safely dead for a number of years.

In solving the "national question," the Yugoslav communists, notwithstanding their amazing and very noncommunist powers of adaptation, still carried over some of their pre-war ideological baggage. The crucial feature of their rule, which affected all judgments on constitutionality in Yugoslavia, was the disdain of laws and legality. In the view of at least Tito and the enormously influential "old guard," statutes were at best mere instruments of rule, and constitutions were largely ornamental. They were not to be taken seriously, since behind them was the inalienable power of the Communist party that would decide or impose its will whenever it deemed necessary. The central paradox of Yugoslavia, reflected in all constitutions, was that while the state was federal in form, it was run or "guided" by the Communist party, which functioned under the principle of "democratic centralism." Thus, although it appeared that the federal authority was not constitutionally empowered to remove leaders in the republics, it did so with relative ease so long as it was the intention of the central party leadership. Of course, Tito's autocratic position as the unchallenged party leader (and as head of state for life) was decisive, which helps explain the turn of events after his death.

There was another inheritance from the pre-war era that was bound to influence the attitude of many Serbs, especially those of a nationalist persuasion, toward the new constitutional order. The pre-war Kingdom of Yugoslavia was characterized by the indigenous as well as the international communists, and by many others, as a centralist state dominated by the Serb elites. The instructions of the Comintern went as far as suggesting to the Yugoslav communists to cooperate even with the rightist non-Serb nationalists, including the Ustashe, in attempts to bring down a state that was controlled by the Serbian bourgeoisie in communion with the treacherous bourgeoisie of the non-Serb nations.[6] In spite of the fact that, outside what was later to become Serbia proper, the rank and file of the Partisans was disproportionally Serb, the obsession with reducing the danger that the most populous nation would pose to the new federation remained. Thus, the lands inhabited mostly by the Serbs were divided into several parts. In addition to Serbia proper (roughly corresponding to the borders of Serbia in 1912), there was a separate republic of Montenegro,[7] and two autonomous provinces were created within Serbia: Vojvodina, with a Serb majority, and Kosovo and Metohija, where the majority of the population was increasingly Albanian.[8] Other Serbs remained in republics defined by the names of other nations, or in Bosnia-Herzegovina, which was the only "a-national" federal unit. Proposals to create an autonomous province in Croatia, encompassing areas where the Serbs were the majority (Krajina), were not accepted.[9] As a result, from the very beginning, many Serbs regarded the overall political arrangement as a solution that was obtained at their expense. The ultranationalists among them have had even wider complaints: for them, Macedonia was also carved out of Serbia (that had annexed it in 1913) and the Macedonians, as well as the later recognized ethnic Muslims, were allegedly estranged Serbs who had been encouraged by the new regime to adopt an "artificial" ethnicity.[10]

The Situation Immediately Preceding the Adoption of the Constitution

Since the framework of the federation was already determined in 1946, the 1974 Constitution cannot be held responsible for it. However, developments immediately preceding the drafting of that document were probably what motivated its drafters and can explain the specifics of that constitution.

In the 1960s there were visible signs of a crisis in Yugoslavia, manifested in economic difficulties, social tension, and sometimes overt nationalism. They were mostly beyond the comprehension of the Partisan ruling elite, but inspired the reform-minded younger generation in the Communist party to look for new solutions. They essentially tried to modernize self-management (nobody dared mention capitalism) by giving it real substance in terms of some kind of market economy, and by freeing it from the constraints of statism. In 1966, two important events took place: the political police were weakened and their conservative chief, Aleksandar Ranković, removed by Tito himself;[11] and at the same time, ambitious economic reforms were announced in order to do away with rigid central planning and most of the state and party tutelage.

The economic reform was unacceptable both to Tito's conservative inner circle and to Marxist intellectuals, who in June 1968 inspired and led a curious revolt of the students in Belgrade and in some other university centers. It was an imitation of similar leftist outbursts in Paris and elsewhere insofar as its thrust was against the "red bourgeoisie," and in favor of a truly Marxist education and full egalitarianism.[12] The students themselves were generally against the regime, but some of their most influential intellectual leaders were neo-Marxists, concerned with doctrinal purity and egalitarianism and who perceived the new "middle class" as the greatest danger to society. While his less clever lieutenants got panicky, Tito defused the crisis quite simply by making a conciliatory and paternalistic speech praising the young generation and inviting students to go back to their classrooms and libraries. Nevertheless, the regime immediately seized the opportunity to scrap the "socially unjust" program of economic reform and to strengthen the police, while the student revolt was blamed on foreign agents.

This is when the modernizers within the party (no other channels were available at the time) shifted the center of their activity to the more economically developed republics, anticipating that the managerial elites there would be stronger in the absence of the federal dogmatists and their primitive supporters from the less developed areas. In some ways, this was a resistance against the center, essentially similar to that of Tito against the Comintern, but this time an association with nationalism was more inviting. This became quite clear in Croatia, where the reformist communists, headed by Miko Tripalo, appealed to the population and almost immediately got unwanted and loud support from Croat nationalists, some of them invoking the memory of the puppet Nazi state in Croatia and the imagery of the Ustashe, which was extremely disquieting to the local Serbs.[13]

At the same time, the Serbian Communist party was in the hands of reformists around Marko Nikezić, who, despite the vulgarity of the nationalist mass movement in Croatia and the formidable challenge of Albanian nationalism in Kosovo, were better at handling Serb nationalism.[14]

In Slovenia, the reformists, led by Stane Kavčič, were most concerned with economic development, which they primarily envisaged within the boundaries of that republic. Nonetheless, they could not have been seriously accused of being nationalists.

After some hesitation, Tito did away with all the reformist party leadership. From the way he and his conservative associates handled the affair it was quite obvious that they were less worried by nationalism than with what they called "anarcho-liberalism."[15] The purge, initiated by a circular letter countersigned by Stane Dolanc,[16] had the makings of a cultural revolution. Directors of the most successful enterprises were sacked (irrespective of self-management), the ablest editors and journalists were dismissed, university professors were removed (in clear violation of the laws), and senior civil servants were demoted to be replaced by docile and incompetent *apparatchiks*, obedient to the new federal and republican party leadership, which now included a considerable number of aged Partisans recalled from retirement or semiretirement. Without satisfying the newly introduced criterion of "moral-political fitness," even junior posts in the administration, schools, and enterprises could not be held. Marxism was (for the first time!) introduced in the obligatory part of the curricula in all schools at all levels. In many cases, but not as a rule, criminal prosecution followed.[17]

The wholesale regression in the early 1970s of the once comparatively attractive Yugoslav approach to socialism, which I believe was the true beginning of the Yugoslav catastrophe, went largely unnoticed abroad. Since it was mostly directed against the liberal elite, the purge did not involve mass persecution of ordinary citizens, who had more rights than the inhabitants of other socialist countries, including the all-important right to travel abroad. This enabled many of them to be migrant workers whose income, together with generous foreign credits that followed, set the stage for the fundamental economic crisis that was to re-emerge in the 1980s.[18] Accordingly, even human rights organizations had to concentrate on the repression of free opinion and expression, which, again in comparison with the Soviet bloc, looked politically irrelevant.[19]

It is very important to note that, at the time of the 1974 Constitution's gestation, communism (in its "real-socialist" version) looked quite alive and well, and the West was perceived as being in moral, economic, and strategic disarray. As a number of selected events will demonstrate, this was the beginning of the end of the cold war, which resulted in détente and the increasing relevance of the nonaligned movement.

In 1970 the Soviet Union tightened its grip on Czechoslovakia, and West Germany normalized its relations with Poland by recognizing the Oder-Neisse border. In 1971, the Beijing regime replaced Taiwan as the representative of China at the United Nations, and the Soviet Union and India signed a treaty of friendship and mutual cooperation. In 1972 President Nixon visited China and the Soviet Union, and both Germanies recognized one another. In 1973 the Western powers recognized East

Germany, and West Germany received Brezhnev, as did the United States and France; West Germany normalized relations with Czechoslovakia, and, after the Yom Kippur war, Arab oil-exporting countries declared an oil embargo against the West. In 1974 Willy Brandt had to step down because of the presence of East German spies in his entourage, India exploded its first atomic bomb, and President Nixon was forced to resign as a result of the Watergate scandal.

In this environment, the regime in Yugoslavia had no reason to believe that the prevailing interpretation of communism was historically doomed or that there was any challenge to its comfortable international position as a tolerable socialist state and one of the leaders of non-alignment, exempt from the anti-Western rage in the developing countries. It is no wonder then that, facing the troubles at home, the Titoist old guard believed that more of the same was the proper medicine. This meant, in the first place, strengthening socialism and the role of the League of Communists and deepening self-management. This universal cure meant that the federal structure would remain intact and that it, too, would be "deepened."

Finally, Tito's "cultural revolution" purged the League of Communists of all liberal and pragmatic reformers and gave prominence in all professions to opportunists and poorly educated followers of the official line. At that time, no important influence on state matters was possible from without the party; nonparty philosophers, political scientists, jurists, and economists were, after 1971, reduced to virtual nonpersons (that is, their professional lives and estates were destroyed), although, to be sure, physical repression was exceptional. There was, on the other side, an army of apologetic hands eager to apply their unimpressive skills in the production of convoluted and long legislative texts and ideological treatises. The tendency, amply confirmed in the 1974 Constitution and the general climate it favored and created, was toward anonymity. A "name" could only be established in areas most remote from politics: as in many other socialist countries, this eventually resulted in strange political elites at the outset of postcommunist pluralism, composed of illustrious personalities devoid of political gifts and with little experience and skill in handling public matters.

The Constitutional Amendments and Public Debates of 1971

The 1974 Constitution cannot be studied in isolation from its corresponding preparatory work, which was already undertaken in 1971 in the form of amendments to the 1963 Constitution. Draft amendments were formulated early in 1971 and, as usual, put to "public debate." This invitation was accepted in good faith in some intellectual quarters, with results reminiscent of Mao's "thousand flowers" campaign. One of the liveliest discussions was held at the University of Belgrade and resulted in the arrest and sentencing of one professor of law, the outright dismissal of several other members of the faculty of law, and still others being relieved of teaching duties. The faculty journal containing the papers and the summary of the discussion was destroyed and the issue was banned.[20] This was a clear indication that the intentions of the authorities were antiliberal and antidemocratic but, in spite of some participants in the debate having been labeled as nationalists, repression was not clearly (or only) antinationalist.

The amendments were perceived by liberal critics as further complicating the political process. Decisionmaking in state organs would become all but impossible without the extraconstitutional intervention of the party and its guidance. There had already been a tendency to fragment self-management and confine it to trivial matters, thus diverting the interest of the population from crucial political issues. Another clear tendency was to weaken the federation in favor of the republics by delegating more power to the legislatures of the latter, and by preventing the federal parliament from making a decision if it was vetoed by the members of a federal unit. This, in addition to the quasi independence of the autonomous provinces, was again an argument in favor of the further deterioration of the position of Serbs, many of whom believed that the nationalists in Croatia had been compensated for their apparent defeat. The overall effect was to strengthen the party leadership in the republics and to transform them into semi-independent fiefdoms of the republican communist elite. This was probably due to the reinstated conservatives being only superficial Marxists, abhorring liberal democracy and capitalist entrepreneurs (or, as they called them, "technocrats"), but not entirely immune to nationalism, if it could serve their autocratic ambitions. The thinning ideology created a void that was to be filled by nationalism.

The 1974 Constitution as Law

After another series of empty public debates (at this point no one really dared to participate) the new constitution was promulgated on February

21, 1974. It was an unusual, enormously long (406 articles), verbose, and confused text, which was nevertheless praised as original and nonlegalistic by apologists in Yugoslavia, as well as by some observers abroad,[21] thus confirming the presumption that its purpose was to hide rather than reveal the true intent of the regime. Mystification was intensified by new jargon, difficult to comprehend in the original Yugoslav versions, and almost impossible to translate.[22] Thus, the old dogmatic communist tendency to rename in order to change was taken to extremes.[23]

The word "delegate," for instance, became one such new term, used not only to indicate parliamentary deputies but also members of intermediary delegations that elected them after being themselves elected by inferior delegations. This concealed a system of multiple indirect elections where the population had the chance to choose only at the lowest possible level, whereas the delegates were fully bound by their mandate and were easily replaceable if they did not follow the instructions of the delegations (which, naturally, were convened only when the party found it opportune). In the jargon, "delegates were responsible to their delegational base." Federal decisionmaking was thus made even more remote than before, when there was at least an illusion that the elections with one candidate presented a real choice, and that the deputy was responsible to his or her electorate. At the microscopic local level, voters were unfamiliar with the names of the proposed candidates for the basic delegations, so the symbolic presence of a few more candidates was meaningless. This charade was called the delegation system and was praised as a major departure from "bourgeois parliamentarism" toward direct democracy.[24]

An examination of the new terms is probably the least tedious way of introducing the 1974 Constitution. The following, therefore, is a discussion and interpretation of its central elements.

The Inherent Inequality of Citizens

The population was divided into the "working class," "working people," and "citizens." "Working class" was not clearly defined, but it was there to indicate the source of power (that is, Article 1), in accordance with Marxist theory. "Working people" were for all practical purposes men and women employed in state ("socially owned") enterprises and institutions. They were also "citizens," but others were "citizens" only and could not fully benefit from the electoral process because they were considered as falling outside "self-managing organizations and communities," which, through their particular delegations, sent delegates to the federal parliament. In theory, ordinary citizens were theoretically able to act, together with "working people," in "socio-political communities," which was the new name given to territorial units, from the federation to the commune, but their real participation was in "local communities" of their immediate neighborhood, where their electoral powers ended with the selection of a "delegation." To the "working people" was reserved the right to join "socio-political organizations" that masqueraded as civil society while in reality were under the firm control of federal authorities. Their creation and activity was dependent on the approval of the Socialist Alliance of the Working People (a successor to the National Front without even the token participation of any political party but the communists, who were the guiding force in the Alliance and formally appointed members of its leading bodies).[25]

The Mystique of Self-Management

The Constitution devoted most of its provisions to self-management in the public sector, which was designated as "associated labor" and included all activities performed with "socially owned" (that is, state) resources. The whole structure was fragmented to the extreme. Self-management became fully universal and covered noneconomic activities, such as the state administration, schools, and theaters. A former enterprise or institution became an "organization of associated labor" and was divided into several "basic organizations of associate labor," which in the frenzy of the implementation of the constitution became ridiculously minute and artificial, such as schools designated by classes or groups of subjects taught, typists representing a separate basic unit from accountancy, and so forth. Organizations of associated labor could then further associate in "composite associations of associated labor," such as railways, or cooperate with individuals in "contractual organizations of associated labor." The whole self-management system was protected by "social attorneys of self-management" and "self-management courts."

A conscious effort was made to dislodge the legislative functions from the parliaments and transfer them to self-managing bodies, which, instead of law, created "self-managing agreements," "social compacts," and "interrepublican compacts."

The "Classic" Political Provisions

In contrast to the self-managing parts of the Constitution, which account for most of its length and which were reinforced in 1976 by the still longer (671 articles!) accompanying Law on Associated Labor,[26] core constitutional matters were addressed with less rhetoric and greater clarity and appeared to allow for a better glimpse into compromises made in the party leadership. Kardelj's and his associates' ideas about the ramifications of integral self-management were not opposed by anyone in the party, either because they were irrelevant to the exercise of real power, or too difficult to follow, or appeared attractively but innocuously learned and original departures from "bourgeois parliamentarism." In contrast, articles relating to the structure of the federation, its competencies, and relevant decisionmaking were easier to understand and became increasingly important as it became obvious that the republican parties gained more independence and that their political arrangements, even if not an exact replica of power relations within the League of Communists, should be protected from the intervention of a federal parliament. It is therefore certain that the important (closed) debate in the supreme quarters of the League was about these matters, and that it was there that some opinions emerged that were denounced as "unacceptable" by Mijalko Todorović,[27] who as president of the Constitutional Commission had introduced the draft, although he failed to identify them explicitly.

The principal message was that, in spite of class rhetoric, the federal state was based on a national arrangement where even nations originally not considered to be the "titular nations" of Yugoslavia came to play a full role. The Slavic Muslims, principally inhabiting Bosnia-Herzegovina, had been promoted in 1971 to a full-fledged Yugoslav people under a religious name, which was not only a misnomer for the nonreligious majority among them, but proved later to be full of dreadful consequences. Others, like the Albanians and Hungarians, got a better status under another new euphemism for national minorities, "narodnost," meaningless in Serbo-Croatian and poorly translatable into English as "nationality."[28] Article 1 defined the Socialist Federal Republic of Yugoslavia as:

> . . . a federal state having the form of a state community of voluntarily united nations and their Socialist Republics, and of the Socialist Autonomous Provinces of Vojvodina and Kosovo, which are constituent parts of the Socialist Republic of Serbia, based on the power of and

self-management by the working class and all working people; it is at the same time a socialist self-management democratic community of working people and citizens and of nations and nationalities, having equal rights. . . .

Self-Determination and Secession

In Article 3 the republics were referred to as states, based on the "sovereignty of the people" and ". . . communities of the working people and citizens, and of nations and nationalities having equal rights." This was a clear indication of a drift toward a confederate structure for the Yugoslav federation. The republics were states but the federation was a "state community" in the context of which, unlike the republics, the term "sovereignty" was not used. All this was accompanied by an ominous statement, in the introductory part of the Constitution:

The nations of Yugoslavia, proceeding from the right of every nation to self-determination, including the right to secession, on the basis of their will freely expressed in the common struggle of all nations and nationalities in the National Liberation War and Socialist Revolution, and in conformity with their historic aspirations, aware that further consolidation of their brotherhood and unity is in the common interest, have, together with the nationalities with which they live, united in a federal republic of free and equal nations and nationalities and founded a socialist federal community of working people—the Socialist Federal Republic of Yugoslavia. . . .

Without indulging in legalistic squabbles about whether the rights to self-determination and secession were or were not extinguished by the creation of Yugoslavia or by the adoption of this or some other constitution, it should be noted that in addition to legitimizing self-determination and secession in this, albeit inoperative, part of the constitution, it remained unclear whether the subjects of this right were ethnic nations, as opposed to peoples in the sense of inhabitants of a state or territory,[29] and whether it also applied to "nationalities" (that is, minorities within a republic or national state). The procedure by which these rights were to be realized was not regulated by the constitution, nor anywhere else. After 1989 this was a complicating factor of extreme importance. The remaining federal authorities declared the decisions of some republics to secede as unconstitutional, but this interpretation was challenged by the argument that Yugoslavia was dissolving.[30] The seceding republics claimed, however, all the territory that had been theirs as constituent parts of Yugoslavia, thus indicating that in this respect they believed that "people" was to be understood in the territorial sense. This was generally opposed by the Serbs, who maintained that the right to self-determination belonged to ethnic nations, encompassing, in particular, Serbs in Croatia and Bosnia-Herzegovina.[31] The term "nationalities" was used by some Albanians in Kosovo to make claims for a separate republic, independent state, or even unification with Albania. The vagueness and incompleteness of the constitution made the process of secession (or dissolution) even more disorderly.

Autonomous Provinces and Minorities

The indication that the autonomous provinces were parts of Serbia was meant to appease some Serbian communists, and these entities were defined in Article 4 not as states but as "sociopolitical communities." Nevertheless, this could not conceal the fact that the autonomous provinces were, for all practical purposes, promoted to the status of full-fledged federal subunits. According to the same article, it was at the level of such subunits that nations and nationalities realized their sovereign rights. Furthermore, the constitution gave a clear mandate for the autonomous provinces' participation in federal decisionmaking conferring territorially based powers. Their role within Serbia was envisaged as their optional participation in the affairs of Serbia without mentioning their subordination to the republic of which they were to be constituent parts. In Article 3, the autonomous provinces were listed, together with the republics, as constituent parts of Yugoslavia. All this led to the widely accepted designation, by the masters of jargon, of the autonomous provinces as "elements of the federation."[32]

Parity in the Federation

The existing tendency toward confederation was cemented in those provisions of the 1974 Constitution relating to the design of the organs of the federation, the decisionmaking process within them, and the hierarchy of legislative acts. As in most federations, the federal parliament (the Assembly of SFRY) was bicameral. The chamber representing federal units (Chamber of Republics and Provinces) was composed, as usual in federal states, of an equal number (twelve) of "delegates" from all republics, elected by their respective assemblies, with the important addition that the autonomous provinces would also be represented, although by a lesser number (eight) of representatives (Article 292). The lower chamber (Federal Chamber), which in federations normally reflects the size of the populations of the federal units, was constituted according to the same principle as the upper: it was to be composed of an equal number (thirty) of delegates from each republic, and of twenty representatives from each autonomous province. They were not directly elected by the population, but were the result of the cumbersome delegation system, the nominations being controlled by the Socialist Alliance of the Working People (that is, the local League of Communists) (Article 291).[33] This arrangement was criticized both by liberals, who complained of discrimination against more populous federal units, and by most Serbs, who found it detrimental to Serbia, as a state in the federation, and to Serbs, the most numerous nation. Fear of Serb domination, traditionally shared by communists and non-Serb nationalists, was undoubtedly the principal concern.[34]

Consensus and Paralysis in the Federal Parliament

The essentially unequal composition of the Federal Chamber was of only symbolic significance. The real and fatal flaw of the constitution was that it prevented any decisions from being adopted if opposed by any single federal unit (including the autonomous provinces). The size of its delegation was irrelevant in this respect. To begin with, the Chamber of Republics and Provinces was unable to conduct business unless all republican and provincial delegations, as well as the majority of delegates, were present (Article 295), which enabled one delegation to formally paralyze the chamber. Furthermore, most important statutes and other decisions, such as the adoption of "social plans," regulation of the monetary system, the total volume of budgetary expenditures, ratification of international treaties, and even the chamber's own procedural rules, could be adopted by that chamber only after it had ensured the "adjustment to the positions" of the assemblies of the republics and autonomous provinces (Article 286). This meant not only long delays but also that, in such cases, the vote in the chamber was by delegation, and not by individual members so that each delegation, including the smaller ones of autonomous provinces, could prevent the adoption of the decision (Article 295). This was a step further than the double majority that had been introduced by the 1971 amendments and that had required majorities *within* each delegation. Consequently, in this house of eighty-eight members the only majority possible was eight to zero! The grip of the republican and provincial party elites was thus made even stronger: by instructing the whole delegation, they destroyed the individuality of the delegates and were fully insured against federalist and liberal mavericks or suprarepublican alliances.

The result was that in the Chamber of Republics and Provinces there was gradually less and less deliberation. The delegates were waiting in the corridors or in the quasi-exterritorial premises of their delegations for the republican and provincial powers to send in their agreements and, if there was no objection, proceed to confirm them by delegational vote. Debate took place only if some of the less rigid republican or provincial authorities had given conditional consent to a decision, allowing some liberty for its delegation to compromise with others. Even to a casual visitor to the parliament it became abundantly clear that things happened elsewhere.

In part IV, chapter I, article 3 the constitution provided for some rules to govern the situation of an impasse caused by lack of consensus among the republics and provinces. It involved new consultations with the federal units, whereupon the Federal Executive Council (the government) could propose to the presidency the adoption of a decree on temporary measures, which had to be confirmed by the Chamber of Republics and Provinces, this time by a two-thirds majority of all delegates (Articles 301, 302). If such a majority could not be mustered, a simple majority was sufficient to allow the presidency itself to adopt a temporary measure, pending the final passage of the statute (Article 302). Given the composition of the presidency, the creation of a majority by a single nation was excluded.

The Chamber of Republics and Provinces was the more important house of the parliament, and was becoming more so with the passage of time. Most matters of relevance were either decided by it or with its consent (Articles 286, 288). To be sure, the Federal Chamber had a number of formal powers that looked important, such as its right to adopt amendments to the federal constitution, to decide on changes to the (external) boundaries of Yugoslavia, to adopt the federal budget, and to declare war; the others were either empty pomposities, such as to "lay down the foundations of the internal and foreign policy" or to "formulate the policy of enforcement of federal statutes or other regulations enacted by it," or largely trivial, such as the power to "discuss reports, opinions and proposals of the Federal Social Attorney of Self-Management" (Article 285). Even then:

> if a bill, draft regulation or draft enactment or any other issue concerning the general issues of a Republic or Autonomous Province, or *the equality of the nations and nationalities* is on the agenda of the Federal Chamber, and if so requested by the majority of delegates from one Republic or Autonomous Province, resort shall be made to a special procedure to consider and adopt such a bill, draft enactment or issue. . . . (Article 294, emphasis added).

This special process was laid down by the rules of procedure and again involved seeking consensus from the power elites in the republics and provinces. Thus each federal unit or "element of the federation" was at liberty to claim that the issue on the agenda raised sensitive federalism concerns, and thereby to reduce further the lower chamber to a negotiation forum for practically sovereign states. In the Federal Chamber, consisting of 220 deputies, eleven votes (the majority of the delegates from an autonomous province) were sufficient for that purpose. Nobody had any illusions as to the possibility that the majority of the delegates of one republic or province (there were no formal delegations, as in the other house) would not represent the views and attitudes of their mentors in the republics and provinces, who, it should be stressed again, until 1990 belonged to the politbureaus and central committees of the only existing political parties; that is, the relevant Leagues of Communists.

In this light, the commotion about the number of deputies was irrelevant, since the real actors in both chambers of the Federal Assembly were republican and provincial delegations, each of them, irrespective of size, able to obstruct work or prevent a decision from being made. On the other hand, there was no chance of any majority playing a meaningful role: even a larger number of delegations could not outvote a minority and this was even less likely to be achieved by a majority of individual delegates, who by definition were not independent but fully controlled either by their assemblies or by their "delegation base" (Articles 291, 296). The only exception was the temporary measures, where a two-thirds majority, or even a simple majority, could play a role; but this was only a theoretical possibility, made dependent on the attitude of the presidency, which was again constituted on the basis of strict parity.

The Presidency as a Negotiating Forum for the Federal Sub-Units

There were in fact two versions of the presidency incorporated in the 1974 Constitution. One was with Tito, another without him. It was fairly obvious that the post of president of the republic was created only for Tito, who was to be elected "for an unlimited term of office" (Article 333).[35] In the whole logic of the constitution, it was not conceivable that a significant federal office could be exercised by an individual since there could be no delegate, or even person, that did not belong to a constituent federal unit (that is, republic or autonomous province). People who declared themselves "Yugoslavs" were not represented anywhere as a group, although in 1981 they comprised some 6 percent of the whole population.[36] The only trusted Yugoslav was Tito, in spite of his Croat and Slovene ethnic origins. While president of the republic, he was at the same time president of the presidency (Article 335). Curiously, there was no provision making him a member of that body: in the case of Tito, that problem was solved by the fact that the president of the League of Communists of Yugoslavia was an *ex officio* member of the state presidency (Article 321) and the League's president was, of course, Tito. Otherwise, the presidency was equipped to act without the president of the republic, and this was the only place where the constitution implied that Tito was mortal. In fact, the relevant Article 321 determined the composition of the presidency without mentioning the president: in addition to the president of the League of Communists, it consisted of one member from each republic and autonomous province, elected by respective assemblies. After Tito's death, Article 321 was amended to accommodate the abolition of the post of the president of the party. Amendment IV of 1981 stipulated that the League of Communists would be represented by the president of its organ "specified by the By-Laws of the League. . .," which was a unique case of a state constitution explicitly depending on the statutes of a supposedly nongovernmental organization. This brought Yugoslavia closer to the African communist model of a one-party state, with the important difference being that in Africa the party has been wider than the state.

Members of the presidency were not independent. They, like everyone else in the organs of the federation, were delegates of the constituent federal units. This was clear from Article 324, which implied a very easy way for the assemblies of the federal units to remove their representatives from the presidency, as well as from the provision, in the same article, that members of the presidency would, in case of incapacity, be deputized by the presidents of the collective heads (presidencies) of the republics or autonomous provinces. On the other hand, there was no control by the organs of the federation over the composition of the presidency. They could not be impeached in any manner. This became abundantly clear at the height of the crisis, when the Serbian-controlled group of the members of that body tried unsuccessfully to prevent the new member, Stipe Mesić, delegated by the noncommunist and nationalist majority in the Assembly of Croatia, from becoming its chairman according to annual rotation. Members of that body rotated as chairmen not on the basis of any personal criteria but, as in the Security Council, depending on the alphabetical order of the republics and provinces (Article 327 in conjunction with the Rules of Procedure of the Presidency of 1975).[37]

In the context of the presidency, there was not even token differentiation between the republics and the autonomous provinces: each had one full member, with the automatic entitlement to be chairman. This went further in making Serbia equal with the autonomous provinces, which were nominally its constituent parts. Sinan Hasani, member of the Albanian national minority who represented Kosovo in the presidency, thus acted as the chairman of the presidency during 1986–87—a gesture that a nationally agitated Serbia viewed as a humiliation.

The Federal Executive Council: Autonomous but Ineffective Executive

The only federal organ that was not based on strict equality of federal subunits was the government; that is, the Federal Executive Council. Its president, elected jointly by both chambers of the Federal Assembly, was, however, by necessity an individual from a federal unit and under the obligation to observe "the principle of equal representation of the Republics and corresponding representation of the Autonomous Provinces" in nominating members of the council, who had to be approved by the assembly (Article 348). For a long while, the candidate for president of the council had been determined by the top of the hierarchy of the federal League of Communists and was known long before the indirect elections for the Federal Assembly even started. As a rule, the new "prime minister" was not from the same republic as the preceding one, but the rotation was not rigid as in other bodies and was free of ethnic considerations.[38] After the adoption of the 1974 Constitution, the presidents of the Federal Executive Council were Džemal Bijedić, a Muslim from Bosnia-Herzegovina; Veselin Djuranović, a Montenegrin; Milka Planinc, a Croat from Croatia; Branko Mikulić, a Croat from Bosnia-Herzegovina; and Ante Marković, a Croat from Croatia.

The Federal Executive Council was heavily constrained by other federal bodies, as well as by the republics and autonomous provinces (Articles 352–362). This was borne out by the council's frequent failure, especially in the last years of the existence of Yugoslavia, to have its draft statutes adopted by the assembly or to effect meaningful change. Constitutional limitations were compounded by the unwritten rule of every communist system that the task of the government is predominantly to deal with the economy, leaving essential political matters, including foreign policy, to the party or the head of state. Nevertheless, some opportunities for initiative and action were there, which paradoxically increased with the intensification of interrepublican and inter-ethnic squabbling. The last prime minister, assisted by a number of federal-minded colleagues in his cabinet, was probably the most enterprising: namely, through government decrees, important economic reform was successfully introduced in 1989. He was soon to realize, however, that he had no true political backing in the existing scheme of things: his unsuccessful attempts to create an independent political basis in the population do not belong to constitutional history, except for the reminder that federal units (Serbia and Slovenia, in the first place) refused to back a constitutional amendment, proposed by the Federal Executive Council and adopted by the existing Assembly on October 8, 1990, to permit direct elections for the Federal Chamber of the Federal Assembly.[39]

The Allegedly Crucial Question: Which Nation Was the Most Disadvantaged?

There is a general impression that it was the Serbs who were most frustrated by the symmetrical, consensual confederal arrangements described previously. This impression has been created by the prevailing assumption that the Serbs have identified with the federal state in order to dominate it, as they did before 1941, and by the vociferous complaints of the Serb nationalist elite.[40] A sober look at the 1974 Constitution will show that *per se*, as a legal text, it further weakened the federation through its confederate elements, but that it was not necessarily disadvantageous to the Serbs under all circumstances. Rather, this depended on the play of political forces, which gave substance to constitutional provisions. The best example was the partition of the Serb people into several federal units, with the overrepresentation of the autonomous provinces. In the original Titoist political climate, which prevailed for quite some time after Tito's death, this in fact meant that only Serbia proper would be represented by "true" Serbs; Montenegro by those who believed themselves to be more Montenegrin than Serb; Kosovo by the Albanian majority; and Vojvodina, if not by Hungarians or members of another minority, by an "autonomist" Serb with questionable nationalist credentials.[41]

From another angle, the proliferation of "Serb" federal units offered a chance to the Serbs, or the Leagues of Communists dominated by them, to appear in the organs of the federation under various hats. This opportunity was in fact seized by the populists around Slobodan Milošević, who, in the sweep of their "antibureaucratic revolution," deposed the leadership of the leagues of communists in Montenegro, Vojvodina, and Kosovo and replaced them with persons loyal to the League of Communists of Serbia and its paramount leader.[42] This had happened before political pluralism was gradually introduced in 1990 and, as a matter of course, resulted in changes in the supreme state organs of Montenegro and the autonomous provinces, and in the replacement of their representatives in federal organs. At the peak of the crisis the regime of Milošević thus controlled four out of eight members of the federal presidency, 100 deputies in the 220-member Federal Chamber, and forty delegates in the eighty-member Chamber of Republics and Provinces (four of eight delegations).

This was not sufficient for a majority; it was a deadlock. Because of the entrenched consensual decisionmaking, even a majority could not predominate. This was another reason or excuse for the (now mostly noncommunist) regimes in Croatia and Slovenia to opt out of the federation, after which other non-Serb entities reluctantly followed suit. This was not due to fear of Serb constitutional domination, as evidenced by the fierce nationalist rhetoric of the recycled dogmatic communists who came to represent Serbia and the Serbs.

This is not to deny that Serbia, according to its own constitution, adopted in conformity with the federal constitution, was not itself in an abnormal constitutional situation. Serbia proper ("Serbia outside the autonomous provinces"[43]) had no organs of its own but was governed by the All-Serbian Assembly, Presidency, Executive Council, and Court, where both autonomous provinces were secured with influential representation. These organs had no jurisdiction in the autonomous provinces, which had their own assemblies, presidencies, governments, and supreme courts. In some important matters, such as social planning, defense, and education, legislation was possible only on the basis of the consensus of the supposedly Serbian legislature and the legislatures of the autonomous provinces. This meant that some indispensable Serbian statutes were not enacted until the very end of Yugoslavia or until the League of Communists of Serbia under the new populist leadership removed the party elite in the provinces and then abolished its autonomy by unilateral acts of the all-Serbian legislature, which the leadership now controlled.

Liberal and Dogmatic Yugoslavism: The Government and the Army

Only the Federal Executive Council remained basically unchanged, creating the illusion that the crisis could be mastered by the actions of this only remaining truly Yugoslav body. It was soon to be discovered that the government was powerless without the loyalty of the army. But the Yugoslav People's Army was never able to forget its late commander in chief, never comfortable with his replacement by a collective presidency, which after 1990 came to include noncommunists. The "technocratic" reformers in the Federal Executive Council, bent on privatization and pluralism, looked utterly unreliable. The military used the constitutional stalemate to elevate its Staff of the Supreme Command, a body not provided for in the constitution and laws, to the de facto position that Tito had held, applying its own criteria as to the trustworthiness and "political correctness" of individual members of the presidency and the Federal Executive Council.[44] This last bastion of Titoism and communist orthodoxy eventually sided with Milošević and his clients, not because, as it has been often suggested, the majority of the officer corps were Serbs and Montenegrins, but for reasons of ideological compatability. The leading generals were replaced in the period between 1990 and 1992 by the now openly nationalist authorities of the new Federal Republic of Yugoslavia. None of them is now active as a pronounced Serb nationalist, while most deplore the fall of communism, in the USSR and elsewhere. Their extreme distaste for the leaders of Serbian noncommunist nationalist political parties is indicative: with some simplification, it could be said that they did not side with the Serb people precisely because, although they were Serbs and the glory or the interests of the nation were their supreme consideration, they "objectively" (to use a favorite communist expression) favored socialism. Had the Communist party prevailed in some other republic, and not in Serbia, it is quite conceivable that many of them would have led the army in another direction.[45]

The Hierarchy of Federal and Republican Norms

Incipient confederalism was to be observed in the 1974 Constitution in many other areas, the most important of them being the hierarchy of federal and republican (provincial) norms. There was an interesting implication in the wording of the constitution that the acts of the federal authorities had to be "in conformity" with the federal constitution and federal statutes (Article 207). This also applied to "sociopolitical communities" and "organizations of associated labor" (Article 206), but not to constitutions and other acts of the republics and provinces, which were required only to "not be contrary" to the federal constitution and statutes (Articles 206, 207), a distinction that had wide implications, since it made it possible to argue about the extent of the departure from federal norms that made a republican norm change from "nonconforming" to "contrary."

However, even where a republican or provincial statute was contrary to the federal law, the inferior republican statute had to be temporarily applied until the decision of the constitutional court (Article 207). According to Article 384, in such cases the Federal Constitutional Court could rule that the inferior statute was contrary to the federal one, but this ruling was without immediate effect: it had to be submitted to the relevant assembly, which had up to one year to remove what was contradictory in the statute. Failing this, the constitutional court had to declare that the contested statute ceased to be valid.

Another growing problem related to the necessary administrative action required to implement federal statutes.[46] Except in the limited jurisdictional field of the federal administration, this was to be done by the administrations of the federal units, which frequently failed to act.

The problem gained such proportions that in 1990 a constitutional amendment was introduced to deal with such cases: the Federal Executive Council was to be empowered to undertake necessary action in the event that the republican or provincial executive had been alerted but again had failed to act. The amendment was not approved by the federal units.[47]

The Poverty of Human Rights

Republics and autonomous provinces thus became very powerful entities. Without the federation, they had no counterweight. For the drafters of the constitution, this involved an experiment with decentralized "associated labor." Their Marxist-Leninist orientation forbade them to look toward the individual and his or her rights. Chapter III of the constitution, devoted to "the freedoms, rights and duties of the citizen" mostly repeated the unsatisfactory provisions of the 1963 Constitution, together with its inherent revulsion for "bourgeois individualism," reflected in the incessant reminders about duties, solidarity, and socialist community, and in the usual order of the rights, with economic rights at the top, close to self-management. The only novelty was the "inalienable right to self-management," which was defined in terms of the new *langue de bois*:

> [It] enables each individual to decide on his personal and common interests in an organization of associated labour, local community, self-managing communities of interest or other self-managing organization or community and socio-political community, and in all other forms of their self-management integration and mutual linkage. Each individual shall be responsible for self-management decision making and the implementation of decisions (Article 155).

Even this inspired vagueness had to be coupled with a socialist duty:

> Everyone shall be bound conscientiously and in the interest of socialist society based on self-management.

As in other constitutions, traditional human rights were granted only grudgingly, and generally submitted to a restrictive socialist *ordre pub-*

lic.[48] Thus, for instance, the freedoms of the press, public expression, association, speech, gathering, and public assembly were lumped together in a short sentence of Article 167, coupled immediately with the duty of the media "to inform the public truthfully and objectively" (Article 168), which was then the "constitutional basis" of criminal law and practice, entailing the prosecution of such offenses as "false information," "the disquieting of the public," and, most famous of all, "inimical propaganda."[49] All rights listed in the constitution were, in spite of the use of the word, "guaranteed" only conditionally and were made wholly dependent on simple statutes and haunted by the typically socialist obsession with the prevention of supposed abuse of human rights:

> No one may use the freedoms and rights established by the present Constitution in order to disrupt the foundations of the socialist self-management democratic order established by present Constitution, to endanger the independence of the country, violate the freedoms and rights of men and the citizen guaranteed by the present Constitution, endanger peace and equality in international cooperation, stir up national, racial or religious hatred or intolerance or abet the commission of criminal offences, nor may these freedoms be used in a way which offends public morals. It shall be specified by statute in what cases and under what conditions the use of these freedoms in a way contrary to the present Constitution will entail restriction or a ban on their use (Article 203).

The most disquieting feature of this part of the constitution was what it failed to provide, in spite of the fact that Yugoslavia was in 1974 a party to both International Covenants on Human Rights and an impressive number of other international treaties.[50] The best testimony to what was missing and incomplete in the 1974 Constitution's "bill of rights" was to be found in the draft Amendment LX thereto, adopted by the Federal Assembly in October 1990, but never ratified by the republics and provinces. The drafters found it necessary to suggest improvement on the principle of nondiscrimination (which conspicuously allowed for discrimination on the basis of political opinion) to ban torture; safeguard privacy and protect personal data; fully guarantee the freedom of conscience and religion; establish the right to organize in political parties; safeguard trade union rights, including the right to strike and collective bargaining; and secure just income from work for everyone, and not only to "working people."[51]

Conclusion

If the 1974 Constitution was to be taken seriously, as a transparent normative act reflecting reality and being truly and conscientiously implemented and implementable, its main features could be described as follows:

—It further weakened the federation by paralyzing the decisionmaking process and removing real authority of federal decisions.

—It made the federal units into sovereign states and the only real centers of power: the federation was run by their consensus.

—It tolerated the existence of two federal units (the autonomous provinces), that were at the same time constituent parts of another federal unit (that is, they were both equal and subordinate).

—As a balance to state power, concentrated in the constituent federal units, it attempted to create a parallel social system of autonomous self-management, atomized and incomprehensible, and, as such, unable to influence political decisionmaking.

—It created an artificial division of the population into "working people" and "citizens" and deprived all of them of the right to vote, except at the lowest level of government and "self-management."

—It totally neglected the individual by denying and restricting his or her rights and allowing him or her to act only within the framework of a collective, as a part thereof, and fully controlled by it.

—It left no basis for political pluralism[52] by preventing the creation of any political organization that was not a "socio-political organization" controlled by the League of Communists, the leading role of which, together with its sister organization, the Socialist Alliance of Working People, was constitutionally recognized.

—In addition to its inherently unliberal spirit, manifested in some of the previously mentioned features, it was openly undemocratic in that it allowed political discrimination and assured the League of Communists the right to nominate all candidates for office and to appoint its own representatives as members of the Federal Assembly and presidency.

—It included a provision for a President for life, but applicable to only one person (Tito).

—In the sensitive field of international relations, it provided for the right to self-determination and secession without envisaging the corresponding procedure.

—It made constitutional changes impossible, except by some kind of international (confederate) agreement.

To leave matters at these observations would be highly unrealistic and naive and would fail to make the most important point, namely that the 1974 SFRY Constitution was an ornamental piece of rhetoric, a justification for dictatorial (even totalitarian) rule, and that its main deficiency, quite apparent in the late 1980s, was that it was not meant as a supreme legal and political text, was not intended to be seriously implemented in the political sphere, and was impossible to implement in other fields. The incisive remarks of Lidija Basta-Posavec, made in regard to the new constitution of Serbia (1990), remain pertinent in relation to the 1974 Yugoslav Constitution and, for that matter, to any communist-inspired constitution:

> . . . the powerholders . . . have consciously foregone their own constitutional legitimacy, remaining consistent in the instrumentalization of law, that is in an *a priori* disparaging attitude to institutions from the standpoint of real political decisions, the people who made them and their content. Institutions are irrelevant as the constitutional area of the decision-making process. Their role amounts merely to achieving subsequent legalization for decisions . . . Therefore, constitutional principles and institutions are important insofar as they will allow political decisions of the first rank concerning constitutional matters to be made outside of the constitutional system.[53]

A proper description of the "outside" can be provided only by detailed analysis of the real structure of power in Yugoslavia and its evolution after 1974, which continued independent of the constitution, and which, at any given time, either gave it political meaning or exposed it as a totally irrelevant document. Such an analysis is outside the limits of this chapter, but some basic indications should nevertheless be made.

In spite of its official depiction, Yugoslavia has in fact never been a true federation. Even with the 1974 Constitution it was, until the death of Tito, a unitary state governed by its centralized Communist party. Top party officials, and above all Tito, were able to make the most important decisions and impose them, regardless of the statutes of the party, not to speak of the constitution. Party members were submitted to the strict discipline of "democratic centralism" and were removable by the decision of the superior party organs, which were obeyed even if they violated the constitution and laws. Their removal could always be portrayed as a "resignation." This is not to say that the party itself was devoid of infighting and a struggle for positions (and the ear of the supreme leader), but this took place according to the murky rules of the game, which had nothing to do with the constitution and laws.

The 1974 Constitution came at a moment when the party structures, cadres, and morale started to decay as a result of the prolonged possession of absolute power. The majority of members and functionaries were opportunist careerists who gradually forgot the Marxist origin of their philosophy and, faced with the lack of enthusiasm in the population, started to seek other sources of support and legitimacy that for them were more comprehensible and natural. By necessity, these sources were parochial and provincial, with a natural tendency to become nationalist. This was to be countered by the largely artificial constructions of self-management, but they were not supportive of any broader unity, relying as they did on minuscule "basic associations of associated labor," which could not resist the meddling of party committees and secretaries from the municipal to the highest levels.

With respect to its handling of ethnic conflict, the political system in Yugoslavia, behind its constitutional façade, was that of consociationalism, to use the taxonomy of McGarry and O'Leary.[54] However, as correctly observed by Schöpflin, "consociational arrangements were never formalised, and with the demise of the party there were no institutional mechanisms to establish democratic consociationalism."[55] The 1974 Constitution, as well as all others, failed to provide them, even as a fallback position.

With Tito no longer there as ruler and powerbroker, the system continued to function for a remarkably long time as a sort of "necrocracy"[56] that morbidly pretended that he was still alive.[57] Inertia was strong enough to overshadow serious economic problems (when the bill for the borrowed life of luxury in the 1970s had to be footed) and ethnic unrest (especially in Kosovo). With the departure of the few stronger Partisan personalities,[58] the party was governed by conservative nonentities who had been recalled by Tito from retirement, in conjunction with the obedient *apparatchiks* who had replaced the liberals and technocrats ten years before and had been promoted on the basis of the criteria of obedience and faithful repetition of current slogans. This "negative" selection produced power-hungry but insecure personalities who, in search of legitimation, became the first converts to populist nationalism, and in fact its leaders.[59] Even the politically and administratively gifted party cadres, especially if they were young, realized then that they had no future outside the nationalist context.

Perestroika and *glasnost* in the Soviet Union and the collapse of the communist empire came too late to boost the reformers in the Yugoslav League of Communists, who believed that democracy and pluralism were the solution. By then, nationalism had become the only conceivable remedy to communism in Yugoslavia: being a communist creation, this state had to disappear.[60]

One can only speculate the extent to which the 1974 Constitution and the constitutional process were responsible for the collapse of the federal state and the nonviability of the democratic option. The safest answer is that it could not have saved something that did not exist. The constitution itself had made it possible for the real government to directly change from an unitary party state to the confederation of party states. The 1974 Constitution did not contain any real basis for democracy. Neither did it pay any respect to human rights, which made it easier for most of the successor states to start their lives with problematic human rights law and still more problematic human rights practice.

The 1974 Constitution was the reflection of its time. Given the internal and international situation and the background of its drafters, it could not have been different. The saddest conclusion, however, must be that these factors combined to produce a category of constitutional experts, political scientists, and jurists who do not seem to have made any effort to provide constitutional solutions for real political difficulties. They failed to establish an alternative decisionmaking process that could function if the party system collapsed. Thus, even if Yugoslavia was to be willingly dismantled, there was no procedure for a controlled transition into explicitly confederate arrangements, or for the peaceful dissolution or separation of the constituent units. For the drafters, this was not only the worst-case scenario, it was unthinkable; apparently, they were whistling in the darkness of self-management.

CHAPTER FOUR

Disparity and Disintegration: the Economic Dimension of Yugoslavia's Demise

Dragomir Vojnić

IN FEW COUNTRIES in contemporary Europe is social diversity combined with a relatively small territory to the extent that it was in the former Yugoslavia. These differences were related to nationality, language, religion, history, tradition, customs, and way of life, as well as the social psychology outlook. Disparity in levels of economic development, linked to demographic and ethnic differences, was an especially important source of conflict. It must be underscored, however, that these differences did not arise in the former Yugoslavia, but were the result of a historical inheritance. While it is common nowadays to speak of Yugoslavia as an artificial entity, it is necessary to distinguish between those differences that are a common characteristic of society, and those that are peculiar to a given context, whether they are clearly defined or not.

The Historical Inheritance

As it is generally known, the former Yugoslavia was constituted by nations and peoples that were conditioned by completely different historical, civilizational, and cultural surroundings over the centuries. For a period lasting several centuries, Croatia, Slovenia, and Vojvodina formed an integral part of the Austro-Hungarian empire while during the same period, Serbia, Macedonia and Kosovo were an integral part of the Turkish-Ottoman empire. In addition, Bosnia-Herzegovina had unique historical characteristics related to the influence of both of the above-mentioned empires. Until the end of the nineteenth century (the Berlin

Congress), it was an integral part of the Turkish-Ottoman empire; it was subsequently incorporated (with the status of a protectorate) as an integral part of the Austro-Hungarian empire. The longest tradition of independent statehood belongs to Montenegro and Dubrovnik. Serbia first attained partial independence during the first half of the nineteenth century, and became completely independent during the second half of the same century.

Considering this historical inheritance, it becomes quite obvious that the former Yugoslavia was characterized by stark contrasts. It is necessary to emphasize that the differences stem not only from nationality, language, and religion, but also from essentially divergent historical and civilizing influences. Historically, the northwestern republics of the former Yugoslavia were under the influence of west European civilization. The influences of Western civilization were manifest in a very broad range of values, from the beginning of the Christian period up to and including the industrial revolution and the development of democracy. In contrast, the southeastern republics of the former Yugoslavia were at the same time under the influence of another civilization that represented a historical mixture of the Muslim religion and the Byzantine tradition and culture.

The historical influences of various civilizations, religions, and cultures were especially apparent in the former Yugoslav republic of Bosnia-Herzegovina. The diversity of historical influences created certain contradictions, controversies, and conflicts. Three nations (the Serbs, Croats, and Bosnian Muslims) and three religions (Catholic, Orthodox, and Islam) had to confront each other on a small territory. Furthermore, the differences in historical inheritance and the influence of various cultures, traditions, and civilizations were compounded by considerable disparity in the level of economic development. In contrast to the former Yugoslavia, other European countries that have had similar differences in the level of economic development of particular regions (for instance northern and southern Italy) have shared a common nationality. The problems arising in such a case are never characterized by the same contradictions and conflicts as those that arise from economic differences in a multinational state.

Gross domestic product per capita is a typical and fairly accurate indicator of economic development. The data contained in tables 4-1 and 4-2 provide the relevant indices for the former Yugoslavia.

It is evident at first glance that there were vast differences in the level of economic development between the republics and provinces of the former Yugoslavia. The extremes can be noticed right from the beginning of the observed period, in 1952. The beginning of the 1950s represented the end of the renewal period and the beginning of important reforms, which through the introduction of the self-management system had a innovative character in comparison with the policies of other socialist countries in that period. As indicated by the statistics from 1952, there were great disparities in the level of economic development, especially between Slovenia and Kosovo. Gross domestic product per capita of Kosovo in that year amounted to no more than one-quarter of the gross domestic product per capita of Slovenia. Furthermore, these differences increased in the years that followed, despite an active policy of accelerated development for the less-developed republics and the province of Kosovo. In addition to the previously mentioned factors related to the former Yugoslavia's historical inheritance and the general level of culture and civilization, demographic movements had a considerable influence on the level of economic disparity. There are many reasons underlying the presumption that within the multinational context of the former Yugoslavia, demographic trends had a significant influence upon the process of disintegration. Consequently, particular attention should be paid to this factor in an analysis of the situation.

Demographic Movements as a Factor of Disintegration

As mentioned above, the historical inheritance and level of economic development of the different republics and provinces of the former Yugoslavia were reflected particularly in demographic trends. This relationship is clearly illustrated by the data contained in table 4-3.

The data in table 4-3 were prepared on the basis of population censuses conducted during the selected years. The last census was conducted in 1991, but adequate data (except for the republic of Croatia) are not available.

The general tendency was such that the less-developed republics and provinces increased their total share of the population while the share of the more developed ones decreased (see tables 4-1 and 4-2). As a more developed republic, Croatia decreased its share of the total population from 27.3 percent in 1921 to 20.5 percent in 1981. Slovenia also decreased its share from 10.3 percent in 1921 to 8.4 percent in 1981. Among the less-developed republics, Bosnia-Herzegovina increased its

Table 4–1. Gross Domestic Product (GDP) per Capita in the Former Yugoslavia, 1952–89

1972 dollars

Year	Yugoslavia	Bosnia-Herzegovina	Montenegro	Croatia	Macedonia	Slovenia	Serbia			
							Total (average)	Serbia proper	Kosovo	Vojvodina
1952	3,356	3,205	2,940	4,074	2,397	6,102	3,105	3,422	1,561	3,005
1953	4,061	3,473	3,033	4,691	2,756	6,549	3,715	3,928	1,873	4,042
1954	4,132	3,436	3,068	5,010	2,729	7,286	3,580	3,780	1,794	3,916
1955	4,628	3,852	3,572	5,666	3,265	8,094	3,975	4,204	1,969	4,333
1956	4,354	3,286	3,243	5,388	3,203	7,912	3,753	3,927	1,858	4,213
1957	5,195	3,855	3,615	6,354	3,504	8,791	4,767	4,990	2,147	5,460
1958	5,246	3,885	3,525	6,476	3,777	9,718	4,578	4,742	2,063	5,389
1959	6,034	4,537	3,743	7,013	3,870	10,202	5,799	6,077	2,351	6,815
1960	6,433	4,886	4,225	7,675	4,108	11,614	5,906	6,201	2,404	6,934
1961	6,728	4,978	4,972	8,189	4,163	12,581	6,050	6,494	2,340	6,836
1962	6,885	4,882	4,846	8,358	4,202	13,025	6,305	6,714	2,328	7,356
1963	7,636	5,407	5,475	9,200	4,884	14,400	7,008	7,448	2,562	8,267
1964	8,428	5,911	6,352	10,018	6,249	15,635	7,722	8,099	3,048	9,313
1965	8,502	6,088	6,473	10,265	5,662	15,602	7,816	8,171	3,102	9,537
1966	9,079	6,506	6,725	10,964	6,099	16,350	8,425	8,779	3,382	10,376
1967	9,205	6,364	6,808	11,293	6,310	16,757	8,500	8,880	3,411	10,465
1968	9,479	6,597	7,102	11,797	6,466	17,726	8,569	9,087	3,267	10,340
1969	10,364	7,127	7,787	12,766	7,109	19,385	9,491	10,080	3,551	11,497

Year										
1970	10,924	7,383	8,342	13,717	7,642	21,154	9,756	10,452	3,764	11,560
1971	11,890	7,950	8,676	15,099	8,217	22,807	10,679	11,263	3,841	13,551
1972	12,277	8,253	9,054	15,426	8,518	23,824	11,049	11,805	3,914	13,757
1973	12,771	8,507	8,947	15,946	8,943	25,172	11,535	12,321	3,986	14,571
1974	13,732	9,060	9,404	17,231	9,351	27,405	12,420	13,196	4,380	15,943
1975	14,102	9,305	9,621	17,632	9,677	28,709	12,685	13,526	4,634	16,181
1976	14,513	9,343	10,030	18,273	9,994	29,133	13,190	14,169	4,598	16,834
1977	15,529	10,020	11,016	19,706	10,511	31,016	14,102	15,173	4,685	18,259
1978	16,458	10,612	11,526	20,079	11,249	33,376	14,764	16,090	4,661	18,899
1979	17,468	11,322	11,431	22,211	11,924	35,625	15,760	17,332	4,851	20,020
1980	17,764	11,722	14,034	22,505	11,946	35,230	15,915	17,453	5,013	20,029
1981	17,891	12,057	13,933	22,743	11,964	34,726	16,088	17,447	5,170	20,918
1982	17,841	12,143	13,531	22,366	11,959	34,598	16,198	17,618	5,031	21,241
1983	17,534	12,046	13,391	21,957	11,554	34,724	15,811	17,234	4,805	20,909
1984	17,759	12,179	13,771	22,396	11,771	35,308	15,932	17,415	4,592	21,359
1985	17,725	12,243	13,748	22,365	11,539	35,558	15,865	17,520	4,847	20,741
1986	18,233	12,587	14,100	22,933	12,205	36,519	16,343	18,103	5,060	21,390
1987	17,917	12,260	13,364	22,875	11,908	36,076	16,003	17,775	4,839	21,138
1988	16,814	11,344	12,417	21,587	10,800	33,932	15,183	16,924	4,535	20,063
1989	16,820	11,424	12,398	21,238	10,891	33,103	15,393	17,429	4,317	20,063

Sources: *Statistical Yearbook of Yugoslavia 1991*, pp. 442, 475; *Yugoslavia 1918–1988, Statistical Yearbook*, Federal Bureau of Statistics, Belgrade, February 1989, p. 105. This table was prepared in the Center for Economic Informatics and Statistics, Economics Institute, Zagreb.

Table 4-2. Indexes of Gross Domestic Product (GDP) per Capita in the Former Yugoslavia, 1952-89

Year	Yugoslavia	Bosnia-Herzegovina	Montenegro	Croatia	Macedonia	Slovenia	Serbia Total (average)	Serbia Serbia proper	Serbia Kosovo	Serbia Vojvodina
1952	100	95.50	87.60	121.39	71.42	181.82	92.52	101.97	46.51	89.54
1953	100	85.52	74.69	115.51	67.87	161.27	91.48	96.72	46.12	99.53
1954	100	83.16	74.25	121.25	66.05	176.33	86.64	91.48	43.42	94.77
1955	100	83.23	77.18	122.43	70.55	174.89	85.89	90.84	42.55	93.63
1956	100	75.47	74.48	123.75	75.56	181.72	86.20	90.19	42.67	96.76
1957	100	74.21	69.59	122.31	67.45	169.22	91.76	96.05	41.33	105.10
1958	100	74.06	67.19	123.45	72.00	185.25	87.27	90.39	39.33	102.73
1959	100	75.19	62.03	116.22	64.14	169.08	96.11	100.71	38.96	112.94
1960	100	75.95	65.68	119.31	63.86	180.54	91.81	96.39	37.37	107.79
1961	100	73.99	73.90	121.72	61.88	186.99	89.92	96.52	34.78	101.61
1962	100	70.91	70.38	121.39	61.03	189.18	91.58	97.52	33.81	106.84
1963	100	70.81	71.70	120.48	63.96	188.58	91.78	97.54	33.55	108.26
1964	100	70.14	75.37	118.87	74.15	185.51	91.62	96.10	36.17	110.50
1965	100	71.61	76.14	120.47	66.60	183.51	91.93	96.11	36.49	112.17
1966	100	71.66	74.07	120.76	67.18	180.09	92.80	96.70	37.25	114.29
1967	100	69.14	73.96	122.68	68.55	182.04	92.34	96.47	37.06	113.69
1968	100	69.60	74.92	124.45	68.21	187.00	90.40	95.86	34.47	109.80
1969	100	68.77	75.14	123.18	68.59	187.04	91.58	97.26	34.26	110.93

Year										
1970	100	67.59	76.36	125.57	69.96	193.65	89.31	95.68	34.46	105.82
1971	100	66.86	72.97	126.99	69.11	191.82	89.81	94.73	32.30	113.97
1972	100	67.22	73.75	125.65	69.38	194.05	90.00	96.16	31.88	112.06
1973	100	66.61	70.06	124.86	70.03	197.10	90.32	96.48	31.21	114.09
1974	100	65.98	68.48	125.48	68.10	199.57	90.45	96.10	31.90	116.10
1975	100	65.98	68.22.	125.03	68.62	203.58	89.95	95.92	32.86	114.74
1976	100	64.38	69.11	125.91	68.86	200.74	90.88	97.63	31.68	115.99
1977	100	64.52	70.94	126.90	67.69	199.73	90.81	97.71	30.17	117.58
1978	100	64.48	70.03	122.00	68.35	202.79	89.71	97.76	28.32	114.83
1979	100	64.82	65.44	127.15	68.26	203.94	90.22	99.22	27.77	114.61
1980	100	65.99	79.00	126.69	67.25	198.32	89.59	98.25	28.22	112.75
1981	100	67.39	77.88	127.12	66.87	194.10	89.92	97.52	28.90	116.92
1982	100	68.06	75.84	125.36	67.03	193.92	90.79	98.75	28.20	119.06
1983	100	68.70	76.37	125.23	65.89	198.04	90.17	98.29	27.40	119.25
1984	100	68.58	77.54	126.11	66.28	198.82	89.71	98.06	25.86	120.27
1985	100	69.07	77.56	126.18	65.10	200.61	89.51	98.84	27.35	117.02
1986	100	69.03	77.33	125.78	66.94	200.29	89.63	99.29	27.75	117.31
1987	100	68.43	74.59	127.67	66.46	201.35	89.32	99.21	27.01	117.98
1988	100	67.46	73.85	128.38	64.23	201.80	90.30	100.65	26.97	119.32
1989	100	67.92	73.71	126.26	64.75	196.80	91.51	103.62	25.66	119.28

Sources: *Statistical Yearbook for Yugoslavia 1991*, pp. 442, 475; *Yugoslavia 1918–1988, Statistical Yearbook*, Federal Bureau of Statistics, Belgrade, February 1989, p. 105. This table was prepared in the Center for Economics Informatics and Statistics, Economic Institute, Zagreb.

Table 4-3. *Population and Household Census Data for the Former Yugoslavia, Selected Years, 1921-81*

Year	Yugoslavia	Bosnia-Herzegovina	Montenegro	Croatia	Macedonia	Slovenia	Serbia Total	Serbia proper	Kosovo	Vojvodina
Total population										
1921	12,545,000	1,890,440	311,341	3,427,268	808,724	1,287,797	4,819,430	2,843,426	439,010	1,536,994
1931	14,534,000	2,323,555	360,044	3,788,571	949,958	1,385,960	5,725,912	3,549,690	552,064	1,624,158
1948	15,841,566	2,563,767	377,189	3,779,858	1,152,986	1,439,800	6,527,966	4,154,175	733,034	1,640,757
1953	16,991,449	2,847,459	419,873	3,936,022	1,304,514	1,504,427	6,979,154	4,463,701	815,908	1,699,545
1961	18,549,291	3,277,948	471,894	4,159,696	1,406,003	1,591,523	7,642,227	4,823,274	963,988	1,854,965
1971	20,522,972	3,746,111	529,604	4,426,221	1,647,308	1,727,137	8,446,591	5,250,365	1,243,693	1,952,533
1981	22,424,711	4,124,256	584,310	4,601,469	1,909,136	1,891,864	9,313,676	5,694,464	1,584,440	2,034,772
Percent										
1921	100	15.07	2.48	27.32	6.45	10.27	38.42	22.67	3.50	12.25
1931	100	15.99	2.48	26.07	6.54	9.54	39.40	24.42	3.80	11.17
1948	100	16.18	2.38	23.86	7.28	9.09	41.21	26.22	4.63	10.36
1953	100	16.76	2.47	23.16	7.68	8.85	41.07	26.27	4.80	10.00
1961	100	17.67	2.54	22.43	7.58	8.58	41.20	26.00	5.20	10.00
1971	100	18.25	2.58	21.57	8.03	8.42	41.16	25.58	6.06	9.51
1981	100	18.39	2.61	20.52	8.51	8.44	41.53	25.39	7.07	9.07
Population per square kilometer										
1921	49.0	37.0	22.5	60.6	31.5	63.6	54.5	50.8	40.3	71.5
1931	56.8	45.4	26.1	67.0	36.9	68.4	64.8	63.4	50.7	75.5
1948	61.9	50.1	27.3	66.9	44.8	71.1	73.9	74.2	67.3	76.3

1953	66.4	55.7	30.4	69.6	50.7	74.3	79.0	79.8	74.9	79.0
1961	72.5	64.1	34.2	73.6	54.7	78.6	86.5	86.2	88.5	86.3
1971	80.2	73.3	38.3	78.3	64.1	85.3	95.6	93.8	114.2	90.8
1981	87.7	80.7	42.3	81.4	74.2	93.4	105.4	101.7	145.5	94.6

Households

1921	2,459,803	336,295	55,463	673,171	146,161	263,494	985,219	573,269	84,889	327,061
1931	2,827,626	399,011	62,836	761,428	164,052	283,045	1,157,254	677,632	108,761	370,861
1948	3,627,024	498,022	83,639	959,857	218,819	380,950	1,485,737	916,021	115,283	454,433
1953	3,963,234	565,212	92,152	1,031,910	246,313	410,976	1,616,671	1,004,731	127,004	484,936
1961	4,648,563	706,107	106,569	1,167,586	280,214	458,853	1,929,234	1,215,899	152,598	560,737
1971	4,087,348	848,545	121,911	1,289	352,034	515,531	2,248,038	1,446,478	188,108	613,453
1981	6,195,826	1,030,689	142,692	1,423,862	435,251	594,571	2,568,761	1,661,576	228,870	678,315

Persons per household

1921	5.10	5.62	6.61	5.09	5.53	4.88	4.89	4.96	5.71	4.70
1931	5.14	5.82	5.73	4.98	5.79	4.90	4.95	5.24	5.08	4.38
1948	4.37	5.15	4.51	3.94	5.27	3.78	4.39	4.54	6.36	3.61
1953	4.29	5.04	4.56	3.81	5.30	3.66	4.32	4.44	6.42	3.50
1961	3.99	4.64	4.43	3.56	5.02	3.47	3.96	3.97	6.32	3.31
1971	3.82	4.41	4.34	3.43	4.68	3.35	3.76	3.63	6.61	3.18
1981	3.62	4.00	4.09	3.23	4.39	3.18	3.63	3.43	6.92	3.00

Source: *Yugoslavia 1918–1988, Statistical Yearbook*, Federal Bureau of Statistics, Belgrade, February 1989, p. 40. This table was prepared in the Center for Economic Informatics and Statistics, Economic Institute, Zagreb.

percentage of the total population from approximately 15.1 percent in 1921 to 18.4 percent in 1981; Montenegro slightly increased its share from 2.5 percent in 1921 to 2.6 percent in 1981; Macedonia increased its share from 6.5 percent in 1921 to 8.5 percent in 1981; Serbia (including the two provinces) increased its share from 38.4 percent in 1921 to 41.5 percent in 1981, while Serbia proper (that is, without the provinces), ranking as average in the level of development, increased its share from 22.7 percent in 1921 to 25.4 percent in 1981; and finally, as the least-developed province, Kosovo increased its share from 3.5 percent in 1921 to 7.1 percent in 1981. Kosovo represented by far the largest increase. In the sixty-year period under consideration, Kosovo doubled its share in the total population of the former Yugoslavia. Such trends changed the basic distribution of population in the former Yugoslavia.

The largest changes occurred in the less-developed republics and in the province of Kosovo. In Bosnia-Herzegovina, the number of inhabitants per square kilometer increased from 37.0 in 1921 to 80.7 in 1981; in Montenegro, from 22.5 to 42.3; and in Macedonia, from 31.5 to 74.2. The largest increase, from 40.3 to 145.5, was in Kosovo. In the more developed republics, Croatia and Slovenia, as well as in the province of Vojvodina, these changes were less marked. In the observed period, certain other significant demographic changes occurred. One such change pertains to the number of households as well as the number of their members, which primarily refers to family members. Generally, there was an increase in the number of households. While on average the number doubled, the increase was even greater in the less-developed republics and the province of Kosovo. With respect to the number of household members, however, there was an opposite tendency, with the exception of Kosovo, where average the number of household members increased from 5.71 in 1921 to 6.92 in 1981. All these differences in population trends were caused by the very different behavior of the population in the various republics and provinces with regard to birth control and family planning. This is best illustrated by the data in table 4-4.

As noted in table 4-4, the rate of natural increase per thousand inhabitants is in inverse proportion to the development level of the various republics and provinces. The biggest rates of natural increase in population occured in the province of Kosovo. Such extremely high rates are rarely experienced by other European countries. Kosovo's percentage of the total natural population in the former Yugoslavia increased from 7.9 percent in 1950 to 38.2 percent in 1990. This increase was simultaneously realized by the other less-developed republics (Bosnia-Herzegovina, Montenegro, and Macedonia), while the percentage decreased in the more developed ones (Croatia, Slovenia, and Serbia without the provinces). In recent periods, Vojvodina experienced negative rates of growth.

As previously noted, the different attitudes toward birth control and family planning in the republics and provinces resulted in differences in levels of development, especially between the various national groups. Consequently, demographic movements during more recent years markedly changed the structure of participation of particular peoples and nations in the former Yugoslavia. The most substantial decrease in the share of the total population of the former Yugoslavia occurred with respect to the largest nations—that is, the Serbs and Croats, as well as the Slovenes. The greatest increases in the share of total population occurred among the Muslims and the Albanians. The degree of these changes in population is, however, very different in the various republics and provinces, as is clearly illustrated by the data contained in tables 4-5 and 4-6.

As the data from these tables illustrate, between 1948 and 1981, the proportion of Serbs and Croats in Bosnia-Herzegovina greatly decreased. In contrast, during the same period, there was a remarkable increase in the proportion of Muslims in the total population of Bosnia-Herzegovina.

The data for Montenegro illustrates a remarkable decrease in the proportion of Montenegrins in the republic, from 90.7 percent of the republic's total population in 1948 to only 68.5 percent in 1981, in contrast to the Muslims, whose proportion in the republic increased from 0.1 percent to 13.4 percent, and somewhat less for the Serbs, who increased from 1.8 percent to 3.3 percent. The percentage of Albanians increased from 5.2 percent to 6.5 percent.

In Croatia there was a decrease in the proportion of the Croats from 79.2 percent of the republic's total population in 1948 to 75.1 percent in 1981, and also a decrease for the Serbs, from 14.5 percent to 11.6 percent. The most noticeable increase was for the Yugoslavs, whose participation rose from an undetectable level in 1948 to 8.2 percent of Croatia's total population in 1981.

Since the data for Croatia are available for 1991, it should be mentioned that the percentage of Croats increased to 78.1 percent; of the Serbs, to 12.2 percent; while the percentage of Yugoslavs decreased to 2.2 percent.[1]

The data for Macedonia show a decrease in the proportion of Macedonians and an increase in the proportion of Muslims and Al-

Table 4-4. *Population Dynamics in Republics and Provinces of the Former Yugoslavia, Selected Years, 1950-90*

Year	Yugoslavia	Bosnia-Herzegovina	Montenegro	Croatia	Macedonia	Slovenia	Serbia			
							Total	Serbia proper	Kosovo	Vojvodina
1950	282,050	66,689	8,222	48,268	31,537	18,657	108,677	67,051	22,231	19,395
1955	271,412	70,353	9,615	46,622	31,174	16,987	96,661	57,342	21,444	17,875
1960	249,902	77,139	9,544	34,795	30,052	12,680	85,692	43,209	28,266	14,217
1965	237,609	73,537	8,902	31,250	29,675	14,600	79,645	36,594	31,802	11,249
1970	181,436	52,941	7,120	16,955	25,432	10,079	68,909	29,778	33,667	5,464
1975	203,130	53,273	7,278	21,376	26,950	11,606	82,647	36,116	39,292	7,239
1980	184,759	44,813	6,839	18,120	26,250	11,082	77,655	27,963	44,238	5,454
1985	153,746	43,756	6,798	10,598	24,314	6,079	62,201	17,756	42,099	2,346
1986	146,477	42,076	6,533	8,486	23,796	6,071	59,515	14,841	44,073	601
1987	144,672	41,516	6,577	6,129	23,928	5,755	60,767	14,425	45,914	428
1988	142,802	41,156	6,529	5,839	23,314	6,083	59,881	13,540	46,026	315
1989	120,911	36,426	5,801	3,082	21,335	4,778	49,489	8,142	43,475	-2,128
1990	119,905	34,877	5,738	2,513	21,124	4,915	50,738	8,271	45,767	-3,300
Percent										
1950	100	23.64	2.92	17.11	11.18	6.61	38.53	23.77	7.88	6.88
1955	100	25.92	3.54	17.18	11.49	6.26	35.61	21.13	7.90	6.59
1960	100	30.87	3.82	13.92	12.03	5.07	34.29	17.29	11.31	5.69
1965	100	30.95	3.75	13.15	12.49	6.14	33.52	15.40	13.38	4.73

1970	100	29.18	3.92	9.34	14.02	5.56	37.98	16.41	18.56	3.01
1975	100	26.23	3.58	10.52	13.27	5.71	40.69	17.78	19.34	3.56
1980	100	24.25	3.70	9.81	14.21	6.00	42.03	15.13	23.94	2.95
1985	100	28.46	4.42	6.89	15.81	3.95	40.46	11.55	27.38	1.53
1986	100	28.73	4.46	5.79	16.25	4.14	40.63	10.13	30.09	0.41
1987	100	28.70	4.55	4.24	16.54	3.98	42.00	9.97	31.74	0.30
1988	100	28.82	4.57	4.09	16.33	4.26	41.93	9.48	32.23	0.22
1989	100	30.13	4.80	2.55	17.65	3.95	40.93	6.73	35.96	-1.76
1990	100	29.09	4.79	2.10	17.62	4.10	42.32	6.90	38.17	-2.75

Natural increase per 1,000 persons

1950	17.3	25.1	20.7	12.5	25.6	12.6	16.1	15.6	29.1	11.5
1955	15.5	23.7	22.1	11.6	23.0	11.1	13.4	12.4	25.4	10.2
1960	13.6	23.8	20.4	8.4	21.6	8.0	11.3	9.0	29.9	7.7
1965	12.2	21.0	17.8	7.3	19.7	8.8	10.0	7.3	29.6	5.9
1970	8.9	14.3	13.6	3.9	15.6	5.9	8.2	5.7	27.6	2.8
1975	9.5	13.4	13.0	4.7	15.3	6.6	9.4	6.7	28.0	3.6
1980	8.3	10.9	11.8	4.0	13.9	5.9	8.4	5.0	28.5	2.7
1985	6.7	10.1	11.1	2.3	12.6	3.2	6.5	3.1	23.9	1.1
1986	6.3	9.7	10.6	1.8	11.7	3.1	6.2	2.6	24.4	0.3
1987	6.2	9.4	10.5	1.3	11.6	3.0	6.3	2.5	24.8	0.2
1988	6.1	9.3	10.3	1.2	11.2	3.1	6.1	2.3	24.3	0.2
1989	5.1	8.1	9.1	0.7	10.1	2.5	5.0	1.4	22.4	-1.0
1990	5.0	7.7	8.9	0.5	9.9	2.5	5.1	1.4	23.1	-1.6

Sources: *Yugoslavia 1918–1988, Statistical Yearbook*, Federal Bureau of Statistics, Belgrade, February 1989; *Statistical Yearbook of Yugoslavia 1991*, p. 443. This table was prepared in the Center for Economics Informatics and Statistics, Economic Institute, Zagreb.

Table 4-5. *Population of the Former Yugoslavia by Ethnic Origin, 1948 and 1981*

Republic or province	Ethnic origin[a]									Total (millions)
	Montenegrin	Croat	Macedonian	Muslim	Slovene	Serb	Albanian	Yugoslav	Other	
Yugoslavia										
1948	425,703	3,784,353	810,126	808,921	1,415,432	6,547,117	750,431	—	1,230,015	15.8
1981	579,023	4,428,005	1,339,729	1,999,957	1,753,554	8,140,452	1,730,364	1,219,045	1,234,582	22.4
Bosnia-Herzegovina										
1948	3,094	614,123	675	788,403	4,338	1,136,116	755	—	17,773	2.6
1981	14,114	758,140	1,892	1,630,033	2,755	1,320,738	4,396	326,316	65,872	4.1
Montenegro										
1948	342,009	6,808	133	387	484	6,707	19,425	—	1,236	0.4
1981	400,488	6,904	875	78,080	564	19,407	37,735	31,243	9,014	0.6
Croatia										
1948	2,871	2,975,399	1,387	1,077	38,734	543,795	635	—	192,909	3.8
1981	9,818	3,454,661	5,362	23,740	25,136	531,502	6,006	379,057	166,187	4.6
Macedonia										
1948	2,348	2,090	789,648	1,560	729	29,721	197,389	—	129,501	1.2
1981	3,920	3,307	1,279,323	39,513	648	44,468	377,208	14,225	146,524	1.9
Slovenia										
1948	521	16,069	366	179	1,350,149	7,048	216	—	17,325	1.4
1981	3,217	55,625	3,288	13,425	1,712,445	42,182	1,985	26,263	33,434	1.9

Serbia (total)										
1948	74,860	169,864	17,917	17,315	20,998	4,823,730	532,011	—	871,271	6.5
1981	147,466	149,368	48,989	215,166	12,006	6,182,155	1,303,034	441,941	813,551	9.3
Serbia proper										
1948	16,221	30,342	8,301	6,586	13,492	3,810,573	33,289	—	218,130	4.1
1981	77,134	31,447	29,033	151,674	8,207	4,865,283	72,484	272,050	187,152	5.7
Kosovo										
1948	28,050	5,290	526	9,679	283	171,911	498,424	—	13,657	0.7
1981	27,028	8,718	1,056	58,562	343	209,497	1,226,736	2,676	49,824	1.6
Vojvodina										
1948	30,589	134,232	9,090	1,050	7,223	841,246	480	—	639,302	1.7
1981	43,304	109,203	18,900	4,930	3,456	1,107,375	3,841	167,215	576,548	2.0

Source: *Yugoslavia 1918–1988, Statistical Yearbook*, Federal Bureau of Statistics, Belgrade, February 1989, p. 44. This table was prepared in the Center for Economic Informatics and Statistics, Economic Institute, Zagreb.

a. Self-declared.

Table 4-6. *Ethnic Structure of the Former Yugoslavia, by Percent of Total Population, 1948 and 1981*

Province or republic	Ethnic origin[a]								
	Montenegrin	Croat	Macedonian	Muslim	Slovene	Serb	Albanian	Yugoslav	Other
Yugoslavia									
1948	2.70	23.99	5.14	5.13	8.97	41.51	4.76	—	7.80
1981	2.58	19.75	5.97	8.92	7.82	36.30	7.72	5.44	5.51
Bosnia-Herzegovina									
1948	0.12	23.94	0.03	30.73	0.17	44.29	0.03	—	0.69
1981	0.34	18.38	0.05	39.52	0.07	32.02	0.11	7.91	1.60
Montenegro									
1948	90.67	1.80	0.04	0.10	0.13	1.78	5.15	—	0.33
1981	68.54	1.18	0.15	13.36	0.10	3.32	6.46	5.35	1.54
Croatia									
1948	0.08	79.20	0.04	0.03	1.03	14.47	0.02	—	5.13
1981	0.21	75.08	0.12	0.52	0.55	11.55	0.13	8.24	3.61
Macedonia									
1948	0.20	0.18	68.49	0.14	0.06	2.58	17.12	—	11.23
1981	0.21	0.17	67.01	2.07	0.03	2.33	19.76	0.75	7.67
Slovenia									
1948	0.04	1.15	0.03	0.01	97.00	0.51	0.02	—	1.24
1981	0.17	2.94	0.17	0.71	90.52	2.23	0.10	1.39	1.77

Serbia (total)									
1948	1.15	2.60	0.27	0.27	0.32	73.89	8.15	—	13.35
1981	1.58	1.60	0.53	2.31	0.13	66.38	13.99	4.75	8.74
Serbia proper									
1948	0.39	0.73	0.20	0.16	0.33	92.11	0.80	—	5.27
1981	1.35	0.55	0.51	2.66	0.14	85.44	1.27	4.78	3.29
Kosovo									
1948	3.85	0.73	0.07	1.33	0.04	23.62	68.48	—	1.88
1981	1.71	0.55	0.07	3.70	0.02	13.22	77.42	0.17	3.14
Vojvodina									
1948	1.84	8.07	0.55	0.06	0.43	50.58	0.03	—	38.44
1981	2.13	5.37	0.93	0.24	0.17	54.42	0.19	8.22	28.33

Source: *Yugoslavia 1918-1988, Statistical Yearbook*, Federal Bureau of Statistics, Belgrade, February 1989, p. 44. This table was prepared in the Center for Economic Informatics and Statistics, Economic Institute, Zagreb.
a. Self-declared.

banians. In Slovenia, there was a noticeable decrease in the percentage of Slovenes from 97.0 percent in 1948 to 90.5 percent in 1981, while all other ethnic groups in the republic increased their percentage.

The data for Serbia including the provinces show a remarkable decrease in the proportion of Serbs from 73.9 percent in 1948 to 66.4 percent in 1981. There was also a decrease in the proportion of Croats and a simultaneous increase in the proportion of Albanians from 8.2 percent to nearly 14 percent. A more substantial increase in proportion is also evident for the Yugoslavs, and somewhat less with the Montenegrins. The data for Serbia without the provinces indicate a decrease in the proportion of the Serbs from 92.1 percent in 1948 to 85.4 percent in 1981. There was also a decrease in the proportion of Croats and Slovenes, while the proportion of Montenegrins, Muslims, Albanians, and Yugoslavs increased. A remarkable increase in the proportion of Albanians, from 68.5 percent in 1948 to 77.4 percent in 1981 can be seen in Kosovo; the Muslim component also increased from 1.3 percent to 3.7 percent.

The data for Vojvodina illustrate the increase in the proportion of Serbs from 50.6 percent in 1948 to 54.4 percent in 1981. An increase also appeared, although at a lower level, in the case of the Montenegrins, Yugoslavs, Albanians, Muslims, and Macedonians. A more significant decrease can be noticed for Croats.

In addition to natural increases, demographic movements and internal ethnic migrations of the population influenced demographic and ethnic changes in the former Yugoslav republics and provinces. Data regarding internal ethnic migrations of the population through various periods for the former Yugoslavia as well as the republics and provinces, based on the 1981 census, are provided in table 4-7.

The statistics indicate that the Serbs and Croats (the most populous nations) account for the largest migrations. However, the level of migration is highest with the Serbs, who in 1981 represented 36.3 percent of the population and 48.8 percent of the total migration. The situation of the Croats is the opposite; they represented 19.8 percent of the population in 1981 and 16.0 percent of the migration. Relatively small migrations occurred in the case of the Slovenes and Albanians. Data from the latest census of 1991 would probably illustrate the continuation of migration for the Serbs, who, considering the data from tables 4-5 and 4-6, are referred to a great deal with respect to the Kosovo-Serbia (without provinces)-Vojvodina relation. This data would also show an increase in the migration of the Muslims and Serbs from Bosnia-Herzegovina to Slovenia.

Economic factors had an important influence on these demographic trends and tendencies to migrate internally. The economic factors primarily relate to the search for better jobs and improved living conditions. Other factors include considerable differences in cultural perspectives and habits in relation to family planning, as well as some psychological traits and influences. The range of these psychological characteristics extends from the wish to participate in the social milieu of a majority nation in a given area to the aversion to, or even fear of, being a national minority.

Such trends are understandable in the context of a national mosaic such as that of the former Yugoslavia, where, despite a formal social ideology that glorified "fraternity and unity" and, consequently, the equality of peoples and nations, national tensions were continually present. The combination of vast differences in tradition and historical inheritance as well as the level of economic development, in addition to a unitarist political constitution that repressed pluralism, contributed to the exacerbation of national tensions and the process of disintegration.

In addition to the foregoing factors, the entire multiethnic framework of the former Yugoslavia was complicated by the fact that the creators of the Yugoslav idea were not the Serbian majority nation, but rather the Croats and Slovenes. The Yugoslav idea and the Yugoslav state were originally connected with the Illyrian movement of Ljudevit Gaj (a Croat) and Stanko Vraz (a Slovene). The representative of the idea was the Croatian spiritual leader, Bishop Josip Juraj Strossmayer, who at the end of the nineteenth century founded the Yugoslav Academy of Sciences and Arts in Zagreb. In the period immediately before the creation of the first Yugoslav state (1918), this prominent role belonged (along with the support of the Catholic church) to the "peoples movement" in Istria (Dobrila, Laginja). In this context, it should be pointed out that the Yugoslav Committee from Trieste played a prominent role in the preparation and creation of a new state of Yugoslavia. However, in the first years of the new state, these facts appeared to be forgotten. Furthermore, although Istria, Trieste, and the Yugoslav Committee in Trieste played such a prominent role in the creation of the new state, they failed to bring about the annexation of Istria to its country of origin, Croatia. Indeed, the new state's majority nation quickly began to play a dominant role in the realization of the Yugoslav idea, in which Serbia became the "Piedmont" of the South Slavs.

Table 4-7. *Internal Ethnic Migration of the Population of the Former Yugoslavia, Various Periods, 1946–81*

| | | | | | | | Serbia | | | |
| | | Percent of population that migrated to: | | | | | | | | |
	Yugoslavia	Bosnia-Herzegovina	Montenegro	Croatia	Macedonia	Slovenia	Total	Serbia proper	Kosovo	Vojvodina
Total population	100.00	18.39	2.61	20.52	8.51	8.44	41.53	25.39	7.07	9.07
Total migration	100.00	8.03	2.56	20.95	4.39	6.36	57.72	30.56	2.87	21.73
1945 and earlier	10.38	7.66	6.55	9.10	7.65	5.94	12.08	12.56	11.50	11.44
1946–60	27.23	24.63	19.49	23.57	34.04	17.02	29.86	25.98	21.28	36.91
1961–70	27.86	26.74	28.68	30.33	32.81	22.61	27.28	28.73	25.99	25.23
1971–81	30.79	37.06	41.43	32.93	23.68	48.38	27.27	30.07	33.67	22.16
Year unknown	3.75	3.91	3.84	4.06	1.82	6.05	3.51	2.66	7.56	4.26
Declared themselves by nationality (total)	87.23	81.07	83.97	82.60	95.12	88.53	89.16	86.70	98.47	91.68
1945 and earlier	9.12	6.50	5.48	8.08	7.32	5.64	10.55	10.53	11.29	10.48
1946–60	23.79	19.80	16.70	19.35	32.40	15.61	26.52	22.12	21.00	33.96
1961–70	24.35	21.61	23.91	25.05	31.40	20.22	24.42	25.05	25.63	23.31
1971–81	26.71	29.99	34.63	26.82	22.27	41.87	24.53	26.73	33.10	20.04
Year unknown	3.24	3.15	3.25	3.30	1.73	5.19	3.14	2.27	7.45	3.89
Montenegrin (total)	5.75	5.09	44.06	1.27	2.46	1.63	6.47	7.39	12.08	4.33
1945 and earlier	0.51	0.21	3.52	0.06	0.16	0.02	0.67	0.40	3.04	0.76
1946–60	1.49	1.35	9.50	0.38	0.84	0.20	1.74	1.58	3.36	1.78
1961–70	1.61	1.51	12.80	0.41	0.83	0.32	1.77	2.35	2.86	0.74
1971–81	1.93	1.84	16.59	0.37	0.59	0.98	2.07	2.88	1.76	0.86
Year unknown	0.21	0.19	1.65	0.06	0.04	0.11	0.23	0.18	1.06	0.19

Croat (total)	16.02	17.35	4.93	47.64	2.51	31.39	4.19	3.72	1.20	5.29
1945 and earlier	1.76	2.29	0.43	5.26	0.15	1.20	0.65	0.61	0.07	0.80
1946-60	4.17	4.57	1.34	11.46	0.87	6.59	1.57	1.37	0.31	2.05
1961-70	4.58	4.19	1.43	14.49	0.80	8.69	1.01	0.90	0.32	1.26
1971-81	4.84	5.54	1.58	14.51	0.64	13.09	0.79	0.74	0.42	0.90
Year unknown	0.68	0.76	0.15	1.91	0.05	1.82	0.17	0.11	0.08	0.29
Macedonian (total)	2.96	0.83	1.17	0.89	21.47	1.71	2.82	3.33	1.36	2.24
1945 and earlier	0.23	0.03	0.05	0.03	2.46	0.01	0.19	0.29	0.09	0.07
1946-60	1.00	0.17	0.20	0.22	7.69	0.15	1.02	1.01	0.16	1.14
1961-70	0.80	0.23	0.32	0.27	6.00	0.32	0.75	0.99	0.40	0.43
1971-81	0.84	0.36	0.56	0.32	4.89	1.13	0.77	0.95	0.63	0.51
Year unknown	0.09	0.04	0.04	0.05	0.44	0.10	0.09	0.09	0.08	0.09
Muslim (total)	4.97	19.04	8.41	4.07	11.24	7.80	2.39	2.42	15.36	0.64
1945 and earlier	0.24	1.39	0.73	0.12	0.13	0.01	0.13	0.15	0.75	0.02
1946-60	1.01	3.79	1.94	0.65	3.70	0.40	0.57	0.57	3.73	0.16
1961-70	1.41	5.32	1.99	1.18	4.96	1.16	0.69	0.65	5.16	0.15
1971-81	2.10	7.85	3.39	1.96	2.31	5.80	0.87	0.93	4.83	0.27
Year unknown	0.20	0.68	0.36	0.15	0.15	0.43	0.13	0.12	0.89	0.04
Slovene (total)	2.68	1.04	0.63	4.40	0.50	19.82	0.66	0.88	0.30	0.37
1945 and earlier	0.69	0.19	0.06	1.40	0.05	4.09	0.21	0.30	0.03	0.09
1946-60	0.83	0.41	0.19	1.36	0.19	5.92	0.21	0.27	0.06	0.14
1961-70	0.53	0.19	0.18	0.72	0.15	4.49	0.12	0.16	0.09	0.06
1971-81	0.50	0.20	0.16	0.73	0.10	4.29	0.10	0.13	0.10	0.05
Year unknown	0.12	0.05	0.03	0.19	0.01	1.04	0.02	0.02	0.03	0.02

Table 4-7. *Internal Ethnic Migration of the Population of the Former Yugoslavia, Various Periods, 1946-81 (continued)*

				Percent of population that migrated to:			Serbia		
	Yugoslavia	Bosnia-Herzegovina	Montenegro	Croatia	Macedonia	Slovenia	Total	Serbia proper	Kosovo	Vojvodina
Serb (total)	48.75	34.18	19.97	20.98	25.26	23.34	66.72	64.86	26.55	74.85
1945 and earlier	5.13	2.25	0.49	0.84	2.54	0.18	8.03	8.32	4.93	8.01
1946-60	13.76	8.60	2.83	4.45	8.32	1.95	20.06	16.32	6.63	27.54
1961-70	13.80	9.32	6.07	7.14	7.61	4.66	18.66	19.00	6.32	19.79
1971-81	14.42	12.69	9.89	7.74	6.51	15.01	17.82	19.70	6.67	16.43
Year unknown	1.63	1.32	0.70	0.80	0.29	1.55	2.13	1.53	2.00	3.07
Albanian (total)	3.40	1.98	2.75	1.06	24.70	1.17	3.09	1.65	38.86	0.57
1945 and earlier	0.15	0.05	0.10	0.01	1.23	0.00	0.16	0.08	2.19	0.01
1946-60	0.77	0.46	0.34	0.16	8.33	0.07	0.56	0.36	6.29	0.10
1961-70	0.97	0.47	0.59	0.25	9.10	0.20	0.79	0.43	9.85	0.15
1970-81	1.32	0.93	1.55	0.60	5.47	0.83	1.37	0.68	17.57	0.29
Year unknown	0.17	0.07	0.17	0.05	0.56	0.07	0.21	0.10	2.97	0.02
Maafri (Hungarian) (total)	0.83	0.46	0.38	0.97	0.24	0.51	0.94	0.60	0.19	1.55
1945 and earlier	0.18	0.01	0.01	0.17	0.02	0.04	0.24	0.10	0.01	0.48
1946-60	0.24	0.17	0.11	0.28	0.07	0.09	0.27	0.21	0.06	0.39
1961-70	0.19	0.12	0.13	0.25	0.07	0.14	0.20	0.14	0.05	0.30
1971-81	0.19	0.14	0.13	0.23	0.08	0.22	0.19	0.13	0.06	0.29
Year unknown	0.04	0.02	0.01	0.03	0.00	0.02	0.04	0.02	0.01	0.08

Other (total)	1.87	1.10	1.66	1.32	6.74	0.16	1.89	1.84	2.58	1.87
1945 and earlier	0.23	0.07	0.10	0.19	0.58	0.08	0.27	0.29	0.19	0.24
1946–60	0.52	0.29	0.26	0.37	2.38	0.24	0.51	0.43	0.40	0.66
1961–70	0.45	0.26	0.39	0.34	1.89	0.24	0.44	0.43	0.58	0.43
1971–81	0.56	0.44	0.77	0.37	1.68	0.53	0.56	0.59	1.07	0.44
Year unknown	0.09	0.04	0.14	0.05	0.20	0.06	0.11	0.10	0.33	0.09
Yugoslav (total)	11.05	17.35	12.62	14.82	3.84	7.26	9.70	11.60	1.13	7.93
1945 and earlier	1.03	1.03	0.47	0.87	0.26	0.23	1.26	1.59	0.10	0.92
1946–60	3.11	4.49	2.21	3.75	1.33	1.03	3.09	3.51	0.20	2.83
1961–70	3.10	4.77	3.93	4.57	1.09	1.58	2.61	3.32	0.29	1.83
1971–81	3.43	6.43	5.62	5.07	1.11	4.00	2.44	2.89	0.47	2.01
Year unknown	0.38	0.64	0.38	0.56	0.04	0.42	0.30	0.29	0.08	0.34

Source: *Yugoslavia 1918–1988, Statistical Yearbook*, Federal Bureau of Statistics, Belgrade, February 1989, p. 44. This table was prepared in the Center for Economics Informatics and Statistics, Economic Institute, Zagreb.

In the period immediately following the creation of the first Yugoslav state, there were two main political movements or parties, one of which was Croatian and the other, Serbian. The Croatian movement was associated with the Croatian Peasant (Republican) party, under the leadership of the Radić brothers. The Serbian movement was associated with the Serbian Radical party under the leadership of Nikola Pašić. These two political movements and their corresponding parties had differing attitudes toward the formation of the new state. The Croatian Peasant party wanted a decentralized federal state, while the Serbian Radical party wanted a centralized unitary state. Because of the circumstances of the time, the political philosophy of the Serbian Radical party prevailed. Thus from the very beginning, there was conflict and confrontation between the Serbs and Croats. The escalation of these tensions culminated in 1928, when a leader of the Croatian Peasant party, Stjepan Radić, was killed in the Yugoslav Parliament. Nevertheless, political confrontations between the Serbs and Croats determined the nature not only of the first, but also the second Yugoslavia. In the midst of the demise of the Bolshevik option and the accompanying process of pluralization and decentralization, the confrontations among the Serbs and Croats escalated considerably, as did the popularity of various nationalist movements among the Muslims, Albanians, Macedonians, and Slovenians. These conflicts culminated in a continuing historical drama that was initiated by Serbian aggression.

The outcome of this drama will depend in part on whether the situation in Kosovo, which was the historical cause of many key incidents during the existence of the former Yugoslavia, will escalate or be contained (with the participation of the international community). The term "contain" is used intentionally because the historical and present conflict pertaining to Kosovo is so complex and difficult that it is very hard to offer even a theoretical, let alone a concrete and viable, solution. Historically, and at present, Serbian nationalism was fed and escalated in large part in connection with the question of Kosovo. It should be remembered that the "Serbian revolution" of 1988 started in Kosovo under the slogan of "people happening" and with the overthrow of the 1974 Constitution of the Socialist Republic of Yugoslavia, which had a confederate character and which gave constitutional rights to the provinces of Vojvodina and Kosovo. These developments mark the true beginning of the disintegration of the former Yugoslavia.

Without excusing aggressive nationalism elsewhere in the former Yugoslavia, it remains a historical fact that, starting with Kosovo, Serbian nationalism initiated and fed all the other nationalisms.[2] Unfortunately, in conjunction with that nationalism, Serbia was and remains the mightiest military power among the nations of the former Yugoslavia. Therefore, despite the positive efforts of the United Nations, the European Union, and the United States, the conflict remains unresolved. Indeed, it may take many decades before its conclusion; we are just witnessing the beginnings of a possible solution to the Palestinian question, and there are many indications that the "question of Kosovo" will not be much easier to deal with.

At first glance, it may seem as if the extensive discussion above does not address the theme of economic disparity as a factor in the disintegration process. Nevertheless, it is not possible to fully appreciate this factor without the other elements; the historical inheritance, demographic movements, internal ethnic migrations, as well as fragments of the historical and present political situation. This is especially true with respect to historical and present relations between the Serbs and Croats, and the corresponding relations between the states of Serbia and Croatia. These relations were fundamental to the determination of the economic and political situation in these respective territories, and there is no doubt that they will continue as such in the future. However, the relations between the Serbs and Croats in the newly independent states of Croatia and Bosnia-Herzegovina will have a decisive influence on the political and security situation on these territories.

Economic Differences and Performance as a Factor of Disintegration

Vast differences in the economic performance of former Yugoslav republics and provinces directly and indirectly stimulated the process of disintegration. Accelerated economic development was a high political priority in the former Yugoslavia, especially following the rift in the socialist bloc in the late 1940s and early 1950s, when workers' self-management was introduced and large-scale investment was required for its realization. The former Yugoslavia belonged to a category of countries that were rapidly developing. This process of development, which during the 1970s (according to United Nations criteria) resulted in Yugoslavia being classified among the ten newly industrialized countries, was expensive and ineffective.[3] The political and developmental policy of the former Yugoslavia placed considerable emphasis on the accelerated development of the less-developed republics and provinces. This policy was reflected in the size of investment efforts, as illustrated by the data contained in table 4-8.

A cursory glance at the data reveals considerable divergence in the levels of investment in the various republics and provinces. In general, investment rates were in inverse proportion to the level of economic development. While investment rates of 20 percent in developed countries are considered very high, during the observed period some republics and provinces had an even higher rate of investment. This especially applies to Kosovo, where in some years the investment rates in relation to fixed assets reached two-thirds of the social product (gross domestic product), so that the share of investment in the social product for the observed period on the whole amounts to approximately 50 percent. Such extremely high investment rates in the less developed republics and provinces were made possible by the Federal Credit Fund for the Development of Economically Underdeveloped Republics and Provinces. This fund centralized and redistributed financial assets from the more developed republics and provinces to the less developed ones. The total redistribution amounted to approximately 2 percent of the social product of Yugoslavia. The amount of redistribution through the federal budget for the purpose of decreasing disparity in the standard of living and living conditions was even greater. The formation and use of assets of the fund are illustrated by the data in tables 4-9 and 4-10.

The trend changed somewhat in 1990, as the inflow of money to the fund decreased. However, the data show a large redistribution of assets from the more to the less developed republics and provinces. This estimation is confirmed by the data concerning the proportion of fund assets to the investment in fixed assets of less developed republics and provinces, as well as the proportion of these assets in the social product of the developed and less developed republics and provinces, as demonstrated in tables 4-11, 4-12, and 4-13.

The data from these tables refer to five-year periods (except a four-year period during 1986–89), as well as to the whole period of the fund's activity from 1966 to 1989. This data, along with the data from tables 4-9 and 4-10, explain how such high investment rates could arise in the less-developed republics and provinces of the former Yugoslavia.

In this connection, it should be pointed out that the whole program of stimulating the rapid development of the less developed republics and provinces caused continuous conflict with the more developed repub-

Table 4-8. *Total Gross Investment Fixed Assets in the Social Sector of the Former Yugoslavia by Subperiods, 1953-89*

Years	Yugoslavia	Bosnia-Herzegovina	Montenegro	Croatia	Macedonia	Slovenia	Serbia			
							Total	Serbia proper	Kosovo	Vojvodina
1953-55	36.2	46.8	101.0	27.8	56.6	34.0	32.8	40.9	26.1	13.8
1953-60	35.3	38.4	89.0	28.9	50.0	29.4	37.5	42.2	43.1	25.0
1956-60	34.9	34.4	82.9	29.4	46.9	27.4	39.3	42.7	51.5	29.1
1961-65	36.4	35.1	65.1	32.0	78.3	29.2	36.6	38.7	63.2	27.5
1961-70	33.3	33.7	50.4	30.0	58.1	25.1	35.0	37.4	62.8	25.2
1966-70	31.4	32.9	43.8	28.5	44.5	22.2	34.8	37.2	63.7	24.4
1971-75	29.0	39.4	52.9	25.0	33.3	26.2	28.0	27.3	53.9	24.9
1966-75	30.0	36.7	49.0	26.5	37.9	24.6	30.8	31.4	57.9	24.7
1976-80	33.1	41.1	57.1	30.0	37.2	28.3	33.2	30.3	66.5	34.0
1981-89	20.2	24.1	31.0	19.1	16.7	18.0	20.7	20.5	36.1	18.2
1953-89	27.4	32.3	46.3	24.8	32.0	23.3	27.9	27.9	49.8	24.1
1953-80	32.4	38.3	57.9	28.6	43.5	27.0	33.0	33.2	59.9	28.1
1953-75	32.1	36.7	58.3	28.0	47.1	26.3	33.0	34.6	56.7	25.3
1953-65	35.8	37.4	74.8	30.3	64.4	29.4	36.6	40.1	53.0	25.9
1956-70	33.8	34.0	58.0	29.9	56.0	25.7	36.3	38.9	61.4	26.4
1961-75	31.5	36.3	52.7	27.8	46.6	25.6	32.2	33.2	59.1	25.4
1961-80	32.1	38.1	54.4	28.6	42.9	26.6	32.6	32.1	62.0	28.6
1971-80	31.3	40.4	55.3	27.8	35.6	27.4	31.0	29.1	61.2	30.1
1976-89	24.4	29.5	39.1	22.7	23.2	21.4	24.7	23.6	45.7	23.3
1966-89	26.0	31.5	41.9	23.8	27.4	22.3	26.5	25.9	49.2	23.7
1956-89	27.2	32.0	45.2	24.8	31.6	23.1	27.8	27.6	50.2	24.3

Source: *Statistical Yearbook of Yugoslavia 1991*, Belgrade, Federal Statistical Office. This table was prepared in the Center for Economic Informatics and Statistics, Economic Institute, Zagreb.

Table 4-9. *Formation of the Federal Credit Fund for the Development of Economically Underdeveloped Republics and Provinces, 1985-90*

Percent

Republic or province	1985	1986	1987	1988	1989	1990
Yugoslavia	100	100	100	100	100	100
Bosnia-Herzegovina	13.05	15.44	17.76	13.32	14.33	21.56
Montenegro	2.14	2.07	1.99	1.62	1.54	2.05
Croatia	25.28	23.08	24.37	24.38	26.42	17.27
Macedonia	6.65	4.99	5.34	5.55	6.52	8.11
Slovenia	14.72	18.00	18.51	20.10	23.77	8.35
Serbia (total)	38.16	36.40	32.03	35.03	27.42	42.65
Serbia proper	26.87	20.83	17.72	26.11	18.57	30.73
Kosovo	1.95	2.85	1.45	2.15	1.61	1.51
Vojvodina	9.34	12.72	12.86	6.77	7.24	10.41

Source: *Statistical Yearbook of Yugoslavia 1991*, p. 501. This table was prepared in the Center for Economic Informatics and Statistics, Economic Institute, Zagreb.

lics and provinces, which had competing interests. Similarly, the more or less decentralized system of foreign exchange also caused dissension. The developed republics of Croatia and Slovenia, as well as the province of Vojvodina, were inclined toward greater market activity, which entailed economic and political decentralization. The less developed republics and provinces, however, saw their interests served through an increased administrative centralization of assets for investment (through the fund) and foreign currency (through the National Bank of Yugoslavia).

Table 4-10. *Distribution of the Federal Credit Fund for the Development of Economically Underdeveloped Republics and Provinces, 1985-90*

Percent

Year	Total	Bosnia-Herzegovina	Montenegro	Macedonia	Kosovo
1985	100	25.18	9.99	25.27	39.56
1986	100	31.05	8.32	14.91	45.73
1987	100	28.52	9.47	17.85	44.15
1988	100	21.30	7.19	16.35	55.17
1989	100	28.32	7.66	18.84	45.18
1990	100	24.11	5.98	16.65	53.26

Source: *Statistical Yearbook of Yugoslavia 1991*, p. 501. This table was prepared in the Center for Economic Informatics and Statistics, Economic Institute, Zagreb.

Table 4-11. *Share of Fund Assets in Public Sector Fixed Asset Expenditure, 1966-89*

Percent, based on 1972 prices

Republic/autonomous region	1966-70	1971-75	1976-80	1981-85	1986-89	1966-89
Yugoslavia	5.8	5.1	5.5	7.1	8.8	6.4
Less developed republics/provinces						
Bosnia-Herzegovina	13.8	12.1	11.3	12.6	15.3	12.6
Montenegro	27.0	19.9	17.9	17.2	28.0	20.3
Macedonia	20.1	22.0	18.8	28.8	30.7	22.9
Kosovo	47.8	59.6	54.2	73.8	95.4	64.1
Average	21.5	20.5	19.4	24.5	29.9	22.4

Source: *Statistical Yearbook of Yugoslavia 1990*, p. 413, and data from the balance sheets of the Federal Credit Fund.

These conflicts of interests and quasi interests greatly contributed to the disintegration process. The term quasi interest is used here because it should have been clear to the less developed entities that decentralization meant the strengthening of the market and an accompanying improvement in economic efficiency, which was without a doubt the interest of both the less- and more developed republics and provinces. In practice, however, this reality was not acknowledged and, instead, efficiency in capital investment in the less developed republics fell even below what was attainable given their less developed economic structures. By using the assets accumulated through administrative redistribu-

Table 4-12. *Share of Fund Assets in the Social Product (GDP) and Investment in the Developed Republics and Vojvodina, 1971-89*

Millions of dinars, 1978 prices

Category	1971-75	1976-80	1981-85	1985-89	1971-89
Social product (total)	1,023,590	1,353,670	1,510,260	1,240,340	5,127,860
Realized investment in fixed assets	188,776	290,925	261,589	166,790	907,080
Fund assets					
Allocated assets	15,049	20,662	20,507	14,033	70,251
Returned annuities	151	2,420	2,977	191	5,739
Net outflow	14,898	18,242	17,530	13,842	64,512
Share of net outflow (percent)					
Social product	1.46	1.34	1.16	1.12	1.26
Investment	7.9	6.3	6.7	8.3	7.1

Source: *Statistical Yearbook of Yugoslavia 1990*, p. 413, and data from the balance sheet of the Federal Credit Fund.

Table 4-13. *Share of Fund Assets in the Social Product (GDP) and Investment in the Less Developed Republics and Kosovo, 1971-89*
Millions of dinars, 1978 prices

Category	1971-75	1976-80	1981-85	1985-89	1971-89
Social product (total)	284,730	373,820	434,120	365,330	1,458,000
Realized investment in fixed					
assets	79,394	114,019	95,874	47,780	337,067
Fund assets					
Inflow from less developed					
republics/provinces	4,001	6,051	6,344	4,588	20,984
Inflow from all	19,050	26,713	26,851	18,621	91,235
Difference	15,049	20,662	20,507	14,033	70,251
Returned annuities	151	2,420	2,977	191	5,739
Net inflow of assets	14,898	18,242	17,530	13,842	64,512
Share of net inflow					
Social product (%)	5.23	4.88	4.04	3.79	4.42
Investment (%)	18.8	16.0	18.3	29.0	19.1

Source: *Statistical Yearbook of Yugoslavia 1990*, p. 413, and data from the balance sheet of the Federal Credit Fund.

tion, the less developed republics and provinces developed bureaucratic structures that became the centers of economic and political power. Their principal objective was to achieve a greater redistribution of assets from the more developed entities, and to oppose market reforms that would weaken their position. In such a political context, the interrepublic and international tensions were continually strengthened. There was a prevailing impression among the less developed republics and provinces that more centralized administrative redistribution of investment assets and of foreign currency was to their benefit. The more developed republics and provinces, however, continually resisted such a policy, not so much because of the magnitude of redistribution, but more because of the legacy of irrational use of assets.[4]

Even worse, the main argument of the less developed republics and provinces in favor of an increase in redistribution was based on the criteria of gross domestic product (GDP) per capita. Measuring economic performance according to this criterion, however, was inadequate for two basic reasons. The first is low return on investment and the second, a large natural increase in population, which created a sort of vicious circle. All felt that the policy was unjust and exploitative toward them. The less developed republics did not adequately appreciate the efforts of the more developed in terms of redistributing assets. The more developed, on the other hand, in addition to critiquing the weak performance of redistributed assets, did not sufficiently respect its benefits in terms of the common Yugoslav market. While redistribution on behalf of the less developed republics could be clearly measured and expressed in terms of statistics, the benefits of the common market to the more developed could only be presumed rather than quantified statistically.

Consequently, all parties were dissatisfied with the status quo. The cumulative effect of such relations and tensions transformed interrepublic confrontations and conflicts to tensions of an international nature. These tensions were further exacerbated because the more developed republics were also obliged to redistribute assets to the less developed regions within their own republic. This especially applied to Croatia and its regions such as Dalmatinska zagora, Kordun, and Lika. In Slovenia as well, the northwest part (Gorenjsko) was much more developed than the southeastern part (Dolenjsko). Therefore, in addition to the other factors previously mentioned, the rise of nationalism in the former Yugoslavia was rooted in relations that created the perception among all of injustice and exploitation. This not only contributed to the process of disintegration, but also destroyed the areas in which cooperation was possible.[5]

The more concrete quantitative expressions of differences in the economic performance of the republics and provinces are illustrated in table 4-14.

Table 4-14 contains data on the rates of economic gross investments in fixed assets, capital coefficients, and growth rates of social products in the former Yugoslav republics and provinces. In order to prepare the relevant data, the Harrod-Domar model was used.[6] The economic logic of that model lies in defining the growth rate of social product as directly proportional to the investment rate and inverse to capital coefficient. The capital coefficient (in this case, marginal) provides the number of units of gross investment (in this case, of dinar) necessary to increase the social product for one unit, relative to a dinar. Consequently, the capital coefficient expresses the efficiency of investment. The differences in that efficiency are extreme; it cost twice as much in investments in Kosovo than it did in Slovenia, Croatia, and Vojvodina to obtain the same results in economic development. However, a relatively large capital coefficient can be noticed even in other less developed republics. An extremely high capital coefficient was noticed during the crisis of the 1980s. It is very important to note in this context that, in spite of great investment efforts, the less developed republics and the province of Kosovo realized relatively modest growth rates in social product.

Table 4-14. *Rates of Gross Investment in Fixed Assets of the Social Sector of the Economy, Capital Coefficients, and GDP Growth Rates, 1953–89 (by subperiods)*

Period	Yugoslavia	Bosnia-Herzegovina	Montenegro	Croatia	Macedonia	Slovenia	Serbia			
							Total	Serbia proper	Kosovo	Vojvodina
Rates of gross investment(s) (percent)										
1953-60	19.3	22.0	52.7	16.7	26.0	16.9	18.9	20.5	18.4	15.0
1961-70	20.4	20.8	36.5	18.8	32.9	16.4	20.9	20.7	39.4	17.9
1971-80	22.7	28.3	39.6	21.0	26.6	21.4	21.5	19.9	42.0	21.5
1981-89	16.3	18.8	21.9	15.7	13.0	14.9	16.4	16.4	25.3	14.6
1953-89	19.5	22.6	32.6	18.2	22.1	17.5	19.2	18.7	32.9	17.6
Capital coefficients (k)										
1953-60	2.2	3.0	8.9	1.9	3.2	1.9	2.0	2.3	2.3	1.2
1961-70	3.2	3.9	4.4	3.0	4.2	2.4	3.4	3.4	5.6	3.1
1971-80	4.0	5.1	6.4	3.9	4.6	3.5	3.7	3.4	7.6	3.7
1981-89	32.3	15.3	1,408.5	297.3	13.9	126.7	26.6	25.7	23.8	30.8
1953-89	3.7	4.7	6.3	3.6	3.9	3.2	3.5	3.5	6.2	3.0
GDP growth rates (r) (percent)										
1953-60	8.9	7.4	5.9	9.0	8.1	9.1	9.7	8.9	7.9	12.1
1961-70	6.3	5.4	8.4	6.3	7.9	6.9	6.1	6.1	7.0	5.8
1971-80	5.7	5.5	6.1	5.4	5.8	6.1	5.9	5.9	5.5	5.8
1981-89	0.5	1.2	0.0	0.1	0.9	0.1	0.6	0.6	1.1	0.5
1953-89	5.3	4.8	5.2	5.1	5.6	5.5	5.4	5.3	5.3	5.8

Source: *Statistical Yearbook of Yugoslavia*, Belgrade, 1991, Federal Statistical Office. This table was prepared in the Center for Economic Informatics and Statistics, Economic Institute, Zagreb.

All this leads to the conclusion that even the considerable investments of the Federal Credit Fund had yielded weak economic results. This situation was also greatly influenced by the economic system, which did not enable the market allocation of investment. That, however, did not in the least help alleviate the dissatisfaction of the developed republics, which rightfully considered the weak economic performance in the less-developed republics and Kosovo to be the result of wrongly directed investment and wrong investment decisions. These investment decisions were influenced considerably by the previously mentioned administrative centers of power, which were given great authority on the basis of assets accumulated through the fund. This exacerbated political tensions between the various republics and nations. The dissatisfaction of the developed republics, especially Croatia and Slovenia, increased, while at the same time the less-developed republics and Kosovo consistently demanded more economic support, which they justified on the basis of social product per capita (see tables 4-1 and 4-2).

Demographic investment rates show those rates that had to be inverted into the republic and province in a determined period in order to keep the social product per capita, with respect to the population increase, at the achieved level. The demographic investment rate is calculated by multiplying the capital coefficient by the growth rate of the population. Considerable differences are evident. Only 1.8 and 2.4 percent of social product had to be invested in Croatia and Slovenia, respectively, whereas in Kosovo, 15.6 percent of social product had to be invested for the same purpose. In other less-developed republics, large differences can be noticed at the lower level.

As early as the 1950s, the economists—particularly at the Institute of Economics in Zagreb—had pointed out these problems, which in a multinational state had not only economic but also political implications.[7] The corresponding United Nations agencies identified these problems in relation to active demographic policy. Nevertheless, perhaps because of political opportunism, the dominant political actors did not show any interest in these problems. The results were crushing: uncontrolled demographic movements and investment in the mosaic of deep historical, national, and economic differences that characterized the former Yugoslavia were among the most important factors in the process leading to serious tensions and eventual disintegration.

Development Strategy and the Economic System as a Factor in Disintegration

As it is generally known, economic reforms in the former Yugoslavia started much earlier than in any other former socialist country. The first major reforms occurred at the beginning of the 1950s through the introduction of workers' self-management. The basic questions of the reform referred to the development strategy and economic system. With respect to the conception and strategy of development, the point of departure was an economic model that started with export promotion as opposed to import substitution, or the so-called open economy model. With respect to the economic system, the point of departure was an economic model that operated on the basis of decentralized economic decisions, free circulation of labor goods and capital, the common Yugoslav market, the freedom of economic enterprises in making business decisions; in short, an economic model that operated on the basis of market institutions, mechanisms, critera, and relations.

It should be said in this connection that, throughout this period of reform in the former Yugoslavia, the conflict between proreform and antireform forces concentrated on the aforementioned questions of development strategy and economic system. The conflicts concerning the division of labor in the common Yugoslav market always existed in the field of development strategy. Under the influence of the Soviet interpretation of the Marxist theory of production, each of the republics wanted to have a self-contained economic structure with an emphasis on heavy industry. These mistakes of developmental orientation and policy became especially apparent during the first phase of industrialization in the 1950s. An immediate consequence was a deformation of the economic structure that could not be easily corrected in the subsequent phases of development. Such aspects of the development strategy jeopardized the unity of the common Yugoslav market and thereby contributed to the existing tensions.

Natural conditions and the inherited development level, along with the tendency of autarchic development not only on the level of Yugoslavia but also on the level of the republics, provinces, and regions, tended to create differing and peculiar economic structures in the various republics and provinces. The more developed republics—Slovenia, Croatia, and, in some respects, Serbia (without Kosovo)—were more involved in the production of final products. The less developed republics and provinces, especially Bosnia-Herzegovina and Kosovo, were more involved in the production of energy as well as intermediate goods and raw materials. In this context, there were continual conflicts concerning pricing policy, customs duties and protection. Final products were under considerable protection while raw materials were subject to few barriers. These conflicts involved the foreign exchange system and the policy of a higher or lower real exchange rate for the dinar; directly or indirectly, they also had the character of conflicts not only between the republics and provinces, but also between peoples and nations. Consequently, it could be predicted that the tendency toward autarchic development at all levels continually weakened cohesion.

With respect to the evolution of the economic system, the basic conflicts related to functional questions and to market development; common agreement related only to the function of a commodity and the services market. The basic differences, dilemmas, and conflicts referred to the development of the institutions of the capital and labor markets. Moreover, although the institutional framework enabled relatively free circulation of labor and somewhat less of capital, neither the institutions of the labor market nor those of the capital market developed satisfactorily. Along with the greater emphasis on the role of the market (especially the commodity and goods and services market) in relation to other ex-socialist countries, a policy of "soft budget constraints" was actually developing, especially so-called selective loans for special purposes such as agriculture, export of machines and ships, and so on. Such a policy represented a constant source of interacting conflicts of republics and provinces. In addition, the fiscal and tax systems, which were mostly based on indirect taxes (sales tax), were resulting in a major redistribution from the developed republics. The biggest part of the federal budget (which figured at approximately 10 percent of the social product, with about one-half for maintaining the army) was financed from the most developed republics and provinces. All of these factors further weakened internal cohesion and aggravated existing tensions among the various peoples and nationalities.

Accordingly, the self-management socialism of the former Yugoslavia suffered the same destiny as the real socialism of the other former socialist countries. The inadequate functioning of the labor and capital markets created conflict among the republics and nations with respect to all aspects of economic system. This especially refers to the system and policy of accelerated development of the less developed republics and provinces as already discussed, as well as to the foreign exchange system and rate policy of the dinar. Although convertability of the dinar was imposed as a fundamental precondition of reform, it was only partially realized, and then only after the disintegration of the former Yugoslavia had already begun.

The first major attempt to bring about reforms to enable the development of the open-market economic model was in 1965.[8] After initial sucesses, the reform was abandoned at the end of the 1960s. The 1970s brought the restoration of the economic system (the agreed economy) and progress in the political system. The Constitution of 1974 provided the institutional framework of political confederation. Given that the constitution contained the economic bases for the 1965 reform and the development model of an open-market economy, the former Yugoslavia can be seen as the first formerly socialist country that definitely broke all the barriers of the Bolshevist framework. That it ended in a tragic and violent disintegration should not decrease the significance of the Yugoslav reform process during four decades of development, and the great influence that it had in the process of decentralization in the other formerly socialist countries.[9] All these developments accelerated the collapse of the Bolshevist option.[10]

The short-lived experience with radical reforms (which were already of a transitional character) at the end of the 1980s and the beginning of the 1990s, when the restricted convertibility of the dinar was introduced, confirms in itself the previously mentioned assessments.[11] Nevertheless, disruptive forces eventually resulted in the collapse of Yugoslavia. Of course, a proper appraisal of these forces calls for a far deeper multidimensional and multidisciplinary study.[12]

Among all the former Yugoslav republics, only Slovenia and Croatia, as newly independent and internationally recognized states (although Croatia is still at war), function normally, at least to a certain extent, although both of them clearly feel the loss of the Yugoslav market. Nevertheless, after all that has occurred during the past years, and especially during the period of Serbian aggression, it appears that the only solution for all the newly independent states on the territory of the former Yugoslavia is independent development according to their specific requirements as a preparatory phase for eventual integration into the evolving common European market.

Some Observations

On the basis of the foregoing discussion and analysis, the following observations may be made:

—Throughout the period of existence of the former Yugoslavia, a broad spectrum of fundamental differences among the republics and provinces contributed to an eventual process of disintegration.

—The multifaceted and fundamental differences were, for the most part, historically inherited, although they continued and intensified during the existence of the common Yugoslav state.

—The differences in the levels of economic development, demographic movements, ethnic structure, civilizational and cultural levels, tradition, habits, psychology, and outlook were key elements in the process of disintegration.

—There are insufficient statistical and empirical indicators to analyze and evaluate the economic effects of the disintegration of Yugoslavia on its former republics and provinces, because, as newly independent states, only Slovenia and, to a lesser extent, Croatia, which is still at war, function with any degree of economic stability.

—The only viable solution for all the republics of the former Yugoslavia as newly independent states is to pursue independent economic policies directed toward eventual integration into the evolving common European market, taking into account the varying requirements and levels of development of each state.

—There are many elements in favor of the presumption that this approach could be applied to all the other former socialist states, especially countries in transition that experience disintegration processes similar to that of the former Yugoslavia.

CHAPTER FIVE

The Linguistic Aspect of Ethnic Conflict in Yugoslavia

Albina Nečak Luk

T O SPEAK ABOUT language and ethnic conflict in the former Yugoslavia is a rather demanding task. The nationality section of the 1991 census, which is composed of twenty-eight categories, is a clear reflection of the great diversity in the ethnic composition of Yugoslavia. This is linked to a complex linguistic reality where a continuum of standard dialect local speech exists within each ethnic entity. It also reveals the very complex sociolinguistic and psycholinguistic implications of contact between languages and linguistic groups. The number of ethnic groups does not correspond to the number of languages. Four Yugoslav nations share what is essentially one common language, although with two alphabets, while several others have distinct languages.

The Historical Development of Languages as an Element of the National Question

The search for a standard written form for some Yugoslav languages that occurred in the late nineteenth century and continued into the twentieth century paralleled the development into modern nations of peoples using these languages (that is, Serbo-Croatian, Slovene). The written form of other languages was settled only recently. Thus, for instance, the first grammar for Macedonian was prepared only after World War II, while the features of a common standard Albanian language were agreed upon only around 1970. Moreover, the languages of some ethnic groups have not yet fully developed a standard written form (for example, Vlach) or have only begun to develop such a form (for example, Romani/Gypsy).

From the point of view of language policy, and especially from the point of view of the legal and political status of language, this historically conditioned variance in the development of individual languages has had a considerable influence on the realization of linguistic rights. At the federal level, relations among three Slavic languages—Macedonian, Serbo-Croatian (spoken by four nations: Croats, Serbs, Montenegrins, and Muslims), and Slovene—received the most attention. At the level of the republics, the languages of the South Slavic nations coexisted with either the Slavic languages of national minorities (Ruthenian, Ukrainian, Slovak, Czech, Bulgarian) or languages of national minorities from other linguistic families (Italian, Romanian, Albanian, Hungarian, Turkish, Romani, and so forth).

The problem of language continuity and discontinuity should also be mentioned. Broken language and sociocultural ties with the nation of origin diverted the development of individual minority languages from the mainstream, thus exacerbating differences in the minority group's speech repertoire. Variations were caused by the differences of dialect, especially where numerically smaller minority groups of a predominantly rural nature were concerned, and also resulted from the influence of intensive contact with a majority language and sociocultural reality. In view of the societal functions of minority languages, the question of repertoire and dialects seems to be of major importance for the linguistic behavior of minority members, as well as for motivating members of majority language groups to develop communicative competence in a minority language.

An approximate typology of the language continuity and discontinuity of minority languages in Yugoslavia is as follows:

—Languages that experienced relatively close contact with mainstream language development: Italian, Hungarian, Albanian;
—Languages that had a loose contact with mainstream language development: Romanian, Bulgarian;
—Languages which were not in contact with mainstream language development: Slovak, Czech, Ruthenian, Ukrainian, Turkish; and
—Languages without a standard written form and those in the course of standardization: Vlach, Romani, Cincari, Arumanian, and so forth.

Another fact to bear in mind is that sociopolitical relations among Yugoslav nations and national minorities have been subject to change during various historical periods. In border regions, changes in the status of individual groups occurred either with outbreaks of war or through peace treaties: a majority in one period became a minority in another and vice versa. Changes to borders and to the balance of political power also brought about changes in the status of the interacting languages and influenced the sociopsychological nature of interethnic relations, together with perceptions and attitudes regarding interacting languages and their role in public use.

The fact that members of one nation or of the same national minority were citizens of different republics or states and were thus subject to different legislation and to different language policies contributed to the complexity of the phenomenon. In addition to the traditional situations where languages of autochtonous national minorities came into contact with languages of other Yugoslav nations, new contacts were created by migration, the largest migratory waves being from the Serbo-Croatian, Macedonian, and Albanian linguistic milieus to Slovenia.

The sociolinguistic features noted above demonstrate the important role of language policy in Yugoslavia as an essential component of Yugoslav policies of interethnic relations. Inter-nation relations played an important role in the very establishment of Yugoslavia as a sovereign state. After all, the very reason for the creation of a multinational state after World War I was the aspirations of the nations that were thereby united to safeguard and develop their national (ethnic, cultural, and linguistic) characteristics. In the multicultural and multilinguistic reality of Yugoslavia, however, the question of how to achieve harmonious coexistence among different ethnic groups has been answered in different ways in different periods. At the beginning of the newly created Kingdom of Yugoslavia after World War I, the regulation of relations among the languages of the three constituent nations—Croats, Serbs, and Slovenes—was the dominant concern. Owing to their ethnic similarity, these three nations were considered merely three tribes of one nation. In fact, language policy reflected the centralist conception of the first Yugoslavia and the basic premise that the concept of a nation was closely related to language. Hence, the four modern nations that spoke Serbo-Croatian in common were considered as a single nation, while the Slovenes with their language were supposed to merge sooner or later into the single, emerging Yugoslav nation. For its part, Macedonian was considered as either a Serbian or a Bulgarian dialect, depending on the nationality of the linguists who analyzed its structure. The smoldering conflict between Croats and Serbs on the linguistic issue was only exacerbated by such a policy. The official centralist policy was well served by the basic premise of the Serbo-Croatian norm, as set out in 1850 in the so-called Vienna Agreement by a group of linguists with pan-Slavic orientation, to the effect that the Serbian and Croatian were but two varieties of the same language.

Subsequent historical developments gave rise to the the gradual emergence of the principle of the equality of nations and ethnic groups. At the rhetorical level, cultural and linguistic differences in Yugoslavia were considered a source of enrichment for the development of ethnic groups, separately and together. Cultural pluralism became the basic principle of interethnic relations in Yugoslavia and "unity in diversity" was proclaimed as a common goal and value. Such an approach was intended to eliminate both ethnic ghettoization and assimilation and to bring about equal opportunities for social advancement to members of both minority and majority nations, irrespective of their ethnic origin. Linguistic pluralism, of course, represents a salient component of cultural pluralism. The role of languages was based on the equality of relations among the various ethnic groups, with the language of each serving as the means for the involvement of the group in all spheres of social activity.

Linguistic Pluralism and Language Policy in Yugoslavia

The language policy model in Yugoslavia was directive in nature, with an admixture of self-management features. Yugoslavia was among those multilingual states that based language policy on the territorial principle but that, in addition, respected the right of an individual to maintain and use his or her mother tongue throughout the state. This right was safeguarded for the dealings of the individual citizen with the authorities, regardless of whether his or her mother tongue was an official language in the area in which its use was at issue, in accordance with the constitution and other legal provisions (the individual right). On the other hand, the languages of nations and ethnic groups were accorded the status of official languages in the regions inhabited by them and for the purpose of interethnic communication (a collective or group right limited to a given area inhabited by a particular group). The territorial principle also meant developing a system of institutional support to enable the language of an individual ethnic group to function on equal terms parallel to the majority language in all channels of public communication, both official and unofficial.

The territorial principle relative to languages in public communication required an agreement on the status and use of individual languages on both the local and wider sociopolitical levels. For the sake of analysis, three levels of linguistic relations can be observed. The first is the level of official Yugoslav political and social life. This comprised:

—Communication on the federal level, where matters of common interest and importance to all republics and autonomous provinces were addressed with respect to certain matters (in the work of various federal organs, the languages of Hungarian and Albanian ethnic groups were also admitted as equal languages);
—Communication between federal institutions and republics and/or autonomous provinces; and
—Direct communication between republics/autonomous provinces.

The second level involved relations between languages of Yugoslav nations and of autochtonous ethnic groups in the territory they inhabited. This was the level of republics and autonomous provinces, but in fact the bulk of these relations were realized at the district level, where the actual interaction and communication between members of a majority and a minority were matters of everyday life and work.

The third level can be designated as the level of contact between the language of a nation and the languages of migratory members of nations and national minorities from other republics or autonomous provinces.

The equal status of a language, however, depends upon the extent that it can be used in social interaction. In this field, the language conflict was the most explicit, manifested as a struggle especially on the part of Slovenes but also on the part of Macedonians to ensure their language had access on an equal level with Serbo-Croatian to all channels of social communication in the framework of the Yugoslav federation. Since the national equality dilemma was supposedly resolved by the mere introduction of the socialist system after 1945, there seemed to be no need to specify the roles of individual languages in public life more precisely. Thus the functions of the Slovene and Macedonian languages, in spite of the principle of explicit equality, were limited not only to communication on the federal level but also to the territory of their own republics.

Besides having an exclusive status for communication between sociopolitical organs at the federal level, in practice, Serbo-Croatian held the status of the language of government. Although this role was not granted formally to Serbo-Croatian, it dominated certain channels of public communication even within Slovene and Macedonian linguistic territory. In addition to Slovene and Macedonian names on public signs on federal institutions in Slovene and Macedonian territory (railway, customs offices, and so forth), Serbo-Croatian was present as well, usually in Cyrillic characters. Instructions for industrial products, medicines, and so forth were usually only in Serbo-Croatian; subtitles for films were in Serbo-Croatian, and so on. Serbo-Croatian newspapers and magazines were traditionally accessible in both linguistic territories while, after the formal regulation of the equal status of the languages of Yugoslav nations, printed matter in Slovene or Macedonian was seldom available even in tourist areas outside these two republics.

In Slovenia and Macedonia, Serbo-Croatian was obligatory in schools even after World War II, while Slovene and Macedonian did not even have the status of optional subjects at schools in Serbo-Croatian linguistic territory. Only in the 1970s did Slovene appear occasionally as an option at schools in border towns. The Slovene public raised the question of regulating relations between the languages of Yugoslav nations by demanding the introduction of Slovene news on television. Initiatives to expand the use of Slovene to all levels of public communication in Slovenia and to the whole sphere of communication on the federal level met with difficulties not only in the broader territory of Yugoslavia but also among Slovenes. Some saw this demand as an unnecessary whim, and there was considerable opposition to the proposal on the grounds that it demonstrated separatist tendencies, a threat to unity, and so forth. Especially untouchable was the language of the Yugoslav army. While Slovene had functioned as a language of command during the war, with the constitution of 1974, Serbo-Croatian supplanted it. According to the provisions of this constitution, Serbo-Croatian remained the only language of command, while other languages could be used in education and other activities, as specified by other legislation.

In spite of this, there was a gradual response to the linguistic problem in Yugoslavia in practice (in 1965 Slovene television started to broadcast the main daily news in Slovene), as well as at the formal level. Macedonia joined the Slovene efforts when legislation was discussed on protecting the status and use of Macedonian in public communication. However, under the pressure of the concept of *zajednistvo* (unity), the idea was abandoned. Constitutional amendments at the end of the 1960s and the 1974 Constitution regulated relations between the languages of the Yugoslav nations on the federal level by declaring them as equal, with no language being superior to others. Macedonian, Slovene, and Serbo-Croatian functioned equally for communication in all spheres of the federation's work, even in international affairs (that is, treaties). In certain spheres at the federal level, Albanian and Hungarian also acquired certain functions. The Slovene constitution of 1974 defined Slovene as the language of business in the territory of Slovenia (and on nationally mixed territories, Italian and Hungarian as well), and thereby denied Serbo-Croatian the status of language of communication in Slovene territory.

Nevertheless, there were misunderstandings and conflicts even after 1974. The question of the language of command in the army remained unresolved. Slovenia earned additional distrust by founding the so-called language arbitration court, whose task was the development of the linguistic culture and the advancement of Slovene in public communication. The fact that the linguistic problem in Yugoslavia had not been satisfactorily resolved was demonstrated during the trial of four Slovenes at the military court-martial in Ljubljana when the demand to use Slovene during the trial appeared among the flowers of the "Slovene Spring." On the other hand, resolution of the Serbo-Croatian linguistic dilemma was far from settled. All the Yugoslav constitutions from 1946 to 1974 dealt with the linguistic situation and the status of languages in Yugoslavia. The provisions, of course, became increasingly detailed and precise.

To better understand the present situation, the names of the versions of the language spoken by four Yugoslav nations (Croatians, Serbs, Montenegrins, and Muslims—the nation constituted in the 1960s) are most interesting and indicative. In the 1946 constitutions of individual republics within Serbo-Croatian linguistic territory, the following were official languages: "Serbian" and "Croatian" in Bosnia-Herzegovina; "Serbian" in Serbia, with the addition of "Croatian" and the languages of national minorities in the autonomous provinces (for instance during court proceedings); "Croatian" or "Serbian" in Croatia; and "Serbian" in Montenegro. With regard to the 1963 constitutions, the language of the four nations is called "Serbo-Croatian" in the constitutions of Bosnia-Herzegovina and Serbia, "Croato-Serbian" in the constitution of Croatia, and "Serbo-Croatian" in the constitution of Montenegro. The 1974 constitutions spoke of "Serbo-Croatian" in Serbia, while in Croatia the Croatian literary language—the standard form of the national language of Croats and Serbs living in Croatia, which is called Croatian or Serbian was in official use. In Bosnia-Herzegovina it was "Serbo-Croatian" or

"Croato-Serbian," while the constitution of Montenegro did not mention an official language.

These classifications reflect the apparent regulation of the status and use of both versions of Serbo-Croatian, which was defined as the common literary language according to the 1850 Vienna Agreement and again by the 1954 Novi Sad Agreement. But for many, the idea of two versions of the Serbo-Croatian literary language is contentious. While many Serbian linguists and writers deny it, a fear prevails on the Croatian side that the Serbian version of Serbo-Croatian is being dictated for public communication. The fear of one version becoming predominant is particularly acute in Bosnia-Herzegovina, where the linguistic situation is by far the most complex. After a heated debate at the 1965 Congress of Yugoslav Slavists, the conflict sharpened, and in 1966 the Declaration on the Name and Status of the Croatian Language, demanding the consistent use of Croatian language and names in schools, press, public, and political life, was published in Zagreb and signed by some 140 Croatian intellectuals, including members of the Central Committee of the League of Communists of Croatia, as well as by eighteen Croatian cultural and scientific institutions. Immediately after the declaration, at the annual meeting of their society, forty-two Serbian writers, among them members of the Central Committee of the League of Communists of Serbia, signed the so-called Proposal for Consideration, in which they acknowledged the professional qualifications of the institutions that signed the declaration to decide on the name and status of the Croatian language. For this reason they considered the Vienna and Novi Sad Agreements of no further use: "the Croatian and Serbian languages will develop as completely independent and equal languages." The attempt to divide the languages was labeled nationalistic and was suppressed through a strong political campaign (many members of the Communist party were expelled or otherwise punished).

While in Serbia and Croatia the language problem was pushed into the background, in Bosnia-Herzegovina the concept of linguistic tolerance and equality began to spring up in the 1970s. Discussions on the status of the languages also began in Bosnia-Herzegovina. As far as the status of national minorities was concerned, language equality was safeguarded on two levels: on one hand, minority languages had the status of official languages, or at least equal languages, in the territory where minority populations lived together with majority populations. This also meant that institutional support was granted for the maintenance of language functions and language use. On the other hand, the language policy of societal and individual bilingualism was practiced in order to bridge the sociocultural gap and overcome obstacles in social interaction and communication.

In actual practice, equal access to all channels of public communication was possible only to a limited extent for the languages of certain linguistic minorities. In particular, it was not possible to include the languages of the numerically smaller ethnic communities in all formal communication situations either because of their level of functional development or because of the characteristic social structure of the minority and other economic and ethno-demographic factors. Especially in smaller ethnic communities, it was possible to notice characteristic generational shifts in the communication competence of their members.[1] But in all of them, even in more numerous and socially better-situated minorities, a two-way bilingualism, which could actually help increase the number of public contexts in which the use of the minority language along with the majority language would be proper, remained unrealized. (The very idea was abandoned at the beginning of the advancement of the "Unified Serbia" concept with the abolition of the previous status of the two autonomous provinces. The decree that Serbo-Croatian would be a required subject in minority schools, first in Kosovo and later in Vojvodina, was one of the first in a series of decrees meant to abolish the concept of linguistic equality in Serbia.) To a certain extent, bilingualism has been successful in Slovenia in the nationally mixed regions of Prekmurje and the three littoral districts, where the use of minority languages in public contexts was increased with the help of institutional support. Nevertheless, it would have been necessary to invest a great deal in order to realize total bilingualism.

CHAPTER SIX

Yugoslav Origins of the Post-Yugoslav Situation and the Bleak Prospects for Civil Society

Žarko Puhovski

THE TERM "postcommunist" is widely but somewhat misleadingly used to describe the period emerging after the decline of communist regimes. The postcommunist world, however, continues to be divided, not only economically or socially, but also politically. Although the world is evidently different as a result of the disintegration of the eastern bloc, most ex-communist countries experiencing so-called postcommunism are still under the direct influence of their communist heritage, which is reflected in practically all areas of their political, economic, cultural, and social life.

The hopes that led intellectuals and activists, thousands of dissidents, and then millions of voters in the first elections to put an end to the decades of communist rule were directly connected with the ideals of democracy, the free market, and the "European way of life." And yet without overlooking the considerable differences among these mainly eastern and central European countries, it is already quite clear that the actual problem is not in the fact (which can be easily explained) that these ideals have not yet been realized (since they were clearly unattainable in such a short period of time), but rather they were is a contrary trend toward premodern and even totalitarian political and social currents.

The Transformation of Collectivism

The keyword prevalent in any analysis of postcommunist situations, irrespective of the political or ideological persuasion of the analysis, is *nationalism.* Even at the phenomenological level, it is rather obvious that nationalism is the essential political ideology, method of historical interpretation, or legitimation of governments in various states. Nevertheless, the essential question concerns the origins of the nationalistic tendencies that have prevailed in the immediate postcommunist environment in contrast to other, primarily west, European countries where nationalism does not have such an important role. In this connection, a central issue is the set of underlying reasons for the different consequences that nationalism has in the various postcommunist countries; in some countries it has led to horrific wars, while in others it is simply a nuisance during a period of transition.

The origins of the specific role and form of nationalism typical of the former communist countries are found in the characteristics of the *ancien régime* of the eastern bloc. The previously mentioned differences in the situation of west European countries in the postcommunist world are at least one reason for making such an assumption. Another reason is that, despite the obvious differences that remain between the former communist states, there is considerable similarity in the basic ideological, political, and social constructs of their respective nationalisms.

Three fundamental elements of postcommunist nationalism have their origins in the old system. Communism was based on an antiliberal ideology that was at the same time collectivist and belligerent in character. The fact that the system was based on ideology is due to a distinctive element of the system; namely, that its fundamental construction was political such that the whole history of communism was a history of dictatorship over society. This type of dictatorship was strictly political in the sense that politics had the possibility not only to regulate, but also to determine basic relations within society.

In such a situation, all attempts to act politically or socially without the omnipresent control of the dominating "ideological apparatus of the state" had to rely upon easily identifiable groups of independent actors that were not subject to ideological manipulation by the state. Therefore, it could not have been just any type of ideology; the obvious and only choice was an ideology that could identify the members of the group more or less automatically. Such group identification was most readily found in ethnicity, which can be demonstrated simply through language (or dialect) or even by name (or family name) in such a way that it cannot be easily stopped or controlled. Accordingly, ethnic membership was a sort of "natural" context for the activities of most dissidents, with the consequence that, in many cases, what was meant to be the (re)birth of civil society turned out to be the renaissance of the ethnonational community.

The antiliberal constitution of the communist political sphere (with its enormous authority) was supported by a similar type of dominant ideology. This system functioned as a sort of giant freezer, literally petrifying all the political currents that were part of the history of states that became communist. The disintegration of such systems led almost directly to the same political situation that prevailed in those countries before communist rule; in the ethnically mixed states of eastern and central Europe, this was a historical and political situation characterized by nationalism and interethnic hostility. Yet there was an additional element that made the situation even worse: on the basis of exactly the same reasons, every ethnic group believed, and still believes, that it was the main victim of the communist system and that, in contrast, the rival ethnic group was a beneficiary.

Class struggle was a dominant ideological doctrine, and for decades society was indoctrinated with collectivist rhetoric. Against this background of an indoctrinated "public sphere," it was relatively easy to transform one form of collectivist ideology into another, even if it was distant in content, so long as the collectivist nature of the ideology was preserved. Therefore, ethnonational collectivism was almost tailor-made to replace the old ideological schema. Another element of this ideological universe that was favorable for elevating the importance of nationalism in the postcommunist states was the element of struggle in the official ideology of communism. Its sequel was the formulation of ideological and political life in terms of an existential struggle between friend and foe, which suited the nationalist world view rather well.

The first postcommunist elections, which in some countries were the first ever, have clearly shown that nationalistic ideologies are predominant. In certain respects, this has been translated into the continuing primacy of the political sphere and, therefore, the secondary importance of the social and economic sector. It has also meant that the new community would be constituted on a very rigid basis. Although many elements of the old system were inherited, the state was organized according to a "new" ideology (which at the same time claims to be ancient). The new ideology is, nevertheless, willing and able to adopt totalitarian characteristics.

This background constituted the formative context of the events in 1989, and it gave rise to a process the outcome of which was remarkably similar to the old system. Instead of the socialist state, the nation-state became the unquestionable framework for the reconstruction of society and, of course, in multiethnic federal entities such as the Soviet Union and Yugoslavia, this implied the inevitable disintegration of the federation.

It is apparent that nationalism as a general doctrine is based on the premise that the highest allegiance is owed to the nation. Therefore, membership in a nation is seen as an essential good for every human being. Nationalist sentiments in political terms are translated into the pursuit of the national interest at the expense of the interests of other nations and without regard for other values such as peaceful coexistence, respect for international law, or the maintenance of international cooperation through bilateral or multilateral treaties and institutions.

In the process of political transformation, the ethnic groups in the old states (including those with ambitions to change the old boundaries to suit their convenience) were consolidated as "peoples" and became the very basis of the emerging democratic order. This process was primarily the result of the rejection of the old regime in favor of the Western democratic model, and the nation served as a vehicle. Nevertheless, although in many respects this was a development worthy of support, there were serious drawbacks in the policy of transforming the leading or majority ethnic group into the exclusive popular base of the newly established democratic order. In essence, this meant that all the other inhabitants of the territory whose ethnicity was different from that of the majority were relegated to inferior status. Even their citizenship—that is, their fundamental right to participate in the political process of their respective countries—became contested through new citizenship legislation. Slovenia, Croatia, Latvia, and Ukraine are examples of this.

The tendency to define the ethnic group that is in the position of majority as "the" people or an exclusive community of citizens leads to an ethnically based definition of sovereignty. Therefore, international recognition of the sovereignty of formerly federated entities such as the Yugoslav republics and provinces, which is the supreme objective of nationalist policies in the contemporary postcommunist period, implicates both exclusion (of ethnic minorities by ethnic majorities) and inclusion (of ethnic groups belonging to the majority group but situated as minorities in the territories of neighboring states that are putative parts of the "mother country").

The minorities are thus divided into "native" minorities, who live in neighboring states and must be "reunited" with the mother country, and "alien" minorities, who live within the mother country and are considered by nationalists as a potential threat to national security, since they could be manipulated in the same manner as their own respective native minorities in other states. Therefore, the so-called historical rights of native minorities are asserted at all costs, while those of alien minorities are denied through repressive measures.

Yugoslavia's "Nonalignment"

Within this conceptual scheme, the Yugoslav situation had certain specific characteristics that help explain the nature of the current post-Yugoslav conflicts. These specific characteristics are: 1) the international position of the Yugoslav state during the cold war period; 2) the ideological "softening" of the original model of the socialist state; and 3) the multiethnic composition of the state and its relatively short history.

Between 1948 and the end of its existence as a single state, Yugoslavia was widely recognized as a sort of intermediary in East-West relations. Indeed, it is well known that, in many respects, this role was decisive for the conduct of international relations during this period as a whole; both sides were ready from time to time to put pressure on Yugoslavia, or to defend the country against pressure from the other side. The interest of both superpowers in Yugoslavia was mixed in nature and included geopolitical, ideological, and propagandistic elements. In general, both sides were in fact satisfied with the status quo as far as the intermediary position of Yugoslavia was concerned. However, there were efforts to influence and manipulate its international position in the world, and even its domestic policies. This was achieved with some degree of success in the case of Western influences linked with consumerism, as opposed to the ideological designs of the eastern bloc.

As a consequence of this situation, Yugoslavia functioned as a kind of arbitrage zone between East and West. This arbitrage existed at all levels: At the military-strategic level, it was present in the way both sides helped the armament of the Yugoslav army in order to strengthen its defenses against the "other side." At the same time, such assistance was used by the superpowers to discover how some of their standard (but not most advanced) equipment compared with the corresponding technology from the opposing side. The equation at the economic level was in a way more complicated, although it functioned along the same lines.

The aid coming from the West (especially in the 1950s, after the break in relations with Moscow) was extremely important, and it led other communist states to view the position of Yugoslavia somewhat pejoratively as a kind of semi-Western liberalized socialism. But, at the same time, it made the Yugoslav socialist model attractive among leftists in the West and in the nations of the third world. Soviet help (primarily in the form of petroleum or other raw materials) also had an ideological rationale, namely to show that the East still had something to give to the Yugoslavs.

The so-called nonalignment policy of the Yugoslav leadership was also one of the essential reasons for Yugoslavia's relative importance in international politics. As a result of this policy, the international pressure upon the Yugoslav leadership was considerably less than that which was exerted upon the other socialist countries, even in situations in which the abuse of power was obvious. At the same time as it led to the relative openness of the country, the relative internal liberalization of Yugoslavia, as well as its international position, made it almost untouchable in the international political arena.

Because of the important international position of Yugoslavia, both cold war rivals were particulary ready to help strengthen the Yugoslav army, because it was—from the viewpoint of the geopolitical and strategic state of affairs that characterized the cold war—clearly a factor of stability in the whole (southeast European) region. In addition, questions related to the internal political consequences of such a campaign of armament were not of concern for the main centers of world power. The Western countries believed that the party had everything under control, thus reflecting a rather cynical approach on the part of the West's intelligence establishment. The eastern bloc believed that, in case of a crisis, the army could be relied upon as a pro-Soviet element within the Yugoslav *nomenklatura.*

Another element that should be added to the list of external stabilizing factors with respect to the situation of Yugoslavia after World War II was the common perception of the Balkan area as the historical powder keg of Europe. Under such circumstances, any element of control over the various ethnic groups of the region that created a sense of security for neighboring and other European countries was welcome. In a way, this perception of Yugoslav affairs has proved to be correct in the last two years, because the period between 1945 and 1990 was some kind of long-term cease-fire within Yugoslavia. Neighboring states were more than willing to countenance the undemocratic character of the system in Yugoslavia as a modest price to be paid for such stability.

Decentralization without Democratization

Yugoslavia's "own socialist way" was known as self-management social-ism. In reality, it simply meant that there was a relative liberalization in the basic structure of society, a corresponding change in the official ideology (including a critique of Stalinist politics and ideology), and a fair amount of decentralization in the organization of the state. This process began as early as Tito's schism with Moscow in 1948. As pre-viously mentioned, the liberalization policy was rather successful in terms of international politics, and it led to a clear change in the official ideology and in the terms used for the legitimization of the state. Never-theless, the virtual political monopoly of the Communist party over the state apparatus remained unchanged.

In economic terms, the official ideology of Yugoslav communists meant more space for certain reform initiatives, so long as they did not threaten the status quo in any way. Therefore, the circumstances pro-vided for the introduction of elements of market economics and the accompanying decentralization, especially after the economic reforms of the 1960s. However, these measures were rather limited in scope and did not establish a systematic basis for a modern market-based economy.

The ideology of self-management contained certain market elements in terms of a level of autonomy for economic actors and an important emphasis on decentralization of federal structures. Within the "eco-nomic and other collectives" that were organized according to the model, certain anarchist tendencies emerged (and, indeed, the model was borrowed from anarchist origins) that were welcomed by the ruling party as an excuse for justifying political intervention in order "to re-store the normal functioning of the system and the general order." However, after more than three decades, the ideology of self-manage-ment had certain consequences for those who were predisposed to believe that they had certain rights, especially within the collectives.

The economic reforms (which, thanks to the logic of the ruling ideology, began much earlier than in the other communist countries) led to the first period of massive unemployment in the mid-1960s, and to the necessity of another type of liberalization or opening toward the West. The economic prosperity of western Europe created favorable circumstances for the export of the Yugoslav labor force, so that in the following fifteen years, hundreds of thousands of *gastarbeiter* went to countries such as Germany, France, and Sweden. The immediate conse-quence was the opening of the borders (which was for decades the most obvious difference between Yugoslavia and other communist countries) and, subsequently, considerable financial aid to the country in the form of the remittance of savings from the workers abroad to their families in Yugoslavia. This eventually led to new working habits, technical abilities, and discipline. In the final analysis, however, it also provided de facto legitimacy for the Yugoslav system in the last two decades of its existence. The gradual convergence between the living standard and working discipline of western Europe and Yugoslavia led to the spontaneous and popular conclusion that there was no country like Yugoslavia, in which one could live so well while working so little.

In effect, this whole context led to a situation in which democratization was replaced with decentralization. This led to the popularity of the Yugoslav system abroad and, in the country itself, to a more relaxed citizen-state relationship (with the exception of specific categories of dissidents). However, it also led to an increasingly noticeable gap between the official ideology on the one hand, and the role of the communist leadership in reality on the other.

The Rise of Ethnonationalism

The trends just described were all occurring within a state that was composed of different ethnic nations with different traditions and—of paramount importance—different territories, mostly defined in historical terms. Indeed, this was the context within which all the political and ideological developments of the post–World War II period took place. Changes in the political and ideological setting were particularly apparent in the field of interethnic relations, which, as discussed previously, were so extremely important for the alternative political life within the existing socialist system.

In such a social and cultural environment, progressive decentralization, which was during the lifetime of Tito a mere legitimation formula, had very particular consequences. Even at a purely ideological level, it meant that the different republics of the Yugoslav federation had certain legitimate claims. Furthermore, as the Constitution of 1974 made quite clear, they were all more or less full-scale, ethnically defined nation-states within a loose federation. However, so long as the League of the Communists of Yugoslavia was a uniform political organization of the ruling elite (that is, as long as Tito lived), the decentralized character of the federation formalized by the constitution was not realized in practice, because the practices of the ruling party were far more important for the political life of the state than the constitution.

The economic impact of decentralization over a period of some thirty years led to the widespread development of specific regional positions and interests, in relation to the center and between the regions themselves. Since the political organization of the regions was more or less ethnically defined (with the notable exception of Bosnia-Herzegovina, which was an obvious error within the political and constitutional framework of Yugoslavia), the economic differences and claims were also defined almost entirely in ethnic terms. Therefore, regional differences led to the perception of exploitation by one ethnic group against another. By the 1980s, every ethnic group had developed an ideology (with supporting historical, economic, social, geopolitical, demographic, and other studies conducted by local institutes) that claimed that the particular ethnic group was the victim of the very existence of the Yugoslav state. The more developed ethnic nations claimed that they had to give too much money for the undeveloped parts of the state, while the underdeveloped complained that at the beginning of the joint state, the developed parts did not have such an advantage compared with them and, consequently, that they had not received their fair share of the country's wealth.

In strictly political terms, the federative structure of the post–World War II Yugoslav state created the first quasi-state entities for ethnic groups like the Slovenes and Macedonians, and in a somewhat different context, the Kosovo Albanians, whose autonomous province was in certain respects equal to the six republics of the federation. Such statelike formations created a basis for the formulation and defense of ethnonational claims and interests against Belgrade, which was identified with the central state apparatus. The disintegration of the League of Communists of Yugoslavia after Tito's death and the increasing independence of the parties at the republican level greatly contributed to this process. In order to legitimize their new circumstances, the republican parties gradually embraced the nationalist ideologies of the majority nation in their respective republics. At this point, the principle of socialist internationalism was no more relevant than any other obsolete communist doctrine, such as the command economy, which had been abandoned in favor of market reforms.

At the same time, the requirement of consensus in the decision-making process at the federal level—which was obviously present in the last ten years of the existence of Yugoslavia—not only paralyzed the essential political functions of the federal government, but also led during the 1970s and 1980s to the development of a linkage between federalism and ethnically defined political differences. At the federal level, officials of the Yugoslav state increasingly were forced to legitimize their functions in terms of the republic to which they belonged, and not in terms of the common good.

The Death of the Yugoslav Federation

The last decade of Yugoslav history was the decade in which the comparative advantages of the Yugoslav model turned out to be serious disadvantages, if not grave dangers, for the political regime, and for the existence of the state itself. Indeed, it ultimately proved to be a tragedy costing thousands of innocent lives. During this period, there were certain developments that played an important role in the disintegration of Yugoslavia. First, the Yugoslav system created all the conditions necessary for the establishment of future nation-states; second, it was characterized by a situation in which the federal (that is, "Yugoslav") political structure was reduced to the Yugoslav army; and third, its external legitimation in terms of its strategic international position was lost with the end of the cold war.

In practice, ethnic pluralism existed only at the federal level, whereas ethnic exclusionism prevailed in the republics. Accordingly, this led to homogenization and the creation of an atmosphere in which the members of other ethnic groups on the territory of each and every republic were regarded as agents of "foreign" interests. Thus, the initial preconditions for ethnonational sovereignty of the future nation-states were already present in the old regime. The republics tended to organize their economies, transportation systems, and foreign contacts as independently as possible in order to reduce the influence of the central authorities as much as possible, and in order to establish alliances needed for the imposition of their interests at the federal level.

The northwestern republics, Slovenia and Croatia, as represented by communist leaderships that were already oriented toward a nationalist ideology and the acceptance of national programs, were strictly against all those decisions of the Yugoslav center perceived to be reinforcing federal authority, even where there were benefits to be gained.

Serbia (with Montenegro and Bosnia-Herzegovina as its allies) wanted to "save Yugoslavia," and therefore its leadership opposed many of the reformist policies coming from the northwestern republics. This is what made the partnership between the Serbian leadership (or rather Milošević) and the army possible. The framework within which they wanted to save Yugoslavia was clearly the framework of the old regime of centralism in Yugoslavia. For the nationalists on both sides, this was a clear indication of the decisive influence of the ethnic group (that is, the Serbs) that had the relative majority among the Yugoslav population. Such a situation of conflict among the republics led to the paralysis of federal decisionmaking exactly during a period in which the role of the center was of crucial importance if the transition from communism to democracy was to be realized without uncontrollable polarization.

The most important problem of such a historical moment was a simple one: if it became obvious that free elections were needed as the first and irreversible step toward democratic reconstruction, the question was whether the elections in the republics would be organized before the federal elections. Paradoxically, this was the only question over which there was a silent consensus between the conflicting factions in the old Yugoslav leadership. On the one hand, the Croatian-Slovenian coalition did not want federal elections, since they were aware that it would result in the direct democratic legitimization of the Yugoslav state, thereby diminishing the prospects of further loosening federal power in favor of greater autonomy for the republics (which, in the period 1988-90, was still the ambition of Croat and Slovene politicians, since independence was not yet a subject under consideration). Those attached to Leninist concepts, on the other hand, opposed free elections on other grounds.

The moment it became clear that free elections were going to be possible only in the republics (Croatia and Slovenia at first, in 1990), the end of Yugoslavia was more or less in sight. The remaining question then was how the partition of the federal state could take place or, rather, whether it could be realized without a war. After the elections in Croatia and Slovenia, the federal level was completely paralyzed. The attempt of the Yugoslav prime minister, Ante Marković, to prevent the breakup of the state through radical economic reforms came too late, and his political position was undermined by both the Serbian and Croatian leaderships. As a consequence of these factors, only one element, albeit the crucial one, of the federal political structure continued to function, namely, the Yugoslav People's Army. However, particularly after the elections in Croatia and Slovenia, the army became associated with Milošević and the Serbian leadership.

In the meantime, because of the end of the cold war, the international community had lost its previous interest in the existence of the Yugoslav state. Yugoslavia was no longer the focus of international political, strategic, and, especially, economic interests. Rather, it was the reintegration of Europe in an atmosphere of triumphalism about democracy and the market economy that was the priority on the international agenda.

The interest in the situation of Yugoslavia was renewed in the summer of 1990, after certain events took place in the country that were already a clear sign of the impending tragedy. However, the Berlin meeting of the Conference on Security and Cooperation in Europe in June 1990 gave the conflicting parties mixed signals by mentioning in the same breath unconditional support for the territorial unity of Yugoslavia, on the one hand, and the right of the nations within Yugoslavia to self-determination, on the other. Tactically, there was strong support for Prime Minister Marković and his economic reforms in the hope of saving Yugoslavia. Generous credits were offered to the last Yugoslav presidency only a few days before the war began, but they came too late, in part because, as previously mentioned, such economic situations were no longer a priority in the postcommunist world.

In fact, the rationale behind the international policy toward Yugoslavia was informed by the assumption that Yugoslavia was important merely as a harbinger or bellwether of the fate of the Soviet Union. Of course, such a policy could not produce anything other than confusion, which came to characterize the international position with respect to Yugoslavia and, subsequently, as reflected in the contemporary period, toward what remains of the former Yugoslav territories.

The Birth of the "Former" Yugoslavia

The post-Yugoslav situation started, in fact, with the onset of war. The events in Slovenia led to the total disintegration of the ideological framework of the army, since its retreat from Slovenia meant: that it had not fulfilled its formal constitutional duty to protect the borders of the state; clear defeat by an enemy that had been understood as militarily irrelevant and incompetent; and the victory of the Serbian nationalists within the army over the Yugoslav socialists (the former wanted control over the areas that were understood to be historically or demographically Serbian; the latter, control over the entire territory of the Socialist Federative Republic of Yugoslavia).

However, the real war began in Croatia after a period of tense relations between the new Croatian authorities and the Serbian minority. The Serbian minority strongly opposed the prospect of greater Croatian autonomy within Yugoslavia, not to mention the already obvious prospect of full independence. This was due in part to the historic memory of the Ustasha crimes against the Serbs during World War II, in part because of the preexisting manipulation of the Serbian minority in Croatia by the Serbian leadership in Belgrade, and in part because of the blatant and not infrequent blunders by the Croatian authorities. Nevertheless, in the direct conflicts between Croats and Serbs in Croatia, relatively few persons were killed in comparison with what was to follow.

After these events, in the spring and early summer of 1991, the Yugoslav army intervened in Croatia, and in the war that followed some 20,000 persons were killed. In ideological terms, there was some (of course, perverse) logic in Serbs killing Croats for Serbia, or Croats killing Serbs for Croatia. On the contrary, there was no logic at all in Yugoslavs killing other Yugoslavs for Yugoslavia. Therefore, the invasion of the Yugoslav army in Croatia, which began with military assistance to Serbian irregulars and was followed by the direct shelling of large Croatian towns and cities such as Dubrovnik, Osijek, and Vukovar, was in fact the end not only of the Yugoslav army, which had clearly become a Serbian army, but also of the Yugoslav state, which had been controlled by the army for years.

The escalation of the war began with the so-called operetta war in Slovenia, followed by the tragedy of the aggression in Croatia, and culminating with the everyday atrocities of the war in Bosnia-Herzegovina that continue to this day. The reason for all these events was obviously the disintegration of Yugoslavia, but it has to be said once again that it was the institutions of the Yugoslav state, and the army in the first place, that in fact started the war and caused the consequent end of the very state they wanted to protect. The independence of Slovenia and Croatia, recognized by the international community, was therefore the most important political result of the first stage of the war.

Slovenia, which was not deeply involved in the war and was able to end it without big losses, oriented its policy toward the West and turned its back on the former Yugoslavia, maintaining only economic relations at a relatively low level. It is somewhat of a paradox to foreign observers that problems exist between Slovenia and Croatia, erstwhile allies in the attempts first to reconstruct and then to dissolve the Yugoslav federation. Although these problems are not substantial, they demonstrate that the fallout from the political absolutism of ethnonational sovereignty eventually leads to conflict, even between traditional allies.

Croatia was and still is under pressure of war, which affects not only its territory (more then 20 percent is still under occupation, even if in principle it is controlled by United Nations peacekeeping soldiers) and its population (thousands of dead, captured, and invalided and hundreds of thousands of refugees and displaced persons), but also its public policies and perspectives. Strong nationalistic tendencies, which have triumphed in the first and second free elections in 1990 and 1992, have been reinforced throughout the course of the war, and especially by its cruelty. All statements about the "other side" (primarily the Serbs) that were more or less obvious prejudices have been somehow confirmed by the events of the war. The fact that some (or rather, many) of the Serbs have organized and committed aggression and atrocities is (and is going to be, at least for the near future) quite broadly understood as empirical proof of the negative qualities of the Serbs as such.

Struggle between Revanchism and Civil Society

In the context of Croatian politics, the popular Croat perception of the Serbs is essential to understanding both internal policy (especially the democratization process) as well as policy in the foreign sphere (especially relations toward Serbia and Bosnia-Herzegovina). Both elements start with the basic premise of Croatian politics; namely, that there are no prospects for real democracy in Croatia except on the basis of the boundaries that Croatia had as part of Yugoslavia at the beginning of the war. It is on this premise that Croatian politics stands or falls. Of course, the majority of nationalists concentrate on the question of boundaries primarily as a symbolic and only secondarily as a pragmatic aim. The small minority of political actors for whom democracy is of central concern also have to support the maintenance of old boundaries, knowing well that with a more or less permanent situation of occupation of parts of Croatian territory, the country will live in a perpetual state of revanchist nationalism without the prospect of arriving at rational political solutions.

Paradoxically, the consequences are not only relevant for Serbo-Croatian relations, but also for the prospect of ending the war in Bosnia-Herzegovina. This happens to be the case because the only immediate way to stop the conflict between Serbia (or Yugoslavia) and Croatia is to partition Bosnia-Herzegovina between the Serbs and Croats. In any other scenario, the end of the war could have only one of two possible outcomes: Croatia is finally liberated from aggression (and of the de facto United Nations protectorate over parts of its territory), which means victory for Croatia and defeat for Serbia; or Serbia manages to retain some parts of Croatian territory (Baranja is most likely going to be the final objective), which means victory for Serbia and defeat for Croatia. In both cases, revanchist sentiments will persist in the region for decades to come.

Therefore, the partition of Bosnia-Herzegovina is the obvious "elegant" solution if the post-Yugoslav war is regarded as an essentially Serbo-Croatian conflict (as many observers have suggested). Of course, such a solution is not accepted by anyone who is concerned with justice, not only for the Bosnian Muslims, but also for the principles of equitable conflict resolution. Yet it could be "sold" to international public opinion with two seemingly solid arguments. First, two of the three sides in the Bosnian-Herzegovinian conflict, the Serbs and the Croats, control most of the arms and troops used in the war and can, therefore, virtually guarantee at least a cease-fire if not long-term peace. It appears that this is exactly what the international community, tired of witnessing the repeated horrors of the war and its own impotence, is eager to achieve. Second, increasing propaganda against "Islamic fundamentalism" in the media of the most influential countries of the world gives Serbs and Croats (as Christians) the chance to claim that they are (once again, after their struggle against Turks) protecting Europe from the Muslim threat.

It is quite obvious that the populist version of Croatian democracy depends on the possibility of the reemergence of a full-scale war in Croatia. That could happen if Croats were to launch a new offensive in the near future (in the region of western Slavonia near Okučani, or somewhere between Karlovac and Petrinja, along the Kupa River). This is quite likely to be the case (and is even politically understandable) if in the near future a solid peace agreement is not signed for Bosnia-Herzegovina. Since this is unlikely to be the case (even the signatures to the peace plan of the International Conference on the Former Yugoslavia cannot be regarded as an endorsement of a realistic plan for peace), the prospects are definitely not very optimistic, especially since the former Yugoslavia is the only postcommunist European country without an effective independent media. Everything appears to point in the direction of the continuation and further deterioration of the already seemingly worst part of recent history.

Two years ago, the movement for pluralism in what was still called Yugoslavia was more or less aware of its objectives: the first really democratic elections in the history of Yugoslavia were certain in the near future. Those elections, however, were not organized as Yugoslav but as "only" Croat and Slovene elections (with elections to be held in all the other republics in the following six months). Every rational and politically informed observer knew at that time that great political problems were yet to come, but practically no one expected a war that would result in thousands of casualties, massive destruction, incitement of collective hatred, and the almost complete loss of any rational perspective in both the private and public spheres.

Of course, only those with an extremely dogmatic orientation are ready to deduce the causes of the war from the first truly free elections in the republics, but the fact remains that there was no real democratization, not to mention the political milieu arising from the war as well as the probable postwar situation. Instead, we face a permanent "prepolitical" status or even a status that precedes the very possibility of civil society. In Croatia this means that all the promises of the government or political parties have to be qualified and, of course, can be (and consequently, were and are) used to undermine not only public discussion about important issues, but also the role of public opinion in general. What helps in this connection is the nationalist ideological persuasion of all major parties and political groups. Using such a legitimation makes it possible to proclaim—for instance, as President Tudjman has done by referring to the recognition of Croatian sovereignty by the states of the European Union—that Croatia is entering a golden age (in a situation of an unfinished war that has involved a loss of some 25 percent of its territory and catastrophic economic damage, not to mention the human cost).

This is exactly the most important point: with so many victims of war, the question of legitimacy becomes crucial. That is why the town of Vukovar has become so important, and that is surely why the government desperately needs something that could be interpreted as a "success." Both the Croatian and Serbian sides try to interpret the deployment of the United Nations forces as their own success, but since there is no propagandistic way to claim real results in economics or in the establishment of democratic institutions, what remains are the spoils of war (which is tantamount to legitimizing the existence of thousands of victims) in the form of new territories, international prestige, and, above all, humiliation of the enemy. But even those fruits are in question, and not only for the Croat side. For the Croatian public, even if there is a way to claim victories of a certain kind in the war with the Yugoslav army, which was vastly superior in military terms; even if there is a constant attempt to persuade the population that they are free because their state is (more or less) independent; even if one employs tricks and deception, such as the frequent claim that, far from losing 25 percent of its territory, Croatia has in fact conquered the other 75 percent (since there was no modern independent Croat state before recent events), all that is not enough.

An ideological consolation will not suffice because there are too many relatives of victims, too many refugees, too many persons who suffer from war in various respects. That is why the boundaries are so important under the present circumstances. It is not "only" a question of principle; in the first place, it is a pragmatic question since there is still a situation of war. There will be no real end of the war until all the fruits of aggression are annulled, and there is no possibility for democracy in Croatia if the state cannot control the territory that was controlled by the Croatian Socialist Republic within the former Yugoslavia. There will be no democracy in Serbia as long as the Serbian state is acting as an occupying power in parts of Croatian territory (or even its own, namely Kosovo). In the case of Croatia, the Croats actually are going to be forced to act out of revenge (or to believe they have to), and in such a highly emotional situation there is no patience for democratic procedures (not to mention the almost "logical" victims of such a revanchist impatience; namely, the Serbian minority within Croatia). In the case of Serbia, it is quite easy to understand that aggression cannot help the democratic process and that the very distribution of looted and plundered goods undermines the rule of law (and raises the crucial question about the punishment of war criminals on all sides, although in the case of the Serbs the entire war of aggression is widely interpreted as a crime in itself).

The ethnonationalistic ideology of the present Croatian establishment makes it even more complicated to justify the fact that Croat territories are under foreign rule (if not under Yugo-Serbian occupation, they will be, at least for a period of time, under the control of the United Nations forces). The way to deal with this—in terms of obvious nationalistic legitimization of the regime—is simple but dangerous: the leaders are, sooner or later, going to say: "Yes, we have lost a (considerable) part of

Croatian territory, but we have established a sovereign and widely recognized state, and we have made it possible to be a state in which only the ethnic Croatian population is relevant, since there are no minorities that constitute more than 5 percent of the entire population." Therefore, the fate of Serbs in Croatia (not to mention the hundreds of thousands of Bosnian Muslim refugees who are not likely to leave the country in the foreseeable future) is really in question: not only as members of an ethnic group that is widely hated in Croatia, but also as the natural obstacle for the realization of the "pure" Croatian community. It is needless to repeat once again what the implications of such a situation are for the prospects of democracy in Croatia (in all the other future scenarios those prospects are questionable, but in this particular case they are nonexistent). That is why there is no room for celebrating the creation of the newly independent states, and an urgent need for rethinking the post-Yugoslav situation.

CHAPTER SEVEN

Piecing Together the Balkan Puzzle

Milorad Pupovać

T HE BALKANS is a complex and diverse region. There is considerable linguistic diversity amounting to some one hundred different languages, ranging from the Indo-European and Turkic families to the Finno-Ugric and other smaller linguistic families. The Catholic, Orthodox, and Islamic faiths are the major religions, while a mixture of some one hundred ethnic groups inhabit common areas. At the economic level, the Balkans has its own developed "north" and underdeveloped "south," which are highly interdependent. In addition, competition for spheres of influence by various powers has been a constant geopolitical feature of the Balkans. Such complexity, however, is not uncommon in the world. Indeed, there are regions far more complex in their elements, such as Nigeria, with over 200 languages, and the Caucasus, with more than seventy linguistic and ethnic groups.

Elements in Balkan Complexity

The peculiarity of Balkan complexity is that it is a strait between seas of homogeneity and archipelagoes of lesser complexity. Indeed, a glance at the linguistic, ethnic, and religious map of the areas surrounding the Balkans will suffice to demonstrate its role as a strait over which significant linguistic, ethnic, and religious tides pass, or have passed, in the course of long historical periods.

Another peculiarity is the internal dynamic of the Balkan region, which is considerably influenced by the process of self-identification and unification of its component nations; that is to say, like the Germans and Italians in the last century, the peoples of the Balkans are belated

European nations whose process of self-identification and unification is only now coming to fruition. This applies especially to the Slavic population of the Balkans and, in particular, to the Serbs and Croats.

According to Johan Galtung, an expert on conflict studies, the first victim of the war in the former Yugoslavia was complexity itself. The political solutions that are offered in response to the conflict tend to be simplistic and one-sided, overlooking the varied elements without which a comprehensive perspective cannot be attained. The consequences of such attempts at conflict resolution are detrimental, both in terms of influencing the character of government (that is, unitarism, statism) as well as the prevailing values of different societies (that is, intolerance and aversion to pluralism).

The Balkan region is an integrated structure in which the interdependence of the components makes it almost impossible to resolve problems affecting any single element without taking into consideration the other elements. Thus, although the conflict in the former Yugoslavia unfolded in different phases and therefore will require resolution in corresponding phases, every particular solution has to be realized in the context of a large, comprehensive solution. It is very difficult, for instance, to settle the Serbian question in Croatia without a solution to the problem of Bosnia-Herzegovina. Likewise, it is difficult to find a solution to the problem of Kosovo Albanians without addressing the problems of Albanians in Macedonia. In addition, every solution has to be reconciled with the interests of neighboring states.

The Balkan region is a heteronomous structure, considerably influenced by external forces. The previously mentioned interdependence of relations, and even more so, the nature of power relations between the Balkan nations and the Balkan states, makes the involvement of a third party, whether as mediator or arbitrator, indispensable to any solution for the future. This assumption rests at least in part on historical precedents such as the Berlin Congress, the Versailles Treaty, and the Yalta Conference. Indeed, the direct or indirect presence of third parties in the search for solutions has been a constant feature of the Balkan political landscape. In the contemporary world, the interests of European powers such as Germany, France, Britain, and Italy, as well as Russia and Turkey, are a vital part of the political equation. Another reason for the heteronomy of the Balkans is, as previously mentioned, its role as a strait that divides the seas and archipelagoes of noncomplexity and autonomy. Each of these seas or archipelagoes is of vital importance, either as an exit point or as a connecting point. The interests of

Russia from the north, the interests of Turkey from the east, the various interests of the European countries from the west are no doubt fundamental to the heteronomy of the Balkans.

Characteristics of the Balkan Conflict

The conflict in the Balkans bears the features of a limited and controlled interethnic war within the context of a state that has disintegrated (that is, the former Yugoslavia) or, in another respect, within the context of states in their early, formative stages (that is, the former constituent republics and provinces). It is fundamentally a conflict between the claimants of equal collective rights for different national groups that have maintained an exclusionist stance since World War II, and between whom there is no readiness for mutual recognition or compromise over the reconciliation of their own respective rights. Because of the inextricable ties between the ethnic and religious identities of these national groups and the corresponding relationship between politics and religion, the conflict in the former Yugoslavia has assumed the characteristics of a religious war.

The conflict in the Balkans has the elements of a limited and specific interstate war. Although mutual declarations of war were never made, some states that were just in the process of formation or were newly constituted waged wars on the territories of other states that were undergoing a similar phase of development (that is, conflicts between Serbia, Croatia, and Bosnia-Herzegovina). These military actions were justified on the basis of "solidarity" with members of one's own ethnic group who were, or were portrayed as, victims of the ruling elites of emerging or newly formed neighboring states that were dominated by other national groups.

Taking into consideration both the existing as well as the potential political and military participants, the conflict in the Balkans, beyond the constituent units of the former Yugoslavia, has the elements of an international conflict. During the first phase of the disintegration of Yugoslavia, the conflict was already internationalized, especially in the form of peace initiatives, peace mediators, and peace conferences sponsored by external actors. In the second phase, the conflict was internationalized through international deliberations concerning the recognition of the Yugoslav republics as independent states. In the third phase, the conflict became internationalized militarily, ranging from the presence of international peacekeeping and other forces to covert military assistance and threats to use armed force in order to ensure compliance with certain demands. Needless to say, the implications of this last phase on the internationalization of the conflict have been and will continue to be far-reaching.

Subjects and Objectives

The process of democratization within the political framework of the former Yugoslavia was led by nationalist movements with the primary objective of establishing nation-states. Between 1981 and 1987, the Kosovo Albanians were the first to make demands for a republic of their own. In 1987 the Serbian leadership called for the formation of a unitary Serbian state, calling for the suspension of the autonomous status of its provinces (Kosovo and Vojvodina). It also encouraged the mobilization of Serbs in other Yugoslav republics in order to create an all-Serbian national movement that had as a point of departure the right of the Serbian nation to self-determination, within or without a Yugoslav state. The Croatians aimed at establishing their own state by transforming the Yugoslav republic of Croatia into a nation-state for Croats, leaving the Serbian population as a national minority, although they had enjoyed the status of a constituent nation in Croatia for a century and a half. In addition, the Croats also mobilized some ethnic Croatians living in other Yugoslav republics and created a nationalist movement whose aim was the defense of Croat national interests throughout Yugoslavia.

At a very early stage the Slovenians stated their preference for self-determination through an independent nation-state. The Muslims also created a national movement whose aim was the national integration of Muslims and the preservation of Bosnia-Herzegovina as a unified state. Following the example of others, the Macedonians established a nation-state in which some of the minority rights of the Albanians in western Macedonia were suspended.

Consequently, the national movements that emerged in the former Yugoslavia had almost identical objectives; namely, the establishment of nation-states. This objective was realized through a similar two-part pattern: the first, by constitution of the republic into a nation-state dominated by the majority ethnic group, and the second, through the attempted unification or integration into this nation-state of members of the ethnic group living in other republics.

The implementation of the similar but conflicting objectives of the national movements in the former Yugoslavia generated a conflict for the following reasons: in the first place, all these movements, whatever the differences among them, either initiated or accepted the destruction of the Yugoslav state before coming to any agreement on its reconstruction or deconstruction; in the second place, most of these movements, and this is most obvious in the case of Bosnia-Herzegovina, sought to maintain their own territorial integrity on the one hand, while on the other, advocating the right of their own nationals in other republics to self-determination through secession and through uniting with the "mother country."

Bosnia-Herzegovina is certainly the most illustrative and tragic example of the policies inspired by such objectives. The initial Muslim position was for a unified Bosnia as a possible confederate unit within a Yugoslav confederation; thereafter, Bosnia as a sovereign and independent state that might enter into a political union with Croatia in the future; thereafter, a regional Bosnia divided into ethnic cantons (that is, the Vance-Owen Plan); and more recently, the ethnic partition of Bosnia through the creation a loose union of three republics dominated by the Muslims, Serbs, and Croats, respectively. The initial Serb position was that Bosnia-Herzegovina remain as a federal unit within the Yugoslav federation (with or without Croatia and Slovenia); thereafter, the cantonization of Bosnia-Herzegovina; and finally, the idea of partition into three national states belonging to the Serbs, Croats, and Muslims, respectively. The initial Croat position was that Bosnia become a confederal state that would be able to conclude a confederate union with Croatia; thereafter, a sovereign Bosnia as the expression of the will of the Muslims and Croats; and finally, Bosnia as a union of three national states.

Both the constant and evolving elements in the positions of the warring sides in Bosnia-Herzegovina demonstrate a complementarity far greater than was evident in the earlier phases. Take, for example, the positions of Serbia and Croatia. Serbia protected its own territorial integrity in the case of Kosovo, on the one hand, while on the other it supported the right of Serbs in Croatia and Bosnia to national self-determination.[1] Croatia, for its part, was unwilling to compromise its territorial integrity in the case of Krajina, where the Serbian majority wished to secede from Croatia, whereas Croatia demanded the right to self-determination for Croatians in Herzegovina, including the creation of their own independent state and its unification with Croatia. In the first instance, the difference between Croatia and Serbia with respect to the maintenance of territorial integrity was that Serbia had sufficient military strength to realize its objectives while Croatia did not. Instead, Croatia relied on the international factor; namely, international recognition and the protection of its territorial integrity by United Nations forces. All other differences are secondary and are essentially of a tactical nature, such as the provisional alliance between Muslims and Croats in Bosnia-Herzegovina.

The cumulative effect of these conflicting nationalist pressures brought into question the very idea of Bosnia-Herzegovina as a multiethnic state, resulting instead in its partition between the Serbs and Croats. The international recognition of Bosnia-Herzegovina, which was in essence an empty declaration, could not prevent the nationalist forces from realizing their objectives. The efforts of the international community to counter or balance these forces always lagged behind events, and arrived too late to save Bosnia.

In some respects, the Macedonian case is similar to the case of Bosnia-Herzegovina insofar as it is situated at the intersection of conflicting spheres of influence, although, fortunately, it is not directly in the zone of conflict between Serbs and Albanians. Indeed, after the Serbo-Croatian conflict, the second most significant source of conflict in the Balkans is Serbian-Albanian relations. And, just as there was a third element in the Serbo-Croat equation (that is, the Muslims in Bosnia-Herzegovina), so there is a third element in the Serbian-Albanian equation (that is, Albanians in Macedonia).

Although, from the viewpoint of interethnic relations, the Macedonian situation is not as complicated as the Bosnian one and does not stand directly in the way of the national-state integration of Albania and Serbia, the situation is complex primarily because of the aspirations of neighboring countries such as Bulgaria and Greece, even if at the early stages of a potentially wider conflict their involvement is rather limited.

Be that as it may, I am ever more convinced that the problem of political relations in the Balkans may be understood in terms of game theory. This is an approach I came across on the occasion of my first meeting with Hakan Wiberg, one of the few Danish experts on Yugoslavia and the Balkans, who related it to the situation in Macedonia.[2] The same approach was echoed in a more comprehensive fashion by Vuk Drašković at a gathering in Geneva in the fall of 1991 in explaining the situation in Bosnia-Herzegovina. Wiberg emphasized that the survival of Macedonia depended on relations between the Serbs and Greeks, the Serbs and Albanians, the Greeks and Albanians, and the Bulgarians and

Albanians. Similarly, in his observation of the situation in Bosnia-Herzegovina, which was at the time far from being one of war, Drašković observed that the political situation was like a card game of "preference": there are three players among which two are playing against the third, but nobody knows who the two are. Surely what he wanted to say was that coalitions were possible in Bosnia in which an enemy enters a coalition with an enemy against a friend, or in which a friend enters a coalition with an enemy against a friend.

Consequences of the Conflict

In every respect, the consequences of the war in the former Yugoslavia are tragic and wide-ranging.

The Human and Demographic Consequences

It is not possible at present to speak accurately about the number of victims because, unfortunately, in addition to the fact that exact numbers are not known, it does not appear that the war is close to an end. Nevertheless, the approximate figure is terrifying. It is estimated that the number of those killed, whether soldiers or civilians, exceeds 300,000 persons. The number of wounded might well be double this figure, and the number of refugees and displaced persons is put at more than 2 million.

The demographic structure, especially the national composition of the newly constituted states of the former Yugoslavia, has changed drastically. Entire communities and whole regions have been "ethnically cleansed." Communities that until recently were multiethnic have become uni-ethnic, or have become ethnically divided. Cities and towns with a multiethnic composition such as Vukovar, Osijek, Karlovac, Zadar, Benkovac, and Petrinje in Croatia, or Banja Luka, Brčko, Mostar, Bijeljina, Bosanski Novi, Bihać, Doboj, and Goražde in Bosnia-Herzegovina have fallen victim to ethnic "cleansing." Regions such as Dalmatia, Lika, Banija, and Slavonia in Croatia, or Podrinje, Posavina, Bosanska Krajina, Middle Bosnia, and East and West Herzegovina have been similarly "cleansed," or have been transformed into regions with an absolute ethnic majority. Hundreds of thousands of people have moved from one town to another, from one region to another, from one state to another. In other words, there has been a massive movement of populations based on ethnicity.

In addition to ethnic movements, there has been generational and labor mobility. Thus, tens of thousands of youngsters left their homes in order to avoid military mobilization, to flee the direct dangers of war, or to escape from the climate of antagonism caused by the war. There has also been an emigration of experienced and highly qualified people; a sort of "brain drain." For example, numerous physicians and professors of medicine have abandoned Belgrade's clinics and institutes and moved to Cyprus. Many entrepreneurs from almost all of the republics of the former Yugoslavia are living in Prague or Bratislava and other cities of eastern Europe. Many leading film directors from Serbia, Croatia, and Bosnia-Herzegovina currently live outside their own countries.

Urban and Economic Consequences

The number of demolished, semidemolished, or seriously damaged communities remains to be accurately recorded. In Slavonia, both eastern and western, in Herzegovina, also eastern and western, many cities, such as Vukovar and Mostar, have been destroyed. Hundreds of villages have been completely destroyed, and in some regions whole agglomerations of village settlements have been systematically devastated. Thousands of homes owned by members of national minorities—for instance, of Serbs in Croatia—located in towns or villages outside the zones of warfare have also been demolished or damaged beyond repair.

Rare are the war zones in which almost all the infrastructure facilities, such as bridges, have not been destroyed. Numerous industrial plants have been severely damaged or completely destroyed. Of course, the destruction of roads, railways, and river communications is an additional and important aspect of the economic disaster. Thus, in Croatia as well as Bosnia-Herzegovina, almost all vital communications in the north-south direction have been broken. The situation is not much better in the east-west direction. The costs of warfare as well as the sanctions that have been applied directly (to Serbia and Montenegro) or indirectly (to Croatia and most of the other Balkan countries) so as to limit the military potential of the parties to the conflict and thereby contain or halt the war are convincing explanations for the internal economic collapse of the newly established states on the territory of the former Yugoslavia.

Cultural and Spiritual Consequences

Every war, and this one is no exception, is a relapse in relation to the previous condition, for a certain time at least. Extreme nationalism before the war and the military bravado during the war have resulted in the confinement of cultural values to an exclusively national and traditional realm, instigating negative emotions, stereotypes, and prejudices toward other nations and their cultural values. Universal cultural values have been stifled by the aggressiveness arising from provincial and intolerant nationalistic values.

Another trend with a profound influence on the world view of people in the former Yugoslavia is the desecularization of social life and the expansion of exclusivist religious ideologies. If this trend continues, it will seriously endanger the long-term viability of civil society and secular values. The impact of religion on gender relations, on family planning, and on freedom of expression is growing rapidly in accordance with the general trend toward desecularization.

Political Consequences

Because of the deterioration of the military situation in the former Yugoslavia, a chaotic political state of affairs prevails. There are four internationally recognized states that were former Yugoslav republics (Slovenia, Croatia, Bosnia-Herzegovina, and Macedonia) in addition to two internationally nonrecognized republics (Serbia and Montenegro and their state union known as the Federal Republic of Yugoslavia, which also has not been recognized). Finally, there is Yugoslavia as a former state, which serves as a framework for the futher disintegration of an already disintegrated state. In this regard, furthermore, there are a number of quasi-states within most of the new states. Although these entities have many of the characteristics of statehood, they are self-proclaimed and do not enjoy recognition. The Republic of Kosovo that emerged in Serbia is backed by the political will (as expressed in a plebiscite) of its predominantly Albanian population. It has its own parallel quasi-governmental institutions that unlawfully operate alongside the "official" Serbian governmental institutions. The Republic of Serbia in Bosnia, the Croatian Republic of Herzeg-Bosnia, and the remainder of Bosnia-Herzegovina, in which the Muslim majority is concentrated, all have their own armies, territories, governments and social institutions. The Republic of Serbian Krajina in Croatia has almost all the attributes of statehood, as do the already-mentioned republics, but, as in the case of the Republic of Kosovo, it lacks adequate internal military power; it has the status of a United Nations protected area. During 1991 in Macedonia, in the area where Albanians are a majority, the Republic of Ilirida was proclaimed. Although it was quickly swept under the carpet, it has not yet been definitely swept away.

Such political consequences are a direct result of the effects of the two principles previously mentioned; namely, the principle of territorial integrity and the principle of national self-determination. Since many entities are attempting to act in compliance with both, the result is the current predicament. At first glance, it seems unresolvable.

Possible Solutions to the Conflict

While it is not possible to continue the process of creating new nation-states and the accompanying policy of national integration and unification, it is equally impossible to stop this process. It appears then that the Balkan nations have reached a stalemate. None of them will be able to attain their desired objectives with respect to ethnic unification. Any attempt to continue in that direction is possible only through a war that would, for many of them, be their last, and for many others would be a tremendous risk with potentially dire consequences. The only possible way out is a solution based on compromise: but by what means is it possible to achieve compromise in the Balkans?

First, it must be recognized that any compromise rests upon the fact that there are two crucial interethnic questions, between the Croats and Serbs on the one hand, and the Albanians and Serbs on the other. It is also crucial to recognize that each of these two questions has a subquestion. The subquestion with respect to Serbo-Croat coexistence relates to the Bosnian Muslims, and in the case of Albanian-Serbian coexistence, it relates to the Macedonians. The first question and its subquestion may be considered the central question of Yugoslavia, or in other words, the relationship between the two largest nations of the former Yugoslavia—Serbia and Croatia, along with the Bosnian Muslims. The second question and its subquestion may be considered as the central question of the Balkans, since in addition to the Macedonians its resolution involves Serbs and Albanians as well as the Bulgarians and Greeks. Therefore, just as it is crucial to provide answers for the first question and its subquestion in order to achieve peace and stability on the territory of the former

Yugoslavia, it is also crucial toward the same end to find a viable solution for the second question and its subquestion.

The answer to the first question may be found by tracing the history of Croatian-Serbian efforts to reach compromise over essential issues. In this respect, the Croatian-Serbian treaty of 1939 is particularly relevant.[3] It should be noted that after the period of Tito's Yugoslavia, and after international recognition of Bosnia-Herzegovina, the position of Bosnian Muslims has become stronger. This means that contrary to the above-mentioned treaty, a new Croatian-Serbian agreement must take into consideration not only the existence of a Bosnian Muslim nation, but also a Bosnian Muslim state. At the same time, it also means that in addition to establishing territorial boundaries (a great part of which has to be determined in Bosnia-Herzegovina), Serbs and Croats will have to formulate the nature of their bilateral political relations. Based on the expressed will of both Serbs and Croats in Bosnia, it would appear that the Serb-held territories will be attached to the Federal Republic of Yugoslavia while the Croat-held territories will be attached to the Republic of Croatia. Accordingly, the relationship of these communities will have to be managed at the interstate level. Of course, the key question with respect to the future of Serbo-Croat relations rests on the eventual status of the United Nations protected areas (that is, Krajina). Although this is a question that cannot be solved quickly or simply, its solution may be found in some form of territorial and political autonomy negotiated between the Croats and Krajina Serbs, which would be endorsed through a bilateral agreement between Yugoslavia and Croatia, and between Croatia and the international community (that is, the United Nations).

Contrary to the first question, the answer to the second question does not have any historical precedents. It is unlikely that the arrangement of the big powers from the early part of this century for the division of the present territory of Macedonia can be repeated. However, as it was not possible to prevent the process of national and state integration in the Serbo-Croat case, neither will it be possible in the case of Albanian-Serbian relations. This means that the process of national integration of ethnic Albanians cannot be stopped, and that there should be an agreement about it between them and other Balkan nations, and above all with the Serbs. As already mentioned, such an agreement would have one basic shortcoming: namely, it may jeopardize Macedonian national interests. However, such interests could be protected if the Macedonians are involved in a negotiating process informed by the spirit of compromise.

The realization of Albanian aspirations for national integration in the same manner as the Serbs and Croats should be avoided because it may result in a new war of tragic proportions, both in terms of the number of victims and the threat to regional peace and security. Therefore, the process of national integration of Albanians in Serbia and Macedonia could take the form of autonomy as a "postponed" right to self-determination. By adopting this gradual approach, it would be possible to bring the process of national integration under control. The procedural mechanisms required for the realization of this postponed right to self-determination should be clearly defined and established. The procedure itself should be based on an agreement on the territory where the autonomy is to be established, as well as an agreement on the duration of the transition period during which the international mechanisms and procedures would operate. An agreement between affected states on the transitional character of the autonomy should also be concluded.

Whether these two questions are solved in the manner described above or in some other manner, the resolution of the problems confronting the Balkans will not be possible without mechanisms for reaching compromise, such as those that have in the past been used with success: preventive diplomacy; negotiation and mediation; international monitoring, especially of human rights, as well as the development of democratic institutions; and the use of United Nations peacekeeping forces. Such mechanisms will have to be present in the former Yugoslavia and the Balkans for a considerable period, although, ideally, only for a transitional period and not as a permanent feature of the region. Furthermore, such mechanisms should be complemented or, better yet, substituted with mechanisms for bilateral and regional cooperation and communication. Mechanisms of bilateral and regional cooperation and communication should primarily deal with two areas: human rights and minority rights, including certain guarantees of security on the one hand, and trade and communications on the other. The first area should be regulated by obligatory bilateral and multilateral treaties that specify the range of human rights and minority rights; regulate the status of armament and military potential, especially among the police forces; and that establish bilateral or regional bodies for monitoring the implementation of these treaties. Insofar as the security situation is concerned, the most appropriate solution would be, if not full demilitarization, a substantial reduction of military capacities in the Balkan region. The second area should be regulated through bilateral and multilateral agreements that reflect the interests of the states concerned. One possible approach would be to group states in two or three potentially overlapping regional alliances. Accordingly, it would be possible to accommodate the intersection of zones of interest, and there would be no reason, for instance, to prevent a country such as Croatia from belonging to both a central European as well as a future Balkan regional association.

Finally, it should be considered that by the time the Yugoslav and Balkan crisis has been contained, its peoples will be impoverished. It is extremely difficult to achieve trust and peace in a poor society with people who have been indoctrinated, and it is even more difficult to build a civil society. Therefore, "sticks" that the international community has used directly or indirectly (that is, economic sanctions) should be replaced with "carrots." In other words, the sanctions should be lifted and, instead, the doors of international economic, trade, financial, and other organizations should be opened as part of a larger program of active and direct assistance to establish democracy in the tormented Balkan region. In this way, perhaps the Balkan puzzle may be pieced together.

CHAPTER EIGHT

Bosnia-Herzegovina: From Multiethnic Coexistence to "Apartheid" . . . and Back

Zoran Pajić

O NLY FOUR YEARS AGO, as Yugoslavia headed toward its first multi-party elections, all options seemed open. Yugoslavia was first on the "waiting list" to join the Council of Europe, and relations with the European Union were expanding rapidly. Market-oriented economic reforms and privatization had begun and were beginning to show significant results. The federal political structures, however, could not be held together any longer; the Communist party establishment was in panic; and the Yugoslav People's Army (JNA) was in total confusion over how to adapt to the changes and to the imminent loss of its privileged position. It was obvious that despite a common Communist party and ideological background, the leaders of the six republics could forge no political consensus on crucial issues for the future of the country.

The global changes in the international community did not give much hope for the continued stability of Yugoslavia either. The fall of the Berlin Wall symbolized the beginning of a new era in which there was no role for a country that was "between the East and the West," a role that Yugoslavia had played well for forty years. The Nonaligned Movement, another trademark of Yugoslavia's world image, was facing increasing marginalization in international relations. These developments had a very strong and disturbing impact on the people, leading to growing frustration and a sense of betrayal. Generations of Yugoslavs had been spoiled by the role their country had played during the cold war period: bridging the iron curtain, leading the nonaligned countries, experimenting with the self-management system, and successfully combining communist rule with some individual freedoms unknown in the rest of the communist world (that is, the freedom to travel abroad, to hold private property, to keep a hard currency bank account, to emigrate, and to return). In the divided cold war world, Yugoslavs believed they were something special.

At the domestic level, for the great majority of people, Yugoslavia offered a predictable life, with a sense of protection and security provided by the "system." Generation after generation followed the same pattern of protected careers and well-planned futures. Tuition from nursery school to university was free, jobs were easily available (before the 1980s), housing was provided by the state, health service was free, and pensions were guaranteed. The system encouraged mediocrity as a way of life, but this "stable stagnation" was a very comfortable environment for ordinary people, happy with the average and protected from changes and challenges. This philosophy was illustrated by the popular wisdom: "We pretend to work, and the state pretends to pay us." This was the way Yugoslavs explained their system and its safe durability.

The enormous changes at the global political and economic level, beginning especially in the late 1980s, required a dramatic alteration of this mentality. And when the change came, it caught Yugoslavia by surprise. The old ideology, good or bad—there is no point in evaluating it now—disappeared almost overnight, but new values had not yet been created. In this kind of moral void, a tremendous gap opened, and one way or another it had to be filled.

In comparison with the previous life, the future offered by the reform-minded political parties was quite terrifying. Their standard election messages included: "open-market economy," "competition," and "the struggle to achieve European standards." People were simply not ready for such a vision. The institutions of civil society could have played a role in soothing people's fears of an unknown future and in solving conflicts, but they were virtually nonexistent. One might argue that after so many years of a comfortably collective identity within the system, the common man was simply unprepared to take on the responsibility to exercise his individual freedom. The easiest option was therefore to seek another form of collective identity, another protective shield against the confusion. This was nationalism. Many politicians quickly realized that the nationalist ticket was a lifeboat for them also. It was an instrument for the homogenization of people and the creation of the constituency that, in the one-party system, they had never had.

In this context it is also important to note Yugoslavia's lack of democratic experience in solving conflicts. During Marshall Tito's regime, social conflicts were solved by two simple means: the more or less indisputable authority of the Communist party, and the personalized role of Tito as the supreme arbiter. Conflicts were solved behind the scenes, by political pressure in prearranged party meetings. From the outside, one could almost get the impression that Yugoslavia was a society without conflict. The truth is that the conflicts were contained, and no democratic institutions and procedures were ever developed to resolve them. At the end, with Tito's death in 1980 and the collapse of the party, conflicts were exploding everywhere, and there were no democratic structures to manage them and to offer a peaceful way out of the crisis.

These factors provide the context for a better understanding of the pre-election period throughout Yugoslavia and the subsequent disaster in the region. Once the nationalist parties with their hardline ideologies had been elected, conflict, especially in Bosnia-Herzegovina, became all but inevitable. After more than two years of the devastating march in the Balkans, it is apparent that democratic governments in Western Europe and elsewhere do not understand nationalism as simply another form of totalitarianism; they fail to see authoritarianism as the crucial factor in the Balkan wars. Former communist politicians, particularly Milošević and Tudjman, as well as ruthless newcomers such as Karadžić and Boban, used nationalism as a pragmatic political option in order to exploit both the postcommunist ideological vacuum as well as the profound sense of personal insecurity among the people. This provides a far more precise and concrete explanation for the divisive politics that have destroyed Yugoslavia than any theory based on the "historic animosities" of the Yugoslav peoples.

Fear, Opportunism, and the Nationalist "Vision"

In the framework of understanding the "new reality" of ethnic majority and minority situations, the case of Bosnia-Herzegovina is of particular interest. By getting the green light for the effective partition of Bosnia-Herzegovina along ethnic lines by the European Union (even agreed to prior to the war, as early as the Lisbon conference in March 1992), all three nationalist parties (HDZ—Hrvatska Demokratska Zajednica, the Croat party led by Mate Boban; SDA—Stranka Demokratske Akcije, the

Muslim party led by Alija Izetbegović; and SDS—Srpska Democratska Stranka, the Serb party led by Radovan Karadžić) have achieved their long-term strategic aims. Long before the war, which "officially" started on April 6, 1992, these parties had heightened the sense of fear and mistrust among different ethnic groups by blaming "the others" for their own "history of oppression and misery." This was followed by hate speech, chauvinistic statements by politicians and loyal intellectuals, and, finally, by tolerating terrorism and encouraging the illegal stockpiling of arms. To a frightened, lonely individual—lacking civil and legal protection, being financially squeezed—salvation was offered beneath the shelter of collective rights.

These developments are the logical outcome of the rise of rival nationalist leaders in a multiethnic community, such as Bosnia-Herzegovina, which was often labeled "Little Yugoslavia" because of its ethnic and religious diversity. It was naive to believe that three nationalist leaders could coexist within a single state. As a rule, the visionary dream of any nationalist leader is to be in control of his or her own national territory, to establish his or her own legal order and economy, to have his or her own military and police force, and so forth. These are the instruments by which one transforms oneself from a leader to an autocratic ruler. This is not unique to Yugoslavia, although its Yugoslav manifestation is one of the bloodiest. Throughout the world, hundreds of different ethnic groups are struggling for statehood under a banner that says "we can't live together." Absolutely everybody wants a state to call their own, or at least to see their (ethnic, tribal) government ruling an autonomous province, if not an independent state.

Preparation for the ethnic division of Bosnia-Herzegovina took a rather long time because it has not been easy to persuade the ordinary man that his friend, neighbor, or even family relation belongs on the other side of the barricade. The nationalist propaganda war, which began long ago between Serbia and Croatia, eventually spread to Bosnia-Herzegovina. There, too, people have been reduced to primitive stereotypes of Serb, Muslim, and Croat zealots. Belgrade media would refer to Croats as "Ustashi," Zagreb would call Serbs "Chetniks," and both would portray Muslims as filthy fundamentalists. The aim of this ferocious and war-mongering propaganda was, and still is, to ease the conscience of people in order to allow them to hate and ultimately to throw themselves into an atrocious war.

Even before the war started, the nationalists were indiscriminate in the means they chose to achieve their ultimate goal of creating ethnic states. They frantically tried to compromise radio and Sarajevo TV and the daily newspaper *Oslobodjenje*. They relentlessly pressured the schools to accept religious education curricula and to classify teachers and headmasters of schools on the basis of their national party membership. The only obstacle they faced was the considerable number of "unreliable and suspicious" people who lived together in ethnically mixed communities and accepted it as a normal way of life.

Euphemism for Apartheid

Although important differences existed among national parties in Bosnia-Herzegovina, there is no doubt that their respective political projects would have brought them to the same end—extreme national homogenization. The political and psychological environment that fostered the March 18, 1992 Lisbon Statement of Principles for the New Constitutional Settlement of Bosnia and Herzegovina, under the sponsorship of the European Community Conference on Bosnia and Herzegovina, was created very skillfully. The ruling political parties had accustomed the people to believe that their leaders could not agree on anything, and that if they did not agree they would have to wage war. With that in mind, the people were prepared to accept anything—even a very problematic and risky agreement—that avoided serious trouble. It seems that today, almost two years later and with the war still going on, many tend to forget that the European Community put all its diplomatic support behind the project of an ethnic partition of Bosnia-Herzegovina; and this idea is still the major political "vision" that Europe is able to offer the region! This is the core political issue and still the only option on the agenda of the International Conference on the Former Yugoslavia (that is, the UN-EU conference in Geneva). It appears that it is based on the principle of "divide and quit," rather than "divide and rule," which has been tried before in some other crisis areas (that is, Cyprus, India-Pakistan in Kashmir, Palestine) but has never worked as a viable long-term solution.

It is clear that in the case of Bosnia, with its ethnically interwoven experience and cosmopolitan cities, this partition plan is a euphemism for an apartheid system. While apartheid, which is based on the total segregation of ethnic groups, is falling apart in South Africa, it is being reborn in southern Europe. The logic of the Lisbon Statement and its subsequent elaboration corresponds perfectly to the idea of a regime in which every individual—from cradle to the grave—has a precisely determined place in society. A person's domicile, the type of education to which he or she is entitled, as well as the conditions for intimate relations are determined on the basis of race, or to use the language adopted by the Lisbon Statement, on the basis of the "national principle." The idea was to achieve the separate development of different ethnic groups and to discourage or even ban any coexistence. Once isolation was achieved, nationalistic propaganda would become much easier to believe, and people would accept such a system as the best solution for all.

For an objective analyst it was easy to assume that from the day ethnic territories or states ("statelets" is the most recent codeword) were proclaimed within Bosnia, individuals from all three "genuine" nations (Serbs, Muslims, and Croats throughout Bosnian history) would find themselves in a "dual" situation depending upon where they lived. In an entity where its people represent a majority, an individual would enjoy the status of full citizenship and all his or her civil and political rights would be guaranteed. Meanwhile, a person of the same ethnicity in a province where the other nation has a majority would become a second-class citizen. Even this absurd outcome seemed acceptable for the majority of voters who endorsed their own ethnic parties, as well as for the European Union. This attitude could be understood as a choice between two evils: war or ethnic partition. They both underestimated the philosophy of nationalism and the idea of ethnic exclusivity. Moreover, they totally overlooked the reality of the Bosnian demographic map (that is, the mixed communities, the regions never before defined along ethnic criteria, the large number of "national atheists"), which, if read carefully, could give them the clear message that the type of partition they had in mind inevitably involved a massive displacement of the population and the redrawing of municipal boundaries.

Finally, the crucial conclusion could be drawn: in Bosnia-Herzegovina it will not be possible to rewrite history without war. In one word, the agreement on "cantonization based on the national principle," signed in Lisbon by three Bosnian national leaders (Izetbegović, Karadžić, and Boban), under the chairmanship of Ambassador Cutileiro, collapsed two weeks later, or it may be more accurate to say that its implementation started with the first wave of "ethnic cleansing" carried out by Serb paramilitary forces and by their shelling and later siege of Sarajevo in April 1992. Karadžić, showed his cards first because he was much better prepared and felt very confident with the full backing of the Yugoslav National Army and the regime in Belgrade. Almost two years after this overture, it seems clear that the lack of political will among democratic governments to understand the substance of Balkan-style nationalistic policies encouraged the architects of Greater Serbia and subsequently of Greater Croatia, and, finally, endorsed the attempt by radicals among the Muslim population to seek their own piece of "ethnic land."

It should not be forgotten that all this has happened at the expense of ordinary people who by pure chance happened to be born as ethnic Muslims, Croats, or Serbs. They have been killed, displaced, raped, "ethnically cleansed," and humiliated only because of their ethnic origin—a fact for which they can take neither credit nor blame. Peoples of the former Yugoslavia have become bearers of the collective guilt for the atrocities committed by a relative few among them. A generation of well-educated, eager Europeans from Bosnia has been sacrificed through either physical elimination or exile. Those who believed in tolerance and pluralism as a normal way of life were labeled "unreliable" by the ethnic leaders and, finally, were left with no country to turn to as their own. Those who stayed or found shelter in besieged towns and "safe areas" have become a strong card in the deadly poker game of power politics. Sarajevo has been under siege since April 1992, and Mostar has been destroyed in the effort to divide it. It is here that the destruction of pluralism shows its ugliest face. For those who experienced and lived through the extraordinary Bosnian amalgam of different cultures, religions, nations, mentalities, and customs, the "unbearable lightness of destruction" of all human values that the democratic world has stood for is beyond comprehension.

The New "Ethnic Constitutionalism"

This political and psychological background represents the stage on which minorities are bound to play their role in the new "ethnic constitutionalism" in the countries that emerged from the former Yugoslavia. The "legal background" has been deliberately excluded from this list of conditions because of a cautious and skeptical approach toward the "normative haven" found in the Yugoslav constitutional tradition. The federal constitutions, as well as those of the constituent republics, were pervaded by statements that gave an ideal picture of society and the political regime. This was remarkably well elaborated in the sections dealing with human rights, which expressed a strong political commitment to the full scope of civil and political, as well as economic, social, and cultural, rights. In reality, human rights issues very much reflected major political trends within the leadership of the Communist party during more than forty years of unchallenged domination. Throughout this period, tolerance and a relaxed attitude toward minorities prevailed as a rule. In this respect, the very modern and generous legal system in this area was not decisive for the social environment, but it nevertheless contributed to the very good reputation of Yugoslavia for the treatment of minorities. The constitutional guarantees were very substantial and covered all areas for the safeguard of minority identity. The protection of native language by minority groups in the former Yugoslavia will remain unrivaled in constitutional practice for a long time. Native language was widely used in the minorities' own printed and electronic media, in schools, in higher education (and at the University of Priština, which was for the Albanian minority), in cultural and art societies, on public signposts, and in public administration. There was, in fact, only one area where minority languages were excluded—the army. And, of course, there was one way in which minorities were not allowed to function as a distinctive ethnic group; namely, they were prohibited from forming their own political parties. However, this was not allowed of any entity in the former Yugoslavia, because the Communist party had a monopoly over the political system.

In spite of its attempt to control everything, the party never abandoned the program of coexistence among different ethnic groups, very often ignoring the criteria of "majority" or "minority." In principle, the 1974 Constitution treated both "nations" and "nationalities" equally. The twofold definition of the Socialist Federal Republic of Yugoslavia takes Yugoslavia as a federal state and as a community. The federation consisted of "voluntary united nations and their Socialist republics and of the autonomous provinces of Vojvodina and Kosovo, which are constituent parts of the Socialist Republic of Serbia." The community was defined as an alliance "of working people and citizens and of nations and nationalities having equal rights." This vocabulary may seem awkward, but it was very common in the Yugoslav legislation, which very often "translated" common terms (minority, people) into more appropriate, politically correct speech. The official interpretation considered the term "minority" offensive and pejorative and, by a stroke of the pen, transformed it into the term "nationality." The same was true for the expression "working people," which in the early stage of communism in Yugoslavia was considered to be a "vanguard" and the "base" for the development of socialism, as opposed to "citizens," which stood for the population in general.

The wording of Article 1 of the constitution (quoted above) was a compromise that left a number of questions unanswered and that eventually led to considerable tension. Two issues appeared to be of crucial importance as soon as the first signs of ethnic homogenization were initiated. The first stumbling block, which shaped much of the later violence and war in the region, was the status of the Serbian population in Croatia after it became clear that this republic was heading toward independence. The second question was, in its condensed form, "To which nation did Bosnia-Herzegovina belong?" Since the beginning of 1990, political movements and parties sprang up in both Serbia and Croatia, claiming large parts of Bosnia-Herzegovina for Serbia or Croatia, respectively. The predominant reaction in Bosnia-Herzegovina was that this federal unit did not belong to any of its constituent nations (Serbs, Croats, and Muslims), but rather to all of its inhabitants ("working people and citizens").

The fall of communism has gone hand in hand with the revival of nationalism. In political reality, nationalism is very often transformed into chauvinism, exclusivity, and militant extremism. This tendency is reflected in most postcommunist constitutions by a very narrow and exclusive definition of the state. The "strategic ideal" of ethnic revival is being literally translated into a pragmatic call for "one state for every ethnic group." The case of the former Yugoslavia can be taken as a paradigm of this phenomenon. The states that emerged from it seem to be "constitutionally owned" by the respective nations, while the presence of members of other ethnic groups is considered an anomaly and a burden inherited from the past. Even if they do not advocate the expulsion or "exchange" of population (as in the case of Bosnia-Herzegovina), nationalist leaders pledge only to tolerate the presence of the others.

The prevailing rhetoric in the respective constitutions of Croatia, Serbia, and Slovenia combines theoretical confusion with an attempt to make it clear beyond any doubt that the state "belongs" to a given nation. The wording of the 1990 Constitution of the Republic of Croatia reflects the ideal of a nation-state:

> The Republic of Croatia is established as a national state of the Croat nation and a state of members of other nations and minorities, who are its citizens: Serbs, Muslims, Slovenes, Czechs, Slovaks, Italians, Hungarians, Jews and others.

It should be noted that this chapter of the constitution contains a brief history of Croats from the seventh century to the present day. This historical saga reads as an argument in favor of continuous Croat state-hood, irrespective of long periods of consociation with others in wider, pluralistic entities. The 1990 Constitution of Serbia also reflects the ideal of a nation-state. According to its preamble, Serbia is "a democratic state of the Serbian people in which members of other nations and national minorities will be able to exercise their national rights. . . ." In addition, one finds a strong emphasis on the "freedom-loving, democratic, and state-building traditions of the Serbian people." In a similar vein, the preamble of the 1991 Constitution of the Republic of Slovenia describes the state as an entity stemming from:

> The basic and permanent right of the Slovene nation to self-determination and from the historical fact that the Slovenes have formed, over many centuries of struggle for national liberation, their own national identity and established their own statehood.

Nevertheless, Article 3 contains a contradiction: "Slovenia is a state of all citizens, based on the permanent and inviolable right of the Slovene nation to self-determination."

The process of consolidation of the new states is still in its initial stage, and it would not be fair to draw firm conclusions one way or the other, particularly for those countries that are still in a state of war. Nevertheless, the tendency toward an ethnically "pure" state is easily noticeable. The common starting point in most of the "new and demo-cratic" constitutions is the idea that the *raison d'être of the state is to serve the nation and not the citizens.* This leaves little room for individ-ual rights. An individual is treated as a member of a group, and rights and freedoms are granted and guaranteed only on the basis of such membership. If an individual belongs to a small group that cannot qualify as a "national minority," there is very little possibility to claim rights on the sole basis of citizenship. Even worse, there are cases where an individual would refuse to be classified as a member of a group for different reasons (mixed ethnic background is very common among "Yugoslavs"; there are many cases of intermarriage, and many who dissent from the "national" leaders and would therefore be reluctant to declare their ethnic background). Not belonging to a recognized group, the individual does not belong anywhere, because the state, as the above-mentioned constitutional provisions suggest, is owned in the first place by the "host" ethnic group and in the second place can serve as a home for people who can qualify as members of a recognized minority ethnic group, and who are treated as "historical guests."

Preventing a Palestine Syndrome

All these tendencies are so frightening for the future of this part of Europe that one has to ask the question: Is there any hope that the present situation will not lead the whole region into a nightmare, that it will not lead into a new phase of apartheid or strict segregation based on the "ethnic principle" and eventually spread further to the east of the continent? Are there no new ideas on the horizon that could show the way out of the atmosphere of hate, warmongering propaganda, ethnic exclusivity, and crime? Are there no instruments in the international community—Europe, in particular—that can at least secure the implementation of a minimum commitment to international law and principles as spelled out in dozens of resolutions and statements concerning the Yugoslav crisis and the situation in Bosnia-Herzegovina?

There is no doubt that, in theory, international law empowers the international community (the United Nations and the European Union, for instance) with more than enough instruments and procedures for conflict resolution, peacekeeping and peacemaking. It is evident, however, that international law is not self-sufficient; it requires a strong political will and determination for its implementation, preferably based on a long-term vision and policy. In the case of Yugoslavia this has not yet materialized. It is easy to agree here that the policy of the international community has been a failure in the sense that the war has not been stopped, war criminals have gone unpunished, and the ethnic map of Bosnia and Herzegovina has been changed through the use of force. However, it could be equally argued that the international community has been very successful in the case of former Yugoslavia, for at least two reasons: "pure" ethnic statelets have been created and international military intervention has been avoided. The lack of political will among democratic governments to view nationalism as an essentially undemocratic, demagogic, and chauvinistic movement encouraged the architects of Greater Serbia and subsequently of Greater Croatia and finally gave the endorsement to radicals among the Muslim population.

Europe's Palestine syndrome may have not been created yet, but there is a lot of evidence that an angry and vengeful people in Europe's midst is being created. Unless something is done to restore trust, this is likely, sooner than later, to undermine what is left of the credibility of the United Nations as well as the highly praised "European standards" of civilization. Europe, whose peace will depend on building a multiethnic, multicultural, and pluralist society, is letting one of the very few operating models of this kind of government, be slowly strangled by the forces of nationalism and fascism.

Finally, reflecting on the future of Bosnia and Herzegovina may require ignoring, at least to a certain extent, the "reality on the ground." So far, this reality has only served the purpose of providing excuses for the international political establishment and government leaders to pursue a do-nothing policy, making it clear for the warring factions that the West does not mean business when threatening military intervention in Bosnia and Herzegovina.

Even before the crisis, I launched the idea of an external system of international administration for Bosnia and Herzegovina in an effort to prevent war. Now, this idea would serve a modified purpose—to give hope to the people of the region and a vision to the rest of the world that such a disaster could be contained. Sooner or later the war will stop, and then what? Reconstruction and rehabilitation of the country cannot be sought under any of the existing regimes in Bosnia. Politically, Europe cannot accept apartheid regimes in its common home, not even in its immediate neighborhood. Economically, such political creations will be dead before they are born, and culturally they would not belong to this era of history. The only way to help reintegrate the people of the region into the international community will be through the establishment of an international trusteeship system as a framework for reconciliation and reconstruction. This will be the only viable guarantee for the future of Bosnia and Herzegovina and the only way to bring about an end to the horrific violence to which the population has been subjected. Without such international involvement, it is difficult to envisage how the people of Bosnia and Herzegovina can be emancipated from the nationalist trap that they have been dragged into by their own leaders.

Notes

Notes to Introduction

1. Francis Fukuyama, "The End of History?" *The National Interest*, vol. 16 (Summer 1989), pp. 3–18; and Fukuyama, *The End of History and the Last Man* (Free Press, 1992). A more sophisticated view of nationalism and its relationship to liberal democracy is evident in some of Fukuyama's more recent writing; see "Comments on Nationalism and Democracy," in Larry Diamond and Marc Plattner, eds., *Nationalism, Ethnic Conflict, and Democracy* (Johns Hopkins University Press, 1994), pp. 23–28.

2. John Mearsheimer, "Back to the Future: Instability in Europe," *International Security*, vol. 15 (Summer 1990), pp. 5–60.

3. Kenneth Anderson, "Illiberal Tolerance: An Essay on the Fall of Yugoslavia and the Rise of Multiculturalism in the United States," *Virginia Journal of International Law*, vol. 33 (1993) p. 429.

4. See Anderson, "Illiberal Tolerance." The best philosophical articulation of a liberal individualist foundation for minority rights and multicultural and multilingual policies is found in Will Kymlicka, *Liberalism, Community, and Culture* (Clarendon Press, 1989). For a legal and policy analysis of federalism and multiculturalism influenced by Kymlicka's work, see Robert Howse and Karen Knop, "Federalism, Secession, and the Limits of Ethnic Accommodation."

5. Slavenka Drakulić, *The Balkan Express: Fragments from the Other Side of War* (Norton, 1993), pp. 135–36.

6. See E. Hobsbawm, *Nations and Nationalism since 1870: Programme, Myth, Reality* (Cambridge University Press, 1990).

7. Stéphane Dion, "Le nationalisme dans la convergence culturelle: Le Québec contemporain et le paradoxe de Tocqueville," in R. Hudson and R. Pelletier, eds., *L'engagement intellectual Mélanges en l'honneur de Léon Dion* (Sainte-Foy: Les Presses de l'Université Laval, 1991).

8. Here, one thinks of Max Weber's account of the defining characteristics of modernity and modernization. See, particularly, *Science as a Vocation* (Indianapolis: Bobbs-Merrill, 1946).

9. "Laziness and cowardice are reasons by which a large proportion of men, even when nature has long emancipated them from alien guidance (*naturaliter maiorennes*), nevertheless gladly remain immature for life. For the same reasons, it is all too easy for others to set themselves up as their guardians. It is so convenient to be immature! If I have a book to have understanding in place of me, a spiritual adviser to have a conscience for me, a doctor to judge my diet for me, and so on, I need not make any efforts at all." Immanuel Kant, "An Answer to the Question: 'What is Englightement?' " in H. Reiss, ed., *Kant: Political Writings* (Cambridge University Press, 1991). p. 54. Many critics of liberalism, from Heidegger to contemporary communitarians such as Alisdair MacIntyre and Mary Ann Glendon, portray liberalism as an ideology of comfort and self-indulgence inherently at odds with the ethos of personal responsibility. Curiously, Fukuyama—the arch-liberal idealist—seems to accept this pejorative characterization of liberal citizens as "men without chests" (*The End of History and the Last Man*, chaps. 27-29). To me, what is most striking is the degree of self-discipline, courage, and personal mastery and order required to make basic life choices without authoritative guidance from religion, parents, or some external ideology in which identity is defined collectively.

10. Gidon Gottlieb criticizes (too gently in my view) the approach of Western mediators and negotiators as reflected in the Vance-Owen plan, with its almost exclusive emphasis on securing an optimal division of territorial sovereignty as a solution and its silence about the possibilities of coexistence between the various peoples in the region even where sovereignty cannot be neatly divided. See *Nation against State: A New Approach to Ethnic Conflicts and the Decline of Sovereignty* (New York: Council on Foreign Relations Press, 1993), pp. 74-76.

11. For the concern over rewarding aggression, see, for example, D. Gompert, "How to Defeat Serbia," *Foreign Affairs* (July-August 1994).

12. A discussion of some of the possibilities of international guarantees is to be found in Gottlieb, chap. 2.

13. The Belgrade Circle is described in Danièle Salleneve, "Des intellectuels courageux et solitaires," *Les Temps Modernes* (January-February 1994), pp. 3-10. A large selection of writings by these individuals has been published in French translation in the same issue of *Temps Modernes* under the rubric "Une Autre Serbie" (Another Serbia).

14. See Immanuel Kant, "Perpetual Peace: A Philosophical Sketch" in Reiss, *Kant: Political Writings*, p. 94; and M. Doyle, "Liberalism and World Politics," *American Political Science Review*, vol. 80, no. 4 (1986), pp. 1151-69.

15. I do not mean to suggest that there is such a thing as liberal nationalism, as Michael Lind has recently argued in "In Defense of Liberal Nationalism," *Foreign Affairs* (May-June 1994). In liberal states, nationalism can be moderated or tamed by the presence of entrenched liberal democratic values and principles. However, because of its core principle, which defines human identity and empowerment in terms of participation in and subordination to the collective power of a homogenous (racially, ethnically, culturally, or religiously circumscribed) *group*, nationalism remains in fundamental tension with and is a radical alternative to liberal individualism. The deeper possibility within liberalism is for

the transformation of nationalism into a model of ethnic justice based on a foundation of individual rights (see Kymlicka, *Liberalism, Community, and Culture*; and Howse and Knop, "Federalism, Secession, and the Limits of Ethnic Accommodation"). But because of the collectivist escape from individual responsibility that nationalism appears to offer, its appeal in times of economic, moral, social, or political uncertainty and destablization will most likely remain powerful, at least to some percentage of the population. The task will therefore always be, at least in part, that of reinforcing liberal values and institutions as a counterweight to nationalism. This goes hand in hand with seizing the initiative to remove conditions of radical uncertainty or destablization, or at least to moderate them.

Notes to Chapter 1

1. For more on this topic, see Janko Pleterski, "Die Sozialistische Foederative Republik Jugoslavien, Ihre Entstehung und Verfassungsform," *Czasopismo prawno-historyczne*, tom XXXII, zeszyt 1 (Warsaw 1980), pp. 265-302.

2. Ibid., p. 267.

3. On December 1, 1918, the Kingdom of Slovenes, Croats, and Serbs came into existence and was the official designation of the Yugoslav state until 1929. The new country was governed from Belgrade for several years, and the Serbian army was its sole means of defense.

4. Pleterski, "Die Sozialistische Foederative Republik Jugoslavien," p. 267.

5. Metohija, a fertile valley between the North Albanian Alps and the Sar Mountains on the Albanian border, was largely agricultural. Until 1913 it was under Turkish rule and was part of the Kosovo viloget.

6. Sandžak or Sanjak of Novi Royal is considered the original home of the Serbs. It was captured by the Turks in the fifteenth century. Occupied in part (1878-1908) by Austro-Hungarian troops, it was under Turkish rule until 1913. The name Sanjak is still applied to the adjoining Serbia-Montenegro frontier region.

7. This was effected by the Treaty of Bucharest (August 1913), which came immediately after the second Balkan war (July 1913). Bulgaria (which had attacked Greece and Serbia in June of that year) was defeated. With the addition of Macedonian territory, Serbia almost doubled in size; Montenegro and Serbia divided the Sanjak of Novi Pazar; and Greece obtained southern Macedonia.

8. Dualism, which occurred in 1867, gave Hungary a great deal of autonomy within the Austro-Hungarian empire (1867-1918).

9. The Nagodba (Agreement on Compromise) negotiated in 1868 established Croatia as a separate political unit within the Kingdom of Hungary, with autonomous jurisdiction over its internal affairs, police, justice system, religion, and education. The Croatian language would be used in domestic administration. The Hungarian government retained strict control over Croatian banking, railroads,

and the conclusion of commerical treaties. The Nagodba was violently opposed by Croats.

10. During the eighteenth and nineteenth centuries, many Russian words were incorporated into the Serbian literary lexicon. This so-called Serbian-Slavonic language, used by the church and by educated Serbs, did not conform either to the spoken idiom or to the standard form used elsewhere in the Balkan-Slavic Orthodox community. The major influence in diverting the language from this course was the work of two scholars, Dositej Obradović and Vuk Karadžić, both of whom wrote in the vernacular.

11. Named after Stephen Dušan, King of Serbia (1331-55), the empire conquered lands to the south (Albania, Macedonia, Epirus, and Thessaly). In 1346, Dušan crowned himself emperor of the Serbs and Greeks and later added the Gulbars and Albanians. Under Dušan's rule, Serbia was the major power in the Balkans. After Dušan's death in 1355 at age forty-six, the Serbian kingdom simply disintegrated, partly because it lacked internal cohesion and partly as a result of foreign pressure.

12. Ilija Garašanin was one of the three leaders of the Constitutionalist party, which was dominant in Serbia during the reign of Alexander (1842-58). In 1844, Garašanin devised a plan called Nacertanije, which illustrates the direction of Serbian nationalist thought at the time. The document called for the unification of the lands that were considered predominantly Serbian and Orthodox, including Bosnia-Herzegovina, and "Old Serbia" (the Kosovo region—Montenegro, Vojvodina, and northern Albania).

13. In 1866 the first Balkan agreement between Serbia and Montenegro (whose inhabitants considered themselves Serbs) was signed. Prince Nicholas of Montenegro was willing to relinquish his throne to Prince Michael Obresnović of Serbia should a union of the two states be possible. The treaty provided for cooperation to prepare an uprising against the Ottoman empire.

The following year Serbia and Greece signed an agreement in which the two states agreed to help each other should either be attacked by the Ottoman empire. The agreement stated that, if circumstances allowed, Serbia would receive Bosnia-Herzegovina while Greece would annex Epirus and Thessaly.

In 1868 Serbia and Romania signed a treaty. It was simply a declaration of friendship rather than a war alliance. However, a war alliance was entered into by Serbia and Bulgaria in 1912. On the surface, this treaty was a mutual defense pact, but secret clauses provided that the land north of the Sar Mountains would go to Serbia, while the area east of the Slnuma River and the Rhodspl Mountains would be given to Bulgaria. It was also established that in a future war with the Ottoman empire, Bulgaria would provide 200,000 troops and Serbia, 150,000.

In October 1912 Montenegro signed agreements with Serbia and Bulgaria. The Balkan states were organized for war. On October 8, Montenegro attacked the Ottoman empire and was immediately joined by its Balkan allies—Greece, Bulgaria, and Serbia. The Ottoman army was easily defeated.

14. Pleterski, "Die Sozialistische Foederative Republik Jugoslavien," p. 271.

15. Svetozar Marković (1846-75) was the leading Serbian socialist of the nineteenth century. His views had a major influence upon the Yugoslav commu-

nists. A Marxist at first, Marković gradually became a left-wing democrat, advocating parliamentary rule and Western institutions. He wanted the people to be concerned with politics; he awakened an interest in economics, influenced the realist trend in Serbian literature, and greatly influenced a number of educated young people. He called for a reorganization of Serbia on the "basis of a community of individuals with equal legal rights. The form of the state is the opstina (commune) and the state is an amalgamation of free opstinas."

16. The Illyrian movement was inaugurated by a leading nineteenth century Croatian intellectual, Ljudevit Gaj. One of his main objectives was to illustrate (by emphasizing commonality of language and history) the existence of a unified Slavic culture. He claimed that the South Slavs were descendants of the ancient Illyrians and thus were the original inhabitants of the land. Accordingly, all South Slavs were basically one people, and should form a political unit. While Illyrism was a great success from a cultural and intellectual point of view, because it minimized linguistic differences, as a political movement it was a failure.

17. On August 2, 1903, the Internal Macedonian Revolutionary Organization (IMRO) called for a large-scale uprising in Macedonia known as the Llinden (St. Elizah's Day) Uprising. In the liberated town of Krusevo, the rebels proclaimed a socialist republic. The proclamation demanded autonomy for all Balkan nationalities within the Ottoman empire and proposed a Balkan federation. The socialist republic was to be short-lived. The Turkish army recovered quickly from the initial setbacks and regrouped; by August 13, it had recaptured Krusevo. The Turks then burned the town and took revenge on Macedonia with their scorched-earth policy.

18. Laza Kostić (1841-1910) attended the Yugoslav Congress of 1870 as the representative of the United Serbian Youth. This organization sought a democratic republic and a Balkan federation. Formally, it devoted its energy to education, while it quietly planned for an uprising in Turkey. It emphasized literary, economic, and political unity.

19. Janko Prunk, *Slovenski narodni programi* (Ljubljana 1986), pp. 12-13.

20. Karl Renner (1870-1950) was an intellectual, reformer, and statesman. In 1900 he became active in the Social Democratic party and soon after became one of its leaders. In 1918 Renner became the first chancellor of the Austrian Republic. At that time, he supported the idea of a union with a democratic federal Germany. On May 12 of the following year, he went to Paris as head of the Austrian delegation. In September 1919, he signed the Treaty of St. Germain, by which an Austro-German union (Anschluss) was prohibited. In October of that year, a second coalition ministry was formed, and Renner was again chancellor (and secretary for foreign affairs). In just over a year, Renner's government raised wages, provided unemployment benefits, introduced the eight-hour work day and collective contracts, and increased the power of trade unions.

When new elections were held in October 1920, the Social Democrats lost their leading position. After the Anschluss in 1938, Renner remained untainted, stating publicly that he had supported the Anschluss in 1918. In early 1945, he obtained approval from the USSR for the formation of the second Austrian

Republic. On December 20, 1945, the newly elected Nationalrat chose him as president of the republic.

21. Otto Bauer (1881-1938) was the leading Marxist theoretician of the Austrian Social Democratic party. In his book *The Nationality Question and Social Democracy* (1907), he devised a scheme (with Karl Renner) for solving the Austro-Hungarian empire's national problem through a complicated system of cultural autonomy based not on territorial units but on community of language.

Bauer returned to Austria in 1917 after his release from a Russian prisoner-of-war camp, where he had studied socialism firsthand. He became the leader of the left wing of his party and lobbied for a republic and autonomy for all nationalities.

In the provisional Austrian government of 1918, Bauer became foreign minister. At that time, he was an advocate of the Anschluss, and on March 2, 1919, he signed a secret Anschluss protocol with German foreign minister Von Brockdorff-Rontgau.

Bauer resigned from the coalition in July 1919 because the assembly's attitude toward the Anschluss was too cautious for him. He then guided the national and international policy of his party, which he preserved as non-Bolshevik but very socialist. After the uprising of the Vienna socialists and workers in 1934, he went into exile (from Czechoslovakia and France) but continued to direct the program of the Austrian Socialist Party.

22. See, for example, Drago Roksandić, "Ljudska prava i gradjanska prava i otvorena pitanja personalne i kulturne autonomije Srba u Hrvatskoj," *Scientia Yugoslavica 1990*, vol. 16 (3-4), pp. 217-28.

23. Rudi Rizman, in *Marksizem in nacionalno vprasanje* (Ljubljana 1980), p. 168.

24. Jurij Perovšek, "Sedemdesetletnica slovenske narodne osvobotive," *Komunist* (November 4, 1988), p. 19.

25. During the Italian *Risorgimento* (the nineteenth century political movement for the unification and independence of Italy), it was Piedmont (a region of northwestern Italy), ruled by King Victor Emmanuel II and his Chief Minister Cavour that led the attempts of 1848, 1859, and 1866 to unite all Italy. In 1862 Victor Emmanuel became modern Italy's first king.

26. Ibid., p. 14.

27. For more on this topic, see *Nova Evropa* (Zagreb, various issues, 1920-41); and Dušan Nećak, *Nova Evropa i Slovenci*.

28. Dušan Bilandžić, *Historija Jugoslavije, 1918-1985*, Glavni procesi, p. 333.

Notes to Chapter 2

1. In this chapter, nationalism is observed as a social and historical phenomenon. It is seen as the conception and implementation of a policy whose main

objective is furtherance of the interests of a particular nation. Such interests are considered absolute and, consequently, the interests of competing nations must be subordinated in their favor. No nation or period in modern history has been immune to nationalism (see Dusan Janjić, "Rečnik nacionaliste," IIGSSO Srbije, Beograd 1988). It is important to note that, owing to Yugoslavia's ethnic diversity, discussing the Serbian, Slovenian, Croatian, or Albanian "nation" or "nationalism" effectively means discussing different political cultures (see John B. Allcock, "In Praise of Chauvinism; Rhetoric of Nationalism in Yugoslav Politics, Ethnicity in World Politics," *Third World Quarterly*, no. 4 (London 1989), p. 216; and William Zimmerman, *Politics and Culture in Yugoslavia* (University of Michigan Press, 1987).

2. Although it is rather difficult to indicate the exact point at which the war in Bosnia-Herzegovina began, analyses of the Bosnian civil war predominantly refer to the following sequence of events. On February 29 and March 1, 1992, a referendum—boycotted by the Serbian Democratic party (SDS)—on sovereignty was held. The results of the referendum confirmed the option for an independent and sovereign state of Bosnia-Herzegovina. On the closing day of the referendum, an assassination took place—a Serb who was a wedding guest was killed in Bas Carsija in the center of Sarajevo. On March 2 and 3, barricades were erected in the streets of Sarajevo, first by the Serbs and then by the Muslims and Croats. After the intervention of the Yugoslav National Army, the situation temporarily calmed down. The real war started in the night between April 5 and 6, 1992, following the celebration of the Muslim Bairam holiday on April 4.

3. See Carl Ulrik Schierup, "The Post-Communist Enigma: Ethnic Mobilization in Yugoslavia," *New Community*, vol. 18 (October 1991), p. 115.

4. Stjepan Gredelj, "Filozofija i Drustvo," *Drustveni Pokreti bez Drustvenih Promena* (Beograd 1990) p. 239.

5. Schierup, "The Post-Communist enigma," p. 115.

6. Ivan Siber, "Psihologijski Aspekti Medjunacionalnih Odnosa," (Psychological aspects of interethnic relations), *Kulturni radnik* (Zagreb 1988), pp. 22–23.

7. Zagorka Golubovi, "Kriza identiteta savremenog jugoslovenskog društva" (Identity crisis of contemporary Yugoslav society), Filip Višnji (Beograd 1988), pp. 325–58.

8. Božidar Jakšći, "Kriza Jugoslavije," *Filozofija i Društvo III* (Beograd 1990), p. 228.

9. Mihajlo Mihajlov, "Can Yugoslavia Survive?" *Journal of Democracy* (Washington, D.C., Spring 1991), p. 90.

10. Jovan Raidević, "Srpski Nacionalizam u Oblasti Društveno-Politićkih Odnosa," *Izvori i Oblici Nacionalizma u SR Srbiji* (Beograd 1974), p. 94.

11. The economic and financial crisis—the largest after the crisis of 1948— that broke out late in the summer of 1983 represented the second shock for post-Tito Yugoslavia. The economic crisis could be defined as stagflation with an extreme drop of the GNP growth rate, which in 1989 amounted to a mere 0.5 percent; 250 percent inflation in 1988; reduction of the purchasing power of the urban population in 1987 to the 1980 level; an external debt of about 20 billion

dollars, with a population of slightly over 23 million, and an equivalent internal debt; and an unemployment rate reaching 15 percent (or about 1 million) in 1989, only to exceed 20 percent some time later.

12. Vladimir Goati, *Jugoslavija na prekretnici: Od monizma do gradjanskog rata* (Beograd: Jugoslovenski institut za novinarstvo, 1991), pp. 11–13.

13. In the 1987–88 period, there was a sudden increase in strikes: in 1987 and 1988 there were 1,685 and 1,002 strikes in the whole of Yugoslavia, with 288,686 and 213,367 participants, respectively (as compared with 1980, with only 235 strikes and 13,505 participants, which is just about the average for the postwar period or, more precisely, the period since 1958). Furthermore, these strikes lose the characteristics of "industrial conflicts" and assume the form of public political conflicts at the level of society at large or individual federal units, and primarily of conflicts where strikes are directed against the party-state bureaucracy. Actually, it is then that the true explosion takes place, followed by a chain reaction of hitherto dormant conflicts (Neca Jovanov, Sukobi, NIO "Univerzitetska Rijeka," (Nikšić, 1989), pp. 28–54).

14. Slobodan Milošević, called Slobo by his fans and followers, took over the leadership of the Serbian Communist party in 1987. He represented himself as being at once the unifier and savior of the Serbs and Serbia, the guarantor of Yugoslav unity, and the "strong man" Yugoslavia had been waiting for since the death of Tito (Jean Philippe Melchior, "De Tito à Slobo: La lente agonie de la fédération Yougoslave," *Les Temps Modernes*, 545–46 (Paris 1991), p. 277).

15. Micheline de Felice, "La Yougoslavie en Question," *Les Temps Modernes* 519 (Paris 1989), p. 91.

16. For the purpose of this article, civil war denotes internal armed conflicts. Other forms of civil disobedience, such as strikes with political motivations, are simply internal conflicts.

17. This division within the LCY was not essentially nationalist. It was announced first in Serbia, where, in the early 1980s, strong criticism developed within the League of Communists itself and from the Marxist intellegentsia, at which time breaking down the mythology of the Partisan past was also initiated. However, it is also in Serbia (the Communist League of Serbia) that the pluralists and reformists suffered their first defeat, which was inflicted on them by the victory of a faction of conservatives and nationalists headed by Slobodan Milošević (the so-called historical eighth session), supported by parts of the then federal and military leadership and initially tolerated by the elites of other republics.

18. The Serbian-Croatian conflict (concentrated in Croatia) was the first to reach the level of large-scale violence and destruction, moving in less than a year from political contention to polarization and segregation. Neither of the parties to this conflict wanted to accept the national identity of the other party or recognize their rights as legitimate, nor were they willing to relinquish a single right of their own. The result was a zero-sum conflict between two nationalistic movements struggling for national identity and existence while at the same time claiming the same territory. Each of the parties believed that the ultimate objec-

tive of the other was to destroy it; it was, in fact, the clash of two nationalist myths (both of which excite divisions, conflicts, and separation) and one destiny (created by intermixing and the impossibility of separation). The triumph of nationalism leads to disintegration, destruction of nations, and a bloody civil war; the only principles for resolution of the present situation still remain in democracy and peaceful coexistence. Nevertheless, the very core of interethnic communication has been destroyed and can be restored only when it is recognized that, in the end, there is no winner. Furthermore, dedication is also necessary. It is true that it will be very difficult to attain interethnic peace in view of the fact that one of the existing mediators (the European Community) resorted to the use of a political tool (recognition of the republics as independent states) that reduced the tensions in some conflicts but generated new and even more dangerous ones (that is, delimitation and adoption of new identities—identities of small independent states on the one hand, and identities of minorities on the other, which is true not only of Serbs in Croatia, but also of Croats in Serbia, and so on).

19. The unilateral act of secession of Slovenia through its declaration of independence on June 26, 1991, was followed on June 27 by the movement of the Yugoslav National Army (JNA) toward the international borders of Yugoslavia, which the leadership of Slovenia sought to assert as its own. On June 28, there was a cease-fire agreement consisting of three articles: 1) cease-fire and return of all troops into barracks; 2) three months' moratorium on activities aimed at the independence of Slovenia and Croatia; and 3) election of Stipe Mesić to the head of the collective federal presidency. It was at this point that the active involvement of the European Community in the Yugoslav conflict began. Despite nonadherence to the agreement, the Yugoslav National Army subsequently withdrew from Slovenia.

20. Many of these were the so-called conglomerate parties—like the catchall parties of the West—which resemble socialist movements and have as their integrative ideas "national harmony," "national basis," "national reconciliation," or "national state." By approaching the electorate as nondifferentiated members of the nation, these parties had outstanding electoral success, although many were simply voting against the status quo. In all, the nationalist movement had a strong influence on the outcome of the first free elections in 1990. In Bosnia-Herzegovina, for instance, national parties (SDA, SDS, and HDZ) won 201 out of a total of 240 seats in the republican parliament.

21. Most parties carefully elaborated national programs, emphasizing attachment to national values. Most of them also had a national designation in their title. Favoring one's own nation was justified by a number of arguments such as providing "economic subordination," "assistance" to economically underdeveloped regions, compensating for past "political denial" by federal regulations and institutions, and so on. In practice, political and national interests were frequently displayed in the form of nationalist and chauvinist rhetoric that had been previously suppressed.

22. The holding of multiparty elections only in the republics and not at the federal level brought about a crisis of legitimacy for the federation, and strengthened the links of voters with their respective republic or nation. In the absence

of an agreement on a loose association of states, this political context provided the basis for an overwhelming majority vote in favor of independence in the Slovenian and Croatian referendums.

23. Bureaucratic, so-called legal nationalism is the mainstay of national socialism. It is established when the national bureaucracy succeeds in subjecting all other interests to its own view, while creating an impression on the outside that it indeed represents the national interest.

24. Dr. Vladimir Goati, Jugoslavija na Prekretnici: Od monizma do Gradjanskog Rata (Beograd: Jugoslovenski institut za novinarstvo, 1991), pp. 12-13.

25. The "national intelligence" always played an important role in the preservation of power. It reemerged from the shambles of the student and youth movements of the 1960s, or at least of its marginal part, which had all the characteristics of traditional "antimovements," such as nationalist and chauvinist programs. This antimovement dramatically revealed the economic, ethnic, and religious divisions of society and reaffirmed xenophobia and resentments that until then had remained dormant. It enabled the system and especially the old elites to resist requests for modernization and democratization by activating nationalism and chauvinism and relying upon these juniors of "national intelligence" and the nouveau riche, who managed to accumulate wealth in the period of liberalized consumption; Stjepan Gredelj, "Društveni pokreti bez društvenih promena," *Filozofija i društvo*, III (Beograd 1990), pp. 251-52.

26. The term political elite is used here to denote all those who take an active part in decisionmaking within relevant political bodies (Leonard J. Cohen, *The Socialist Pyramid: Elites and Power in Yugoslavia* [Toronto: Tri-Star Press, 1989], p. 69), while "national elite" refers to those who make decisions of overall importance at the level of the constituent republic or province, or in connection and with the authentication of one of the ethnic groups.

27. During the 1970s and 1980s the ethnic representation of the Yugoslav elite (at the supraregional or Yugoslav level) endeavored to use the national formula or "ethnic quota" to fill vacancies at the highest positions. Each of the regions is responsible for the election of leadership that should reflect its ethnic structure. However, there was considerable ethnic imbalance in important areas such as the army and the state security apparatus, which, by tradition, employed a high percentage of Serbs and Montenegrins. (That, however, cannot be attributed to the intentional efforts of the regime or to any official discrimination.) In light of the ethnic complexities at the regional (republican or provincial) levels, the ethnic structure and composition of elites became an exceptionally important factor. This was particularly true of Croatia, Bosnia-Herzegovina, Kosovo, and Vojvodina (Cohen, *The Socialist Pyramid*, pp. 297-314).

28. This is also demonstrated by the effects of the rule of new political elites: 1) propagating fear of an imperiled national existence; 2) encouraging xenophobia and aggression; 3) closing ranks behind national parties and leaders (that is, transition to the system of presidential power); 4) emphasizing an absolute priority for the collectivity, national programs, and values, accompanied by the

suppression of differences, individuality, autonomy, and regionalism; and 5) encouraging political exclusivity and the intensification of ethnic conflicts that could, as in the case of Serbia and Croatia, lead to armed conflicts.

29. The nationalist leader, especially in the mass psychological structure of petit bourgeois, represents the embodiment of the nation, while the ties with the nation correspond to family ties. If the leader personifies the nation pursuant to the expectations and feelings of the masses, further personal bonds to him or her are developed. The more helpless a member of the masses is, the stronger his or her identification with the leader and the stronger his or her childish need to rely on someone, to be one with the leader.

Notes for Chapter Three

1. It is to be noted that, until his death, the main architect of all constitutions and amendments was Edvard Kardelj, a close associate of Tito and the chief ideologue of the Communist party (later League) of Yugoslavia. He was always at hand to "scientifically" justify changes in Tito's policies and has therefore been compared to an "ideological tailor" George Schöpflin, "The Rise and Fall of Yugoslavia" in John McGarry and Brendan O'Leary, eds., *The Politics of Ethnic Conflict* (London: Routledge, 1993), pp. 186, 189. Kardelj was an ethnic Slovene. I resent having to making reference to the ethnicity of former Yugoslav political actors, but I find it necessary to do so in view of the deplorable tendency of many writers on Yugoslavia to explain the motivations of the former predominantly on the basis of their national affiliation. I shall therefore indicate ethnicity whenever it can be established without doubt.

2. Dimitrije Djordjević, "The Yugoslav Phenomenon" in Joseph Held, ed., *The Columbia History of Europe in the Twentieth Century* (Columbia University Press, 1992), p. 328.

3. Asolute authority in one corporate body as, theoretically, in Italy under fascism.

4. Djilas was Montenegrin.

5. For some time, we have to be reconciled to the fact that we know very little about what really went on in the inner circles of the communist decisionmakers until Tito's death, and even thereafter. There is no order in the archives of the party (parties), and some of them have been pilfered; memoirs are self-indulgent and unreliable, and the now highly regarded "patriotic" historians are selective and partial. Ordinary state archives are of little help since the most relevant disputes and the most important decisions took place in party conclaves.

6. Djordejević, "The Yugoslav Phenomenon," p. 321.

7. The ethnic nature of Montenegro is somewhat complicated. The most simple statement is that some Montenegrins believe they are only Serb, whereas others feel that they are Montenegrin and Serb simultaneously. Often these attitudes have been conditioned by the prevailing political climate.

8. Kosovo and Metohija was originally a region (oblast). Later, with its promotion to a province, the "Metohija" part of the name was dropped—to please the Albanians, it was believed. It is not surprising, then, that the nationalist-populist movement in Serbia, together with practically abolishing the autonomy of the province, restored "Metohija" to its title. This is only one of the examples of the war of words so dear to dogmatic communists and nationalists alike. In fact, "Kosovo" is a very Serb word indeed, derived as it is from the name of a bird, whereas "Metohija" has non-Slavic (but not Albanian) roots. The Kosovo Albanians insist, in their turn, on the albanized version, "Kosova," and, naturally, reject "Metohija."

9. Schöpfin, "The Rise and Fall of Yugoslavia," p. 181.

10. The complaint about "invented" or "artificial" nations is common to nationalists throughout East and Central Europe. See Vojin Dmitrijević, *The Insecurity of Human Rights After Communism* (Oslo: Norwegian Institute of Human Rights, 1993), p. 36.

11. Tito did so principally because of his own interests and not in order to liberalize the system. Ranković was a Serb, and for some Serbs his deposition (including criminal charges, later dropped by Tito's decision in his capacity as president of the republic) was another anti-Serbian gesture. This led to the grotesque consequence that the funeral, in 1983, of this erstwhile dreaded chief of secret police, best known for his persecution of noncommunist Serbs, attracted huge crowds in Belgrade.

12. The proposal was to rename the University of Belgrade "The Red University—Karl Marx."

13. Miko Tripalo is now an opponent of the nationalist regime in Croatia and belongs to human rights groups denouncing the persecution of Serbs. *Vreme* (Belgrade, December 27, 1993), p. 29.

14. It was at that time that the famous nationalist writer and later (impeached) president of the new Federal Republic of Yugoslavia, Dobrica Ćosić, lost his position in the Serbian Communist party for warning against the Albanian menace and thus gained most of his political popularity. Appealing to the visceral Serbian fear of Albanians seems to be the surest way to obtain political support; this is how Slobodan Milošević was catapulted into prominence in 1987.

15. Stalinist and neo-Stalinist communists have always been masterful at devising invectives that combine incompatible adjectives; in this case, a possibility for an anarchist to be liberal. Given the repeated statements of Tito between 1969 and 1971 that he did not observe any important signs of nationalism in Croatia, he decided to act when Croat "anarcho-liberalism" became confused with Croat nationalism, as indeed in the "Croatian Spring" insistence on Croat identity came to be identified with nationalism. If only nationalism was at issue, Tito would have spared the communist leadership in other republics. Nobody has ever hinted that Nikezić and his associates were nationalists. The views on one of the surviving prominent Serbian leaders of the time are expressed in Latinka Perović, "Yugoslavia was Defeated From Inside" in Sonja Biscako, ed., *Yugoslavia: Collapse, War Crimes* (Belgrade: Center for Anti-War Action–Belgrade Circle, 1993), p. 57.

16. Then secretary of the federal League of Communists. This close associate of the aging dictator remained very powerful after Tito's death. In the state hierachy, he was the federal minister of the interior and head of security services. He was a Slovene.

17. It has been suggested that the repression of nationalists was harsher than that of "Marxist humanists, modernists and universalists in the glorious sense." Kenneth Anderson, "Illiberal Tolerance: An Essay on the Fall of Yugoslavia and the Rise of Multiculturalism in the United States," *Virginia Journal of International Law*, vol. 33 (1993), p. 414. However, the example given does not seem convincing: a group of neo-Marxist philosophers and sociologists in Serbia was "only" thrown out of their teaching positions and spared prison, not because they were not nationalists but because they were not identified with the reformists and modernizers in the party. The peak of their rebellion had been in 1968–69, when they considered the "anarcho-liberal" Nikezić group as principal advocates of the "red bourgeoisie." The identical group in Croatia was treated accordingly. Harsh punishment was, in both republics, meted out to intellectuals who were not, or did not identify themselves as Marxists, especially if they could be labeled as nationalists, which made criminal prosecution easier.

18. Paul Shoup, "Crisis and Reform in Yugoslavia," *Telos*, vol. 79 (1989), p. 129.

19. Anderson, "Illiberal Tolerance," p. 415.

20. A reprint was published in 1990. *Anali Pravnog fakulteta u Beogradu,* 3/1971 (1990).

21. Jovan Djordević, "La Constitution de 1974," *Questions Actuelles du Socialisme*, 1984, p. 12; Miodrag Zečević, *Ustav Socijalističke Federativne Republike Jugoslavije* (Beograd: Privredni pregled, 1978), p. 5; and Gisbert H. Flanz, "Yugoslavia" in Albert P. Blaustein and Gisbert H. Flanz, eds. *Consitutions of the Countries of the World* (Dobbs Ferry, N.Y.: Oceana, 1986), p. 6.

22. I will be using the valiant translation into English by Marko Pavić, in Blaustein and Flanz, *Constitutions of the Countries of the World.*

23. After the adoption of the constitution, "newspeak" permeated all legislation, public discourse, and administration. There were no wages and salaries anymore: "working people" had "personal incomes," schools became "educational centers," peasants and farmers were replaced by "agricultural producers," tenants were promoted into "bearers of tenant rights," and so forth.

24. Ivica Lovric, *Delegatski Sistem—Uloga Znaaj i Pretpostavke za Njegovo Funkcionisanje* (Sarajevo: Oslobodjenje, 1994), p. 3; Paule Nikolić, "Basic Characteristics of the System of Delegates," *Review of International Affairs*, no. 576 (1974), p. 8.

25. Marjan Rodić, "The Delegation System and the Socialist Alliance," *Review of International Affairs*, no. 589 (1974), p. 5.

26. Blaustein and Flanz, *Constitutions of the Countries of the World.*

27. Todorović is a Serb.

28. The intended meaning was probably closest to the German "Völkerschaft."

29. The word "narod" conveys both meanings in many Slavonic languages.

30. Compare the decisions of the Federal Constitutional Court regarding the constitutions and declarations of independence of some republics adopted in 1991. *Borba*, specijalno izdanje (November 1991), p. 21.

31. Some of these disputes were later brought before the Arbitration Commission of the Conference of Peace in Yugoslavia (the Badinter Commission), which advised that Yugoslavia was engaged in a "process of dissolution" and that Serbs in Bosnia-Herzegovina and Croatia were minorities without the right to self-determination. Opinions nos. 1 (1991) and 2 (1992).

32. Alexsandar Fira, "Federalism Under the New Constitution of the SFR Yugoslavia," *Review of International Affairs*, no. 574, 1974, p. 4.

33. On the role of the Socialist Alliance see Rodiće, "The Delegation System and the Socialist Alliance," p. 5.

34. That this was a complaint of the Serbian leadership was demonstrated by its proposals for constitutional amendments in 1990 and 1991. However, a compromise solution, which would make the number of deputies correspond to the size of the population but within a maximum of thirty and minimum of ten, was flatly rejected. *Borba*, Specijalno izdanje (November 1991), p. 34.

35. This wording has been sarcastically interpreted to mean that Tito remained president even after his death. One of the reasons was that in Slovene, the language of Edvard Kardelj, the notion of a life term cannot be expressed without referring to death ("dosmrtni" meaning "until death"). In the 1970s, the cult of Tito's personality reached its peak, and he was treated as immortal.

36. *Statistiki Godinjak Jugoslavije 1988* (Beograd: Savezni Zavod za Statistiku, 1988), p. 122. Contrary to the prevailing opinion that "Yugoslavism" was promoted by the Communists (Schöpflin, "The Rise and Fall of Yugoslavia," p. 186), such allegiance has been discouraged since the late 1960s; this was visible from the instructions given to the census takers (André Liebich, "Minorities in Eastern Europe: Obstacles to a Reliable Count," *RFE/RL Research Report*, vol. 1, p. 36). Yugoslavs were not a nation, not even a "nationality." It is often forgotten that the first Yugoslavia of 1918 was not created, but opposed, by the communists. The greatest proponent of supranational Yugoslavism was King Alexander, a staunch anti-communist (Djordjević, "The Yugoslav Phenomenon," p. 316).

37. *Sluzbeni list SFRJ*, 6/1975.

38. In practice, special attention was given to the distribution of the posts of greatest political significance. Thus, as a rule, the presidents of the Presidium of the League of Communists, of the Federal Assembly, the Presidency, and the Federal Executive Council should not have been of the same nationality.

39. Proposed amendment 65. *Borba*, specijalno izdanje (November 1991), p. 29.

40. The text to which most authors refer is the controversial Memorandum of the Serbian Academy of Sciences and Arts of 1985. It cannot be quoted, however, since it has never been published by the academy itself and has repeatedly been disowned by its officers, who have maintained that it was only a leaked

draft of a working group. Several versions are in circulation, some of them published in periodicals.

41. Autonomist ("autonomac") became a frequently used invective in the late 1980s for those Serbs favoring strong autonomy of the province of Vojvodina.

42. Vesna Pešić, "Nationalism, War and Disintegration of Communist Federations: The Yugoslav case," in Sonja Beserko, ed., *Yugoslavia: Collapse, War Crimes* (Belgrade: Center for Anti-War Action—Belgrade Circle, 1993), p. 49.

43. Commonly ridiculed as "Serbia beside itself."

44. Veljko Kadijević, *Moje Vidjenje Raspada. Vojska bez Drave* (Beograd: Politika, 1993) pp. 6, 109.

45. For a long while Milošević was actively protecting the cult of Tito's personality primarily to please the army (Pešić, "Nationalism, War and Disintegration," pp. 48-49). The memoirs of the last federal minister of defense, Veljko Kadijević (born in Croatia of mixed Serbo-Croat parenthood), who was also the head of the staff of the Supreme Command in 1990 and 1991, are extremely revealing (Kadijević, *Moje Ridjenje Raspada*). He remained convinced that the collapse of Yugoslavia was the result of a devilish plot of the "actors of the new international order . . . Bush's administration and Germany" (p. 7), that "the destruction of the regime in Yugoslavia was only a segment of the unified plan to topple all 'Communist' regimes in the world, above all in the Soviet Union" (p. 31). Gorbachev was a traitor who lead the way to "classical restoration of capitalism" in all former socialist countries, with China remaining the only hope (p. 55). In the Federal Executive Council, of which he was formally a member, Kadijević trusted only the minister of the interior, a retired general (p. 109).

46. Vlado Kambovski, "Od Ideala do stvarnosti," *Borba*, specijalno izdanje (November 1991), p. 3.

47. Amendment 70. *Borba*, specijalno izdanje (November 1991), p. 30.

48. Vojin Dimitrijević, "Freedom of Opinion and Expression" in A. Rosas and J. Helgesen, eds., *Human Rights in a Changing East-West Perspective* (London, New York: Pinter, 1990), p. 73.

49. On this see the symposium volume *Misao, rec, kazna* (Thought, speech, punishment) (Beograd: Institut za kriminololočka i socioločka istraivanja, 1989).

50. Vojin Dimitrijević, "Medjunarodno za Tena Ljudska Prava i Jugoslavija," *Anali Pravnog Fakulteta u Beogradu*, 1987, p. 715.

51. *Borba*, specijalno izdanje (November 1991), p. 29.

52. According to Kardelj, this was to be substituted by the depoliticized "pluralism of self-management interests." Edvard Kardelj, *Pravci Razvoja Socijalistckog Samoupravljanja* (Beograd: Komunist, 1977), p. 112.

53. Lidija Basta-Posavec, "Constitutional Requirements of Democracy and a Non-Democratic (Consititution of) Society, Serbia under the Constitution of 1990," *Bulletin of the Australian Society of Legal Philosophy*, vol. 17 (1992), p. 110.

54. John McGarry and Brendan O'Leary, *The Politics of Ethnic Conflict* (London: Routledge, 1993), p. 35.

55. Schöpflin, "The Rise and Fall of Yugoslavia," p. 182.

56. Mileta Prodanović, *Pas Prebijene Kime* (Beograde: Plato, 1993), p. 56.

57. Schöpflin, "The Rise and Fall of Yugoslavia," p. 190.

58. Apart from Kardelj, the most important was Vladimir Bakarić, a Croat.

59. Bogdan Denitch, *The End of the Cold War* (University of Minnesota Press, 1990), p. xv.

60. This also seems to have become the common wisdom of "instant" foreign experts on Yugoslavia. It disregards the existence of pre-World War II noncommunist Yugoslavia and fails to give a convincing criterion for the alleged artificiality of the Yugoslav state, except its multinationality. For a critique, see Anderson, p. 386, and Sabrina Petra Ramet, "War in the Balkans," *Foreign Affairs*, vol. 71 (1992), p. 80.

Notes for Chapter Four

1. Popis Stanovništva (population Census) 1991. Zagreb: Republicki zavod za statistiku, 1992, p.9

2. In this connection, it is necessary to point out the tragic role played by the memorandum of the Serbian Academy of Sciences and Arts, which was announced in Belgrade in 1986.

3. Low investment efficiency can be clearly illustrated by making comparisons. If the economic investment efficiency in the period 1960-80 had been equal to that of some countries with similar structural characteristics (Greece, Turkey, Spain, and Portugal), Yugoslavia would have almost doubled its gross domestic product by 1980. For more detailed information, see Aleksandar Bajt, *Samoupravni Oblik Društvene svojine* (The self-management form of social ownership) (Zagreb: Globus, 1988), pp. 13-21.

4. Observing the complexity of conflicts arising from these problems, the European Center for Peace and Development of the United Nations University initiated (on the occasion of the twenty-fifth anniversary of the formation of the Federal Credit Fund) the preparation of a special study. The authors of this study, which was published by the Federal Credit Fund under the title "Fond Federacije" (Fund of Federation) Belgrade, 1991, are Branislav Olanović (a Serb) and Berislav Šefer (a Croat). The reviewers of the study are Dragoslav Avramovic (a Serb), Spasoje Medenica (a Montenegrin), and Vladimir Stipetić (a Croat). The study gives well-documented analyses of a broad range of problems, covering the complexity of this controversial area.

5. More detailed information about these questions can be found in the writings of Zvonimir Baletić: "Osnove Politike Privredno Nedovoljno Razvijenih Republika i Autonomnih Pokrajina" (Elements of Policy of Economically Insufficiently Developed Republics and Autonomous Provinces) in *Problemi Privrednog Razvoja i Privrednog Sistema Jugoslavije* (The problems of economic development and economic system of Yugoslavia) (Zagreb: Globus, Ekonomski institut Zagreb, 1989), pp. 312-21; and *Razvoj Privredno*

Nedovoljno Razvijenih Krajeva SR Hrvatske (Development of economically insufficiently developed territories of SR Croatia), Republički fond za razvoj privredno nedovoljno razvijenih krajeva SRH, Ekonomski institut Zagreb, 1985, p. 228.

6. These are, in fact, two similar models and starting points by their constructions. See R. F. Harrod, "An Essay in Dynamic Theory," *Economic Journal* (June 1939); and E. D. Domar, *Essays in the Theory of Economic Growth* (New York: Oxford University Press 1957).

7. The author of this chapter was one of the first (more than three decades ago) to point out the complexity of the problem in his paper, "Neki Aspekti Problema Demografskih Investicija" ("Some aspects of demographic investment problems"), Ekonomski pregled, br. 4, Zagreb, 1960, pp. 222-49. A decade later, "Demografske Investicije i Ekonomski Razvoj" ("Demographic investment and economic development") was published in the journal *Ekonomske studije*, no. 5 (1970), pp. 87-128. In it, the author pointed out these problems and presented them at the Annual Conference of the International Association for Research in Income and Wealth held in Nathan, Israel, August 24-31, 1969. The paper also was published under the title "Demographic Investment and Economic Development in Yugoslavia" in *The Florida State University Slavic Papers*, Center for Slavic and East European Studies, vol. 4, Tallahassee, Florida, 1970. As the chairman of the Federal Economic Council, the author continually pointed out these problems, especially during the 1980s, as deputy chairman of Kiro Gligorov's working group for the Preparation and Realization of The Long-Term Program of Economic Stabilization.

8. For more detailed information, see *Problemi Provodenja Društveno-Ekonomske Reforme*, Rikard Lang, ed. (The problems of realization of the socioeconomic reform) (Ekonomski institut Zagreb, 1969).

9. In that context, see author's works published in editions of the Academy of Sciences of the Russian Federation: "Nekotorye Problemy Reformi Socializma v Svete Jugoslavskogo Opyta," *Voprosy ekonomiki*, Moskva, 2, 1990; "Pluralizam Sobstvennosti i Razvytie Modely Rynochnoj Ekonomiki," *Vestnik nauchnoj informacii*, Moskva, 2, 1992; "Problemy Ekonomicheskoj Reformi v Svete Razvytia Modely Rynochnoj Demokratii," *Vestnik nauchnoj informacii*, Moskva, 2, 1992; as well as Dragomir Vojnić and Rikard Lang, "Reformy Ekonomicheskoj Sistemy Socializma v Jugoslavii," *Mirovaja ekonomika i mejdunarodnye otnošenija*, br. 5, 1990, str. 110-116.

10. See Dragomir Vojnić, "Opča Kriza Socijalizma, Krah Boljševicke Opcije i Razvitak Modela Trišne Demokracije" ("General crisis of socialism, the break of the bolshevist option and the development of the model of market democracy"), *Ekonomski pregled*, br. 1-2-3 (Zagreb, 1990). pp. 3-24.

11. *The Laws on Economic Reform in Yugoslavia*, Federal Executive Council Secretariat for Information, Jugoslovenski Pregled (Beograd, 1990), p. 275.

12. For information on a broad spectrum of the issues discussed, See Dragomir Vojnić, ed., *Problemi Privrednog Razvoja i Privrednog Sistema Jugoslavije* (Problems of economic development and economic system of Yugoslavia), (Zagreb: Globus, Ekonomski institut Zagreb, 1989), p. 883. That study

was the starting point of the International Scientific Meeting held on the occasion of the fiftieth anniversary of the Institute of Economics, Zagreb, on November 15, 1989.

Notes for Chapter Five

1. U. Weinreich, *Languages in Contact* (The Hague: Mouton, 1963), ch. 4.

Notes for Chapter Seven

1. Within the context of a disintegrating multiethnic state, the explanation that on the basis of constitutional law Albanians were "only" a national minority in the former Yugoslavia and not a state-building nation like the Serbs in Bosnia-Herzegovina is not convincing.

2. See, generally, Hakan Wiberg, "States and Nations as Challenges to Peace Research" *Journal of Peace Research*, vol. 28 (1991) pp. 337–43.

3. In this treaty, signed by the president of the Yugoslav government, Dragića Cvetković, and the president of the leading Croatian political party, Vlatko Maček, agreement was reached about mutual territorial boundaries between Croats and Serbs. What this treaty did not define was the position of Bosnian Muslims and, of course, final political relations between the Croatian and Serbian states.

Index

Albanians in former Yugoslavia, *xiii*, 14; autonomy movement, 26, 142; demographic trends, 50, 85–92; interpretation of 1974 Constitution, 59; language, 112; majority provinces, 50; political significance, *xx*, 148–50; religious diversity, 17; Serb relations, 23–24, 38, 144, 148–49
Anderson, Kenneth, 5
Andrić, Ivo, *xxvi*
Austro-Hungarian empire, 16, 21, 22, 75, 76
Austro-Marxist thesis, 21–22, 24
Balkans: conflict resolution in, 140–41; cultural diversity, 139; ethnic challenges, *xix–xxi*; game theory perspective, 144–45; nature of current conflict, 141–42; prospects for resolution, 148–51; sociopolitical complexity, 139–40

Bauer, Otto, 21
Bijedić, Džemal, 65
Birth control/family planning, 85
Boban, Mate, 154, 157
Bosnia-Herzegovina: autonomy movement, 37; in communist period, 27, 50; in Constitution of 1974, 57; costs of war in, 146; cultural influences, 75–76; current political structure, 147; demographic trends, 77, 84, 85, 93; economic development in communist period, 108–09; ethnic conflict in, *xvi*; historical development, 16, 18, 19, 75–76; language, 118, 119–20; Muslims in, *xx*, 9, 12, 148–49; nationalist strategies in, 154–56; nature of conflict in, *xiii*, *xxiii*, 14, 133, 143–44; partition plan as apartheid, 156–58; per capita gross product, *xv*; prospects

for, *xxii–xxiii*, 134–35, 145, 163; in resolution of Serb-Croat conflict, *xviii–xix*, 9–10, 134–35, 148–49
Boundaries and borders: Croatian policy, 134, 137; future of Yugoslavia, *xviii*, 10; historical development, 16; linguistic analysis and, 113–14
Bulgaria, *xx*; Macedonia and, 20

China, 52
Class struggle, *xvii–xviii*; postcommunist nationalism and, 123; in Yugoslavian conflict, 35–36
Communist period: anonymity of policymakers, 53; decline of party, 73; economic development/mamagement in, 27, 99–102, 105, 107, 108–10; ethnic conflict in, *xii*, 34; language policy, 159; nationalist movements in, 47–49, 51–52; national questions in, *xii*, 13, 25–28; origins of nationalism in, *xiv*, 3, 121–25; political functioning in, *xv*, 72–73; postcommunist period, 1, 121; reform movement in 1960s, 50–52; regional economic disparities in, 100–105; self-management socialism, 45–47, 54, 56, 99, 108, 127; status of Serbs in, 49–50, 51, 66; survival of *nomenklatura*, 40–41; world standing in early 1970s, 52–53; Yugoslavian constitutional law, 53–54; Yugoslavian experience, 13
Conference on Security and Cooperation in Europe, 132
Consociationalism, 73
Constitution of 1974: anti-liberal orientation, 4–5; autonomous provinces in, 59; decentralization